Elusive Unity

ELUSIVE UNITY

**Factionalism and the Limits of
Identity Politics in Yucatán, Mexico**

Fernando Armstrong-Fumero

UNIVERSITY PRESS OF COLORADO
Boulder

© 2013 by University Press of Colorado

Published by University Press of Colorado
5589 Arapahoe Avenue, Suite 206C
Boulder, Colorado 80303

 The University Press of Colorado is a proud member of
the Association of American University Presses.

The University Press of Colorado is a proud member of the Association of American University Presses. The University Press of Colorado is a cooperative publishing enterprise supported, in part, by Adams State University, Colorado State University, Fort Lewis College, Metropolitan State University of Denver, Regis University, University of Colorado, University of Northern Colorado, Utah State University, and Western State Colorado University.

∞ This paper meets the requirements of the ANSI/NISO Z39.48-1992 (Permanence of Paper).

Library of Congress Cataloging-in-Publication Data

Armstrong-Fumero, Fernando.
  Elusive unity : factionalism and the limits of identity politics in Yucatán, Mexico / Fernando Armstrong-Fumero.
    pages cm
  Includes bibliographical references and index.
    ISBN 978-1-60732-238-2 (hardback) — ISBN 978-1-60732-239-9 (ebook) —
  ISBN 978-1-60732-353-2 (pbk)
    1. Mayas—Mexico—Yucatán (State)—Ethnic identity. 2. Mayas—Mexico—Yucatán (State)—Politics and government. I. Title.
    F1435.3.E72A76 2013
    305.897'427—dc23

                    2013009235

Cover photograph by the author.

To the agriculturalists, artisans,
and parents of Oriente,

in their respective and overlapping *luchas*.

Contents

List of Figures ix

Acknowledgments xi

1. Peasants and Maya, Solidarity and Factionalism 1

2. "How It Happened That We Fomented This Town":
Tensions between Family Autonomy and Community
Solidarity during the Agrarian Reform 23

3. "Back Then, There Was No Order": The Early
Twentieth Century in Collective Memory 51

4. "Now There Is More Culture": Rural Schools as
Monuments to Revolutionary Culture 77

5. "When I First Went to Study": Pedagogy, National
History, and Bilingualism 95

6. "That Time of Change": The Limits of Agriculture and
the Rise of the Tourist Industry 113

7. "What Does 'Culture' Mean?": Progressivism,
Patrimonialism, and Corporatism in Vernacular Discourse
on Maya Culture 137

8. The Realpolitik of Yucatecan Multiculturalism 161

References 183

Index 197

Figures

1.1. Reynaldo Mis Dzib at Chichén Itzá 3

1.2. Map of the towns and villages of Oriente 15

3.1. Making posole 55

3.2. Public monument on the
Paseo Montejo of Mérida 56

5.1. Doing tich' 109

6.1. The road to Popolá 121

6.2. The electrical cables leading to Nicté Há 124

6.3. Main street and municipal hall of Pisté 131

7.1. The OXXO chain convenience store in Pisté 151

Acknowledgments

All academic books are the result of collaborative endeav-
ors, but the debts that one accrues in writing a historical
ethnography like this one are particularly numerous. First
and foremost, I would like to thank the many families from
Pisté, Xcalakdzonot, Popolá, Nicté Há, Kaua, Ticimul,
Xkatun, and elsewhere in Oriente who have been informants, friends, and gracious hosts over the years.

There are, as well, individuals to whom I owe particular
thanks. First, there are Don Víctor Tun and Doña Jacinta
Cimé, who rented me a room in their home during my
first visit in 1997, and began referring to me as an adoptive
son soon after. Most of my earliest knowledge of the Maya
language was learned in Doña Jacinta's kitchen and Don
Víctor's work area through countless hours of conversation
with them and with the members of their very extended
household: Ignacio, Lilian, Cristina, Emiliano, Aurelia,

Magdalena, Amalia, Jorge, Víctor Manuel, Luis, Antonio, Mario, Gloria, the Twins, Betty, Chucho, Mercedes, Giovani, and the younger grandchildren.

Don Reynaldo Mis and Doña Ediwilma Cimé are another pair of dear friends from Pisté who provided a great deal of help and emotional support over the years, along with their children René, Hugo, Papo, Gabriela, Juan, and their respective spouses and children. Other members of their extended families to whom I am especially indebted include Don Olegario and Doña Elda, Maricela, Patricio, Sergio, Gloria, Fernando, and many others.

Other friends in Pisté to whom I owe a strong debt of gratitude for the completion of this work include Víctor, Hilario, Isauro and the other members of the Olalde family, José León and Luis Tuz Kituc and their circle of artisan friends, Wilberth Serrano Mex and his family, Gilberto Yam and his family, Jorge Pool Cahuich, Ramón Quijano, Juan Gutiérrez, and many others. In Popolá, I am especially indebted to the family of Don Feliciano Dzul. In Xcalakoop, I am grateful to Julio Hoil Gutiérrez (more on my debt to him below), Manuela Un, the late Don David Dzib, and his family. In Xcalakdzonot, I owe a very hearty collective "jach dios bo'otike'ex" to the *ejidatarios* and their families.

My field sites for this research included various archives, and I gained access to the texts that are cited throughout this book with the gracious and expert help of the staff of the Archivo General de Yucatán, the historical archive of the Registro Agrario Nacional in Mérida, the Centro de Apoyo para Investigaciones de la Historia de Yucatán, and the Archivo Histórico de la Secretaría de Educación Pública in Mexico City.

Over the years, I have also accrued major debts to the fellow scholars with whom I have interacted in Yucatán. First among these is Julio Hoil Gutiérrez, who besides becoming one of my closest friends has helped me as a Maya language tutor, co-investigator, and most recently as coauthor on a number of scholarly publications. Just as his warmth and wit provided constant encouragement, our intellectual collaboration has been a major influence on many aspects of my work, including this book. As I finish this book, he is completing his own PhD, and I look forward to many more years of friendship and collaboration.

I also owe a significant debt to Lisa Breglia, Carlos Bojorquez Urzaiz, Juan Castillo Cocom, and Quetzil Castaneda.

I should also thank a long list of mentors who supported and shaped my work away from the field. At the University of Pennsylvania, these people include Wendy Ashmore, Julia Paley, and Christine Kray. At Stanford, they include Renato Rosaldo, Miyako Inoue, Paulla Ebron, and (as visiting faculty and external committee members) Roger Bartra and Mauricio Tenorio Trillo. During the later stages of developing this book, I received invaluable help and support (once again) from Wendy Ashmore, Julia Paley, Renato Rosaldo, and Mary Louise Pratt.

As this book reached completion, I received a great deal of help from the staff at University Press of Colorado, particularly Darrin Pratt and Jessica d'Arbonne. I'm also grateful to the anonymous external reviewers the press chose for this manuscript.

Finally, one of my greatest debts in life is to my parents, Fernando Armstrong Rivera and Dafne Fumero Pugliesi, for their support over many years, and for raising me in a Spanish-speaking household even as the entirety of my formal education was in English. Without that particular gift, I'm sure that my trajectory in life would have been very different, and far less fun.

Elusive Unity

1

Peasants and Maya, Solidarity and Factionalism

This book is a study of the dichotomous nature of identity politics. It documents how the same forms of politicized self-labeling that members of local communities use to build large-scale coalitions can also fuel factional disputes. The rural inhabitants of Oriente, a region of the Mexican state of Yucatán, have had some of their most important dealings with their nation's government as self-identified "peasants" and "Maya." In the early twentieth century, peasant identity played a key role in a series of institutions through which communities secured title to collectively held lands and free public schools, and asserted their rights as a special class of Mexican citizens. Today, amid vastly different economic and political realities, the descendants of these same people are experimenting with the use of Mayan identity as a means of securing other concessions and collective rights (see Figure 1.1). Yet both of these periods also

1

DOI: 10.5876/9781607322399.c01

involve a second dimension of identity politics: the narratives and labels that help local people to imagine different forms of collective action and solidarity also figure in intracommunity feuds that fragment larger coalitions.

Throughout this book, I will argue that this dual tendency is an element of local experience that transcends the differences between the agrarian politics of the early twentieth century and contemporary mobilizations of Mayan identity. My goal in stressing these parallels is not to provide a comprehensive linear history of the evolution or transformation of identity politics in Oriente. Rather, I will use ethnography, oral history, and closely targeted archival research to examine how local experiences of peasant and indigenous politics are shaped both by ambiguities built into the vernacular language of identity and by tensions within the social organization of rural communities. In some cases, the parallels between agrarian and ethnic politics are due to a direct historical continuity in certain institutions or ideas. For example, the collective memory of political processes associated with the agrarian reform of the 1920s and 1930s has shaped the expectations that many people have for newer forms of indigenous identity politics. The heritage of early twentieth-century institutions is less evident in other political phenomena, such as the new importance given to the term "Maya" by the market for cultural tourism. Even in these cases, however, processes of factionalism and solidarity—like those that shaped the agrarian reform— are also shaping multicultural politics.

In my comparison of these two periods, I will use a fairly expansive definition of phrases such as "identity politics" or "politics of identity." That is, I will use these terms to refer both to the negotiation of older state-sanctioned social identities such as "peasant" and to more contemporary uses of Mayan ethnic identity. This approach runs somewhat against the grain of a tendency in contemporary literature, which often draws a contrast between the "class-based" peasant organizing of the early and mid-twentieth century and the explicitly ethnic "identity politics" of post–Cold War indigenous movements (Alvarez, Dagnino, and Escobar 1998; Castañeda 1994; Hale 1994; Yashar 2005). But as social histories of other parts of Mexico have demonstrated (Boyer 2003; Purnell 1999), the meaning of the term "peasant" was as ambiguous to rural agriculturalists in the 1920s and 1930s as notions like Maya are today. In many ways, early twentieth-century peasant-based organizations were also experienced by local communities as a form of identity politics, in which rural people and urban bureaucrats negotiated a working definition of these politically resonant labels. Then and now, who can claim specific rights and privileges often hinges on local disputes over who "counts" as a member of a given social or ethnic category.

This kind of ethnographic history, like the expansive definition of identity politics that I will use throughout the text, helps explain how the ethnic movements of post–

FIGURE 1.1. Reynaldo Mis Dzib at Chichén Itzá, 2010. One of his grandfathers was among the first people to introduce Presbyterianism to the community of Pisté. His other grandfather was the first tour guide at Chichén Itzá. He himself has helped to administer Pisté's collective landholdings as director of the local agrarian committee (*comisario ejidal*). He and his family are active participants in an organization of local vendors of handicrafts who have asserted their rights to sites of sale in the ruins of Chichén Itzá as descendants of its ancient builders. The range of engagements with peasant, Mayan, and other identities that are implicit in his and his family's experience is typical of the complexity of self-labeling in the political life of Oriente. Photo by author.

Cold War Latin America are understood by their rank-and-file constituents. Changes in political culture that seem significant from a top-down perspective can—but often don't—have a significant impact on the everyday speech and common sense of rural people. Especially since the 1990s, anthropologists have demonstrated how the application of a broad identity label such as "Maya people" tends to obscure a range of localized identities and loyalties that have a more tangible presence in the everyday life of rural communities (Gabbert 2004; Hervik 1999; Restall 1997; Gabbert 2004; Hervik 1999). The fact that grassroots movements have begun employing the idea of

Maya culture and other broad ethnic rubrics in new ways seems to imply that these essentializing "Mayan" identities are transforming older localisms.[1] In the Mexican case, this shift in local forms of identity has often been explained in terms of a dynamic between the decline of twentieth-century welfare institutions and peasant organization, and the rise of ethnic mobilizations that have sought to adapt to new neoliberal realities (Mattiace 2009; Yashar 2005).

Although a top-down analysis of large-scale mobilizations and formal political institutions suggests that post–Cold War identity politics is changing local forms of identity, these processes can seem more fluid and ambiguous in the conversations that take place at the kitchen tables, agricultural fields, and storefronts of rural communities. In these spaces, people make sense of new political possibilities with oral narratives that commemorate earlier moments of local history. As in other parts of Mexico,[2] rural people in Oriente often associate their collective rights as self-identified indigenes with the heritage of agrarian institutions that were developed in the 1920s. But it is important to note that defining the local body politic and the nature of these "communities" during this earlier period was as much marked by conflict and semantic ambiguity as the definition of politicized Mayanness is today. This heritage of ambiguity (Armstrong-Fumero 2009a) tends to blur the distinctions between "peasant" and "ethnic" politics that can seem clearer from the analysis of formal and large-scale institutions.

These local contexts for the language of identity politics also provide important insights into the reasons why larger-scale mobilizations *don't* come together, or why coalitions tend to fragment into factional groups. The everyday narratives that help people imagine large-scale political mobilizations also bear the seeds of a parallel series of processes that tend to reinstate differences of interest between communities, families, and individuals. These tensions between communal solidarity and factionalism have a long history in Mexicanist and Mesoamericanist ethnography. Perhaps the most important were early critiques of Robert Redfield's idyllic image of a "folk" community, which he thought was defined by egalitarianism and a shared class and territorial identity (Redfield 1941; Redfield and Villa Rojas 1934). From Oscar Lewis's (1960) discussion of class differences in Tepoztlán to George Foster's (1987) analysis of individualistic behaviors that were conditioned by the "idea of limited good," scholars writing since the 1950s seem to revel in unveiling the factionalism and hierarchies that exist beneath the surface of the "little community."

In returning to this old debate I intend to apply the kind of ethnographic insights that Redfield, Lewis, and Foster derived from the quotidian experience of rural people to the larger question of why and how groups mobilize around certain state-sanctioned identities. Narratives about Mayanness, peasantness, and other identities don't just emerge during the kind of public events and mobilizations that receive international recognition. They can also be heard in the much more intimate public and private spheres of rural communities, spaces in which ethnography can provide a perspective distinct from that which can be derived from more top-down analysis of formal state or nongovernmental organizations. It is in these spaces that semantically ambiguous concepts such as Maya culture enter the speech and consciousness of the rank-and-file constituents of different regimes of identity politics.

The ambiguity and semantic flexibility that mark everyday invocations of "peasant" and "Maya" constitute a discursive space in which divisions between peasant and ethnic politics are far from clear-cut. This discursive space also enables the almost simultaneous emergence of solidarity and factionalism. I took part in a conversation in 2003 that provides a good example of these two phenomena. I posed the question "How would you characterize the culture of this community?" to a gathering of several generations of a well-to-do family of Maya speakers from the town of Pisté. Doña Petrona Chan de Mukul, the seventy-year-old matriarch of the family, responded in Maya, as many people of her generation did, "Today there is more culture, more education" (*Behlae, mas yan kúultura, mas yan éedukasion*). She expounded on how the building of the first school in the town around the time that she was born and the expansion of public education in the decades since had given local people "more culture" and "more order." When she was a young girl, she noted, "There was no order! There were cattle in the village square" (*Mina'an orden! Yan wakax* t[*i l*]*e k'iwiko!*).

Mario Mukul, her fifty-year-old son, agreed with his mother. Switching between Maya and Spanish, he mentioned that old marriage customs and respect for elders were once commonplace, but "Now there is not as much old Maya culture as before" (*Behlae . . . Pues, ahora, no hay tanta cultura antigua de los Mayas como antes*). Doña Petrona smiled and nodded. Like most people her age, she welcomed the coming of "order," but lamented the loss of older traditions.

Something that struck me but that Doña Petrona seemed *not* to notice was that Mario defined "culture" in a way that was quite distinct from her use of the term. She associated culture with the Westernized education and habits that brought order to unruly peasant lifestyles, while he associated the term with traditionally Maya ways of being that were lost with the advent of modernization. Although I initially thought that the different ways in which they used the term "culture" would be a source of friction between their two narratives, Doña Petrona and Mario Mukul were in essential agreement about the moral content of modernization. As in many examples that I heard over the course of my fieldwork, the representation of local identity as a dialectic between pride in modernization and nostalgia for the loss of tradition is far more important than the exact semantic content of a powerful word like "culture."

Just as this ambiguity of the term "culture" allows Doña Petrona and Mario to agree while making very different kinds of arguments,[3] this same term creates a conceptual space in which a speaker can imagine either an egalitarian solidarity or a series of elitist hierarchies. Mario's reference to "old Maya culture" means a heritage that is shared by people of all social classes in town and a collective memory that can be used as the basis for cross-class solidarity. In contrast, Doña Petrona's iteration of "culture" as something that some people have "more" of refers to a process through which whole communities became "cultured." But it also hints at differential access to intellectual goods that have allowed some local families to become more "cultured" than others. Similar assumptions about being cultured are often applied in discussions of who speaks the "best" Maya. Through these and other everyday performances of indigenous identity, the same labels that become a metonym for ethnic solidarity can also become tools for factional and individual competition.

This book will examine the history and texture of this dynamic between solidarity and factionalism in three sections. Chapters 2 and 3 will look closely at the experience of communities in Oriente during the early 1920s, and at how this period is remembered today. The collective memory of the early twentieth century—or the way in which the period is retrospectively understood—constitutes a series of precedents for collective action and factionalism that are cited in everyday narratives about the politics of Mayan identity today. Chapters 4 and 5 turn to rural education, focusing on the foundation of the first public schools in the 1930s and the pedagogical techniques that diffused a series of key narratives about national and linguistic identity to students. As I will show, rural education translated the pact that had been established between Maya-speaking agriculturalists and the state into the idiom of "culture," instituting a series of assumptions that continue to play a role in the contemporary politics of ethnicity.

Chapters 6 through 8 turn to transformations in vernacular narratives about "culture" that have taken place in the last three decades. I will focus on some cases in which local people successfully use this discourse in articulating different political projects, and others that show a growing disconnect between popular expectations conditioned by the heritage of peasant politics and the more limited possibilities of neoliberal multiculturalism. I will also stress ways that the contemporary politics of indigenous identity figures in processes that are just as likely to reinstate existing hierarchies and factional disputes as they are to forge new kinds of political coalitions.

Before entering into substantive discussion of local experiences of the agrarian reform, the remaining sections of the current chapter will provide additional background for three topics that will occur repeatedly in this book. The first is the ethnic labels used in the everyday speech of Yucatán. These labels form the basis on which rural people make sense of the discourses on ethnicity diffused by formal political organizations, and they differ in significant ways from the assumptions of many foreigners and urban Mexicans. Second, this section will be followed by a brief discussion of the broader political context of twentieth- and twenty-first-century Mexico, an important backdrop for many of the local processes that will be discussed later on. Third, I will close this introduction with a general summary of some of the specific sources and methods that figure in the research that contributed to this book.

Ethnic Labels in Yucatán

Identity labels that seem straightforward to many foreigners and urban Mexicans tend to be far more contentious or ambiguous in rural communities such as those of Oriente. In much anthropological literature written from the nineteenth century until the 1960s, rural people who spoke Yucatec Maya are referred to as "Maya Indians." Today, in most if not all of the communities where I have conducted research, "Indian" (Sp. *indio*) is more an insulting reference to poor manners and low education than an ethnic or racial label. Similarly, the term "Maya" is rather ambiguously linked to ideas of race or ethnicity. In the early twentieth century, the vast majority of rural Yucatecans would only have used the term to refer to *maya t'aan*, or the Yucatec Maya language. This language is spoken by a diverse community of rural and urban social groups, many of which are identified with the heritage of Europe as much as they are with the indigenous (see Armstrong-Fumero 2009b). This disjuncture between academic writing and local ethnic categories is compounded by the fact that the concept of "Maya Indian" has no simple cognate in maya t'aan. The term *máasewal*, translated as "Indian" in many contemporary dictionaries, tends to refer to poverty more than to ethnicity as such. Likewise, the term *ts'ul*, used to refer to "white" foreigners and Spanish-speaking urban Yucatecans, is also applied to wealthy Maya speakers from rural communities who have cultivated urban habits and speech.

Other terms for describing ethnicity common throughout Mexico are just as awkward a fit for the native social nomenclature of Yucatán. In other parts of Mexico, the term *mestiza* or *mestizo* refers, respectively, to the female or male member of the "national" society who has a mixed European and native genetic heritage. But since the mid-nineteenth century (Gabbert 2004), Yucatecans have tended to use the term *mestizo/mestiza* to refer to people who wear a kind of traditional dress that people from other parts of the republic would characterize as "Indian" (see also Hervik 1999; Thompson 1974). Along with the fact that the Maya language was historically spoken by a socially and ethnically diverse regional society, this definition of *mestizo* precludes the kind of clear-cut distinctions between "Indians" and *ladinos* that is common in the highlands of Chiapas and Guatemala.

One final dimension of vernacular discourse on Maya identity is the notion of "race" (Sp. *raza*). From José Vasconcelos' (1926) classic *La raza cósmica* to a range of popular celebrations of Mexican nationalism, "race" has been a common term for the blending of indigenous, European, and African people that defines the essence of Latin American identity (Miller 2004). This conflation of identity with "blood" is still common in the everyday speech of many of the communities where I have conducted fieldwork. This usage should not, however, be interpreted as the heritage of eugenics or other twentieth-century forms of biological determinism. Instead, it reflects a romantic narrative that tended to conflate language, culture, and biological makeup into a national gestalt that grew and died through a humanlike life cycle (Stocking 1968, 65). This narrative of the racial life cycle took on special significance for urban Yucatecan authors in the 1840s, who saw the Spanish conquest as the "natural" ascendancy of the Hispanic race amid the decline of the Indians.[4] Today, many people still refer to poverty, lack of education, and so on as signs of the "weakness" of Maya people's "blood" or "race," or refer to the perseverance of rural communities as a function of a similarly "racial" strength. Multicultural institutions that refer to the "breath" of the Maya language (*u yiikal Maya t'an*) or to an "Awakening of the Maya people" (*u Yahlal maaya winiko'ob*) are broadly consistent with the anthropomorphized narrative of collective identity.

By the late twentieth century, terms such as "Indian," "mestizo," and "race" were being supplemented by an explicitly "cultural" idiom of Mayan identity. Today, the phrase "we represent the Maya culture" is part of a lexicon used on a daily basis in most of the communities where I have conducted research. Still, as the conversation between Mario Mukul and his mother shows, the actual semantic content of words such as "Maya" and "culture" tends to be ambiguous and quite flexible in the everyday speech of Oriente. Older people, who attended rural schools from the 1930s to 1960s, tend to use a somewhat more conservative definition of this term. That is, they are far more likely to characterize "culture" as something that one has more or less of, depending on one's exposure to the Western habits and education of the *ts'ulo'ob* (plural of *ts'ul*). In contrast, people in their twenties, thirties, or forties, who reached adulthood during the burgeoning of the tourist industry, often invoke "culture" to refer to a concatenation of language, belief, and habits that makes Maya speakers distinct from Europeans and urban Mexicans.

The gradual diffusion of these new uses of "culture" into the everyday lexicon of people in Oriente reflects a combination of local and external factors. One local factor is the experience of new political and economic possibilities offered by the widening market for cultural tourism and by an emergent series of formal multicultural institutions. External factors include changes in federal policies that have accompanied the neoliberal transformation of Mexico, the development of a transnational indigenous movement, and the changing place of the southeast of the republic in the global economy. Both of these elements, and their implications for quotidian identity politics in Oriente, will be the focus of the next section.

Neoliberalism and the Heritage of the Mexican Revolution

As noted earlier, the neoliberalization of national economies has been one of the most common factors in interpretations of post–Cold War indigenous identity politics in Latin America. Throughout the region, neoliberal reforms have undermined many older forms of collective political participation or corporate citizenship, and have limited the tactical mobility of class-based grassroots organizations (Alvarez, Dagnino, and Escobar 1998; Castañeda 1994; Warren and Jackson 2002; Wiarda 2003; Yashar 2005). In national contexts ranging from Central America (Hale 2005; Warren 1998) to Ecuador, Peru, and Bolivia (Albó 2002; de la Cadena 2000; García 2005; Postero 2006; Sawyer 2004), these changing possibilities for local political agency were one motivator in the emergence of ethnic movements. In Mexico, this process was epitomized by the concurrent rise of multicultural discourse and the decline of agrarian institutions that had bound the peasantry to a populist state for over half a century. Given that this process took place against the backdrop of a series of political crises that led to the end of seventy years of single-party rule by the Institutional Revolutionary Party (Partido Revolucionario Institucional, PRI) in 2000, it tends to be associated with the ambivalent blend of neoliberal and democratic reforms that have marked the last two decades of Mexican history.[5]

That said, the experience of Yucatán presents a series of factors that contradict the expectations of this literature on indigenous identity politics, which predicts some transformations in the nature of local political identity in the post–Cold War period. The growing political cachet of indigeneity was certainly notable in post-1960s Yucatán, where a tourist industry that revolved around pre-Hispanic ruins turned "the Maya culture" into a source of economic as well as political capital (Breglia 2006; Castañeda 1996, 2004; Mattiace 2009). But in contrast to the Mexican states of Chiapas and Oaxaca—hot spots of ethnic activism that have been the focus of most recent research (see below)—the transition from "peasant" to "Maya" identity politics in Yucatán is far less clear-cut. This ambiguity is due, in part, to the rather indistinct ethnic boundaries to which I referred earlier. It also seems to be especially difficult for many people in Oriente to extricate their own notions of territoriality from the forms of land tenure that developed in the aftermath of the Mexican Revolution. The social organization of eastern Yucatán is difficult to reconcile with the ideas of historical continuity used by groups such as the Zapatista Army of National Liberation (Ejército Zapatista de Liberación Nacional, EZLN) to assert the autonomy of "traditional" forms of local leadership that preceded the incorporation of indigenous communities into the modern state. Yucatecan communities lack clearly constituted elders' councils or civic-religious hierarchies (Sp. *cargos*), which are present in highland Maya communities (Cancian 1965). In Oriente, the collective memory of most rural communities also tends to lack the deep roots in historical and mythological time that mark consciousness of local identity in many of these highland ethnic groups (Gossen 1998), or even in communities in other parts of the peninsula (Eiss 2010). Given this loose relationship between community and territory, the historical memory of much of rural Oriente tends to blur the boundaries between "Mayan" identity and the heritage of Revolutionary-era agrarian institutions. As I will discuss in Chapter 3, the foundation stories of most of the communities where I have conducted fieldwork are intimately tied to how the agrarian reform created a new pact between communities and the Mexican state in the 1920s.[6]

Although many discussions of indigenous politics in Latin America have tended to stress that ethnic and national identities underwent significant transformation in the post–Cold War era, the kind of continuity that is evident in the idea that land rights are guaranteed by the Revolutionary state has also been a consistent theme in analyses of contemporary Mexican politics. The transformation in notions of identity and citizenship is, in a sense, a large-scale political and cultural process that rural people in Oriente are experiencing alongside the diverse urban and rural populations of Mexico. Some scholars, such as Roger Bartra (1987, 2002a, 2002b), contemplated the waning years of PRI hegemony as the slow "decay" of the massive and all-pervasive body of social, economic, and ideological institutions that had dominated national politics for seventy years (see Baños Ramírez and Sabido Méndez 2008; Collier 1987). But this is only part of the story. Neoliberal reforms and the North American Free Trade Agreement (NAFTA) notwithstanding, the heritage of the agrarian reform and similar institutions still has a significant role to play in the lives of many Mexicans, and no model of collective identity has emerged to compete successfully with the canons of Revolutionary nationalism (see Beer 2002; Benjamin 2002; Fox 2000; Gawronski 2002; McDonald 1997; Morris 2003; Tenorio-Trillo 2009).

This kind of continuity is an important factor in the success of some mobilizations of indigenous identity, even if the idiom of multiculturalism represents a relatively novel way of redefining Mexican citizenship. For example, by invoking the Revolutionary hero Emiliano Zapata and other elements of a nationalist iconography with roots in the early twentieth century, the EZLN of Chiapas created a vision of social justice that was widely intelligible to indigenous and nonindigenous Mexicans alike (Collier and Quaratiello 2005; Gutmann 2002, 143–56; Stephen 2002). From 1994 to 1999, the rhetoric of the movement shifted from an emphasis on agrarian politics to a politics of indigenous identity and rights.[7] Though many authors have viewed this shift as a radically new form of subaltern politics (Rabasa 2004), ethnographic studies have shown that many of the rural constituents of neo-zapatismo continue to use this as a contemporary iteration of corporate political traditions with roots in twentieth-century institutions (Mattiace 2003; Stephen 2002).

This phenomenon brings us back to the rural Yucatán, where I conducted ethnographic research between 1997 and the present. Multiculturalism in Oriente emerged in an ambivalent place between the heritage of Revolutionary-era institutions, the political capital of contemporary indigenous movements such as the EZLN, and the economic promise of a tourist boom. In spite of being a state where a significant majority of the rural population fits the criterion of "indigenousness" used by official institutions (Ruz 2002b), Yucatán is remarkable for the relative lack of grassroots organization based on indigenous identity (Armstrong-Fumero 2009a; Castañeda 2003; Castillo Cocom 2005; Mattiace 2009), which is due, in part, to some of the factors I noted earlier, including the absence of traditional civic-religious hierarchies and the ambiguity of the Indian/ladino boundary on the peninsula. Other important differences between identity politics in Yucatán and Chiapas boil down to economics, and to the particular experience of late twentieth-century politics in regions such as Oriente.

Access to land, one of the primary motivators for the EZLN rebellion (Collier and Quaratiello 2005), has been far less of a problem for agriculturalists in Yucatán in the second half of the twentieth century. Since the 1970s, the primary crisis for agriculture in the state's western henequen-producing zone has hinged more on access to credit than on land (Mattiace 2009). Meanwhile, the relatively poor development of commercial agriculture in "maize zones" such as Oriente made land accessible for peasants through much of the twentieth century.[8] As Chapters 2 and 6 will show, a number of calamities *did* affect peasant communities in the second half of the twentieth century, but these tended to involve a range of natural disasters and intercommunity disputes that did not lend themselves to the development of organized resistance to the Mexican state.

Rural people in Oriente are also blessed with a number of workable alternatives to agriculture. Even as the traditional cultivation of maize, beans, and squash ceased to be viable for local self-sufficiency, rural families had other safety nets through relatively free access to nonagricultural labor in the tourist sector. Seasonal wage labor in construction and other tourism-related sectors has provided rural Yucatecan families with direct access to the cash economy since the 1970s (Castellanos 2010b; Warman 1985). The transformation of Chichén Itzá into a major world attraction has been especially important, as it created markets both for labor in the tourist sector and for the sale of artisanry that can be produced by full-time craftspeople or as a peripheral activity for agriculturalists.

Perhaps ironically, recourse to other sources of income in Oriente has diminished people's dependence on agriculture, but it has also provided additional motivations for preserving Revolutionary-era agrarian institutions. Many scholars predicted that the 1992 amendment to the Mexican Constitution, an act that allowed peasant communities to parcel and sell state-titled collective landholdings (*ejidos*), would seal the fate of a peasant sector that had enjoyed certain protections from the state throughout the post-Revolutionary period. But in the communities where I have conducted research, as in many other parts of the Mexican countryside (Castellanos 2010a; Stephen 2002), the parceling and sale of ejidos are uncommon. In the smaller villages, the cultivation of maize, beans, and squash provides a degree of security amidst the ebb and flow of the tourist market, and the local agrarian committee continues to be the principal body involved in campaigns and other local political rituals. Even in larger communities such as Pisté, the preservation of the ejido serves as a guarantee that potentially valuable real estate—given the proximity of the town to the tourist zone of Chichén Itzá—is maintained under some degree of collective local stewardship.

Religious activism, another factor that elsewhere has contributed to the formation of grassroots political networks that figure in active resistance to neoliberal reforms, has played a less obvious role in the development of explicitly ethnic politics in the communities where I have worked. The politicization of ethnic identity in response to the perceived acculturation promoted by some Protestant missionaries (Montejo 2005; Warren 1998), or in tangent with politically progressive organizing associated with both Catholic and Protestant congregations (Falla 2001; Kovic 2005; Nash 2001; Rus et al. 2003), has played a significant role in the emergence of Mayan-identified organizations in Guatemala and Chiapas. However, religious diversity seems to have a different political texture in Yucatán. There, Protestant conversion became an important factor in many communities by the 1920s, and played a major role in a series of conflicts that I will discuss at length in Chapter 2. However, there seems to be little direct correlation between the heritage of religious strife and the emergence of politicized Mayan identity. Though the Archdiocese of Yucatán has employed a number of catechistic programs to counteract the work of Protestant conversion, these make little, if any, strategic use of indigenous culture in the communities that I have studied. In Chapter 7, I will discuss a few projects by local Presbyterian congregations that have placed a special emphasis on Maya-language writing. However, I would not characterize these as "prime movers" in the politicization of indigenous identity. Given the degree to which the tourist industry is one of the prime motivators for local appropriations of indigeneity, the narratives of Maya identity that permeate these local missionary projects have a broad currency that crosscuts denominational and secular/religious divisions in these communities.

One final factor in the development—or lack—of ethnic mobilization in Oriente is the tendency for class and factional divisions to crosscut the constituency of peasant and Maya identity politics. Today there are significant economic hierarchies within the community of people who can make credible claims to Mayan identity. The tourist trade has drastically altered the economic and political organization of large towns such as Pisté and Xcalakoop, which are located near the major site of Chichén Itzá (Breglia 2006; Castañeda 1996; see also Castellanos 2010b). Though a substantial portion of both communities is dedicated to the cultivation of traditional subsistence crops, both communities are home to many full-time artisans and a large middle class composed of skilled tourism professionals. These transformations of the local economy are less evident in communities that have more limited access to work in the tourist economy, and where the majority of the residents still depend on agriculture in spite of participating in part-time labor in the tourist industry or in handicrafts production. Many of the more isolated agrarian communities become dependent satellites of larger and wealthier towns as sources of farm and forest products and cheap unskilled labor that is often exploited by rural capitalists who are themselves native speakers of Yucatec and self-identified Maya. In many of the cases that I will describe in later chapters, these divisions of class and occupation undermine the cohesion of coalitions based on use of the Maya language and other shared markers of indigeneity.

To summarize, the Maya-speaking population of rural Oriente is a diverse community with a strong investment in Mayan identity but an ambiguous relationship to many of the social and cultural markers that have defined indigenous identity politics on a national and an international level. Members of different communities share the historical experience of participating in the agrarian reform and other processes that guaranteed certain kinds of collective rights to self-identified "peasants." The tourist market and other regional economic factors have contributed to new political possibilities based on claims to the "Maya culture." But many of the economic pressures that motivated grassroots movements such as the EZLN of Chiapas seem to have been experienced less keenly in Yucatán. What's more, the economic transformations associated with tourism have also contributed to a series of class hierarchies that produce fractures and conflicts in Maya-speaking rural society. In many ways, rural people in Oriente must make sense of the possibilities of contemporary multiculturalism by negotiating between these realities and official discourses that often posit a far simpler picture of the "indigenous community."

Sources, Scope, and Objectives

Understanding how rural people in Oriente navigate the possibilities and limitations of agrarian and indigenous politics involves two sets of problems. The first regards documenting a society that is composed of diverse economic sectors, and in which community membership has historically been porous and relatively fragile. A second series of problems involves understanding the processes through which individuals learn and perform the narratives that give a tangible form to different political identities. The research that informs this book has involved a careful and ongoing negotiation of these two broad issues.

I have addressed the first of these problems by adopting a microregional approach to ethnography and history, thus incorporating a broader range of distinct experiences of peasant and Maya identity in Oriente (see Figure 1.2). This has entailed more than a decade of research in towns and villages in the municipalities of Tinúm, Chan Kom, Cuncunul, and Yaxcabá. Though all of these communities were villages of peasants in the early twentieth century, today they range considerably in size and in the internal diversification of labor sectors and class structure. The smallest of the communities that figure in this book is Popolá, a village of 200 Maya-speaking peasant agriculturalists that—at least on the surface—might remind a visitor of the "folk" villages studied by Robert Redfield in the 1920s and 1930s. The largest community in this study is Pisté, a town of around 5,000 souls strategically located near the tourist mecca of Chichén Itzá. Whereas all adults in Popolá still tilled the soil at the turn of the millennium, Pisté is home to several generations of old-money families and nouveaux riches, a merchant and a laboring middle class, unionized tour guides, taxi drivers, and a large underclass devoted solely to the production and wholesale of tourist art. Though most adults in Pisté are bilingual, children who begin primary school speaking Maya there are immediately marked as stemming from the peasant or artisan lower class. Between the extremes of Pisté and Popolá lie a number of communities that, in the words of many locals, reflect varying and debatable degrees of "culture" and "civilization."

As a microregional study, my research represents some departures from the tradition of Mesoamerican "community studies" (Hawkins 1983) that are based on extensive research in a single town or village. The communities that feature in this book

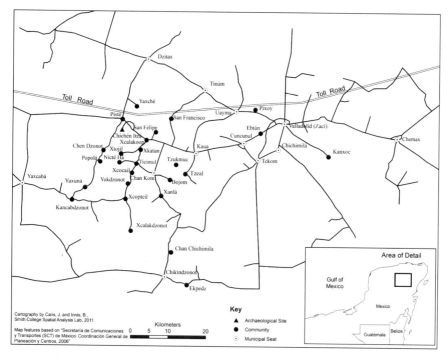

FIGURE 1.2. Map of the towns and villages of Oriente.

were selected based on their situation within a given microregion and the fact that all had left fairly equal, if thin, documentary footprints in the various archives that I consulted. My ethnographic research in the various communities was uneven. I have lived in Pisté every summer since 1997 and spent over a year there continuously from 2003 to 2004. I also spent significant time working in Popolá for several months over two summers. I have had extensive interactions with people in Xcalakoop in the municipality of Tinúm, where I taught English for a summer and have many friends and acquaintances. More recently, since 2007, I have been engaged in extensive collaborative fieldwork with the *ejidatarios* of Xcalakdzonot. However, my direct research in other communities—such as Kaua, Ticimul, Nicté Há, and Xkatun—has been limited to a few interviews and brief stays. My knowledge of some of the communities that figure in this book, Chan Kom and Xtojil, for instance, is based almost entirely on archival materials, oral news gathered from sources in other communities, and a few secondary sources.

In the end, the social dynamics of this part of Yucatán both justified a microregional study and facilitated the gathering of data about a number of different communities.

Writing about roughly the same communities in the 1920s, Robert Redfield and Alfonso Villa Rojas (1934) defined this microregion as a "folk state" that represented the geographic boundaries of the world that were familiar to the residents of individual villages. Whether selling livestock or produce, attending masses, burying their dead in consecrated ground, or visiting relatives, residents of any given village in the so-called folk state were likely to have extensive ties with people in other communities. This is still the case, particularly as growing numbers of rural people seek temporary work in the tourist industry focused on the ruins of Chichén Itzá. As will be evident in Chapters 2 and 3, Redfield's folk state was marked by a striking degree of internal mobility and migration at the beginning of the 1900s, with villages splitting apart as some families sought their fortunes in unclaimed stretches of bush. In fact, the very notion of "the closed, corporate community" (Wolf 1959), a mainstay of Mesoamericanist ethnography, is often difficult to reconcile with the reality of settlement patterns in this part of Yucatán (see especially Alexander 2006).

The second problem to which I alluded at the beginning of this section, understanding the processes through which individuals learn and employ narratives that give a tangible form to political identity, also reflects a recurrent part of my own experience in the field. My movement between the archive and contemporary engagements between rural people and multicultural institutions brought a series of fascinating historical continuities and transformations into sharp relief. Days after wading through a sheaf of moldy papers that chronicled the application for a land grant that had taken place almost eighty years earlier, I might speak to an artisan who was applying for federal funds for the maintenance of traditional crafts. On a number of occasions, I sat in on meetings of handicrafts cooperatives and community agrarian associations that were seeking a range of development grants. More than once, I was asked to take dictation or to type and print letters to be sent to agencies that ranged from a regional handicrafts association known as the Casa de las Artesanías to the office of the governor of the state.

In some sense, the letters that were composed on my computer screen were quite different from those written in the 1920s and 1930s. The terms "Mayans" and "Mayan agriculturalist" are common now, but were virtually nonexistent in documents written by representatives of local communities during the first two-thirds of the twentieth century. The nature of the transactions referred to in these letters—soliciting legal title to collective lands in the 1920s versus providing tools for carving handicrafts to sell to tourists at the turn of the millennium—also reflected some of the ways in which the economic realities of these communities had changed. Still, there were other elements of these letters that were remarkably consistent across decades and generations. One of the most striking continuities was the use of a collective voice, a

"We," to address representatives of the state. Whether in the agrarian committees of the 1920s or in the more vaguely defined "Mayan communities" of today, the power of these territorial and political entities is based on their status as corporations that address the state in a voice of organic consensus. Letters from both time periods tend to represent the responsibilities of the state as part of a pact in which the need of the local corporate group and its willingness to work toward improvement oblige urban officials to provide certain materials.

Many of these continuities reflect a relationship between the written and spoken word that plays an important role in the political culture of rural Oriente, which I will discuss in more detail in Chapter 3. I first got a sense of the mechanisms that motivated this relationship between speech and writing during a series of observations that I made of a honey-production cooperative in the village of Popolá. Many adults and young children in Popolá are monolingual in Maya. In keeping with local custom, every letter received from the state office in charge of disbursing funds for the honey cooperative—like every letter written by the secretary in the name of the local agrarian committee members—was carefully examined in the presence of the entire group. One of the better-educated young men in the cooperative first read every document out loud in Spanish, and then explicated it in Maya. This was followed by a period of commentary and debate, after which consensus was reached.

This kind of ritualistic reading of letters and other bureaucratic texts was a common occurrence in my ethnographic experience. I had a very personal encounter with the document-reading ritual in 2007, when I began to conduct collaborative research on landscape memory with the ejidatarios of the village of Xcalakdzonot, a process that required a series of negotiations with the agrarian committee to gain access to their collective lands. The accord that I signed with the ejidatarios in 2008—a document based on an Institutional Review Board Non-Medical Human Subjects Protocol that detailed the access and obligations my coresearchers and I would have while working in the ejido—includes a list of those present and voting at the meeting, along with their signatures or thumbprints. The names of all the signers—including mine and those of the other researchers—were read out loud at the close of the meeting by the secretary of the agrarian committee. Similar lists of names, signatures, and thumbprints are appended to most of the petitions that I saw in the archive, which are dated from the 1920s to 1940s. Those texts were probably read aloud in the same way, for the benefit of committee members who could not read and write.

Political rituals like this become an important site of contact between the bureaucratic protocols of statist institutions, such as the agrarian reform, and the oral narratives that manifest collective identity in more quotidian spaces.[9] For example, many of the oral narratives that I have recorded about the foundation of ejidos in the 1920s and 1930s cite specific letters and transactions with urban bureaucrats. They even include detailed lists of the names of the different individuals who were involved, producing an effect much like the reading of signatures at the end of letters. In a number of examples that I will discuss later, this kind of parallel between the written and spoken word plays a central role in how individuals establish their own credibility or narrative authority by referencing bureaucratic procedures that have a formal legal charge. More often than not, this carefully honed drive to establish the kind of credibility that will hold up in legal proceedings or in the courts of public opinion is a defining factor in even the most quotidian statements about Maya identity.

Summary

Throughout this book, I will look at the social contexts in which oral and written texts are performed as a key site in which rural people in Oriente come into contact with state-sanctioned identity politics. Just as written texts become irrefutable and legally binding testaments to collective pacts with the state, oral narratives invoke this aura of sanctity in more spontaneous and ephemeral contexts. When people talk about emergent forms of Mayan identity politics, they employ many tropes, genres, and stories that already have a venerable history in earlier iterations of the relationship between rural Maya speakers and the Mexican state. Many of the same narratives have had a complex life cycle in which they figure in the different realities of twentieth-century agrarianism and twenty-first-century multiculturalism. Given the ambiguity of many key identity labels, these stories can also function alternatively as tools for creating communal solidarity or for drawing factional divisions.

In the next chapter, I will turn to the foundation of ejidos in the 1920s. As a legal and bureaucratic process that transformed the political geography of Oriente, this development plays a crucial role in the collective memory of interactions between local people and the Mexican state and in the imagining of new forms of collective rights. A complex interplay of family loyalties, state-sanctioned bureaucratic protocols, and indigenous forms of landscape perception, this process also set an early standard for the interplay between factionalism and solidarity that is a recurrent theme in the identity politics of Oriente.

Notes

1. The first generation of Mayanist ethnographers observed how the communities that they identified as "Maya Indians" tended to characterize themselves simply as "Indians" or "peasants," by the name of their town, or with a host of other locally relevant social categories (Gabbert 2004; Tax 1937). For scholars in the 1990s, the fact that people in the same com-

munities were explicitly self-identifying as "Mayas" for the first time reflected new kinds of "strategic essentialism" (Fischer 1999; Fischer and Brown 1997; Spivak 1987; Warren 1998) and "tactical" appropriation of anthropological narratives by Maya-speaking communities (Castañeda 1996; Nelson 1999).

2. For a discussion of Chiapas, see Mattiace 2003. For a good ethnographic study of similar processes in Chiapas, see Stephen 2002.

3. This is a phenomenon that I have elsewhere referred to as "non-disruptive ambiguity" (Armstrong-Fumero 2009a). When the semantic flexibility that characterized this kitchen table discussion is transposed into the context of dialogues between rural Yucatecans and urban representatives of government institutions, this phenomenon parallels the kinds of intercultural interactions that the colonial historian James Lockhart has referred to as "double mistaken identity." Lockhart (1999) observed how the descendants of the Aztecs and Spanish colonists in sixteenth- and seventeenth-century Mexico had fundamentally different notions of community and governance, even as both groups were complicit in the emergence of a fairly stable and long-lasting series of political institutions. Likewise, individuals in rural Yucatán, and the urban Mexicans and foreigners with whom they interact, often have very different understandings of what "community," "Maya culture," and the like mean. But these ambiguities did relatively little to hinder the consolidation of a series of key "peasant" institutions in the early twentieth century, or the more recent participation of rural Yucatecans in a range of multicultural institutions.

4. A number of foreign and creole authors attributed the magnificent ruins of Chichén Itzá and Uxmal to an extinct race that had been exterminated by the inherently "barbarous" ancestors of the Yucatecan Indians. This narrative seems to have appealed to Sierra O'Reilly and other writers who saw the Spanish conquest as the "natural" ascendancy of the Hispanic race. These writers identified this ascendancy amid the decline of the Indians, who had themselves exterminated the ruin builders. After the Caste War and the disastrous defeat of Mexico in the 1846–48 war with the United States, this same model became the basis for anxious musings about the fate of Yucatán's "white" race as the Anglo-Saxon neighbor to the north emerged as a regional power. These anxieties were eloquently expressed by Sierra O'Reilly himself during this especially trying period. In 1846, Yucatán was a provisionally independent republic after a protracted conflict with the Mexican regime of Santa Ana, and Sierra O'Reilly was sent to Washington to seek recognition from the United States Congress. A year later, after the outbreak of the Caste War, he received orders to make an ultimately unsuccessful bid to have Yucatán annexed to the United States in return for military aid. Faced with the humiliating defeat of Santa Ana's armies in Mexico and the seemingly impending doom of his own Hispanic Yucatecan civilization, he wrote:

> It has been three centuries since the Spanish race, after having been the strongest, proudest and
> most vigorous, has been walking the path of degradation and defeat. That race, adulterated a bit
> in México where a soft climate and the ease of making a living has helped make it meek and sloth-
> ful, that race has begun to take its end. The stupendous and incredible triumphs of the Americans
> can almost not be explained in any other way . . .

The providential destiny of the United States will be fulfilled sooner or later, the same with Mexico, it is only a matter of time. Peoples [Sp. *los pueblos*] are not like individuals in this respect: the life of the peoples is longer, as is their infancy, their puberty, their virility and decadence. And how rare are those peoples that, upon reaching the last period, are able to regenerate themselves! (Sierra O'Reilly 2002, 43)

5. As I noted earlier, many Mexicanist scholars associate the emergence of grassroots indigenous identity movements and official multiculturalism with a set of transnational processes that transformed the Mexican state in the last decades of the twentieth century. This is by now a familiar narrative, focused on the decay of a powerful bureaucratic and ideological apparatus that had legitimated an essentially authoritarian state for seventy years. The concatenation of modernizing projects, peasant-and-worker corporatism, and political patronage generated popular loyalty for the official party (the PRI), which itself guaranteed peaceful electoral transitions while limiting the participation of oppositional groups. Popular dissent grew in the 1970s, when the more authoritarian mechanisms built into the PRI were increasingly criticized by Left-leaning scholars, activists and students, and as middle-class Mexicans experienced a steady decline in their standard of living. The last three PRI presidents began a series of political and economic reforms that paved the way for the transformations still under way after the turn of the millennium. The administrations of Miguel de la Madrid (1982–88) and Carlos Salinas de Gortari (1988–94) sought to curb an economic downturn with a range of neoliberal interventions that included decentralizing a massive federal apparatus, privatizing a number of previously state-run sectors, and negotiating the North American Free Trade Agreement (Ai Camp 2002; Aguilar Camín and Meyer 1993; Rodríguez 1997; Russel 1994; Turner 2002). These reforms included a 1992 revision to the Constitution that permitted peasant communities to parcel and sell their state-titled collective landholdings, undermining the material and symbolic pact that had bound rural communities in Yucatán to the state since the decades after the Revolution. But even if these neoliberal reforms gained international praise and initially succeeded in curbing inflation, accusations of electoral fraud and corruption haunted the PRI. When Ernesto Zedillo, the last PRI president, took office in 1994, he inherited a new financial shock that undid many of the gains of the previous administrations, as well as an armed rebellion by the Ejército Zapatista de Liberación Nacional (EZLN) in the state of Chiapas.

6. In this sense, oral narratives in Maya or Spanish told in these communities are often very consistent with a Revolutionary nationalism in which communitarian ideals were rooted in a dual commitment to popular sovereignty and material or intellectual progress (see Bonfil-Batalla 1987; Córdova 1973; Gamio 1916; Knight 1997; Tenorio-Trillo 2009).

7. The evolution of the movement is itself telling of the processes that facilitated the reformulation of early twentieth-century populism into the idiom of indigenous ethnic politics. The EZLN originated as an essentially agrarian movement based on a coalition between radicalized intellectuals from Mexico City and local peasant organizations. The timing of the revolt, on January 1, 1994, was meant to coincide with the start date of the NAFTA agreement, as a protest against the undermining of Revolutionary-era institutions that served as an

important social safety net for peasants. Hopelessly outgunned but symbolically powerful, the EZLN entered into negotiations with the Mexican government that transformed the members into icons of grassroots politics in Mexico and abroad, in spite of the ultimate breakdown of talks by 2001 (Collier and Quaratiello 2005; López Bárcenas 2005; Nash 2001).

8. Mattiace (2009) makes a vague reference to how "ecological conditions" made communities in the maize zone as dependent on federal subsidies as those in the henequen zone. I am not certain what she means by this, but what will become clear from my discussion in later chapters is that the relative absence of large plantations at the beginning of the twentieth century made the course of post-Revolutionary agriculture in Oriente very different from the better-studied case of the henequen zone. Similar correlations between the retention of landholdings and the emergence and development of collective action have also been documented in other parts of Mexico, as in the study of 1930s Michoacán by Purnell (1999).

9. From a more abstract theoretical perspective, the role that this tradition of written and oral narrative plays in shaping different local experiments in identity politics suggests some insights into the nature of agency in local communities like those of Oriente. Borrowing from Valentin Voloshinov, Raymond Williams, and other Marxian scholars of language and literature (see Jameson 1972; Williams 1977; Voloshinov 1973), we can view the formal elements of oral narrative as materialized signs that are distinguished more by their tangible presence in social space than by their semantic content in any given act of communication. That is, the meaning that people ascribe to such words as "culture" and "community" might change or become ambiguous, but the narratives in which these terms are uttered have a fairly unequivocal presence in human experience through the social and material processes of talking and writing. From this perspective, the choices or strategies of individuals and groups aren't the only site of agency that shapes political mobilizations. The narrative repertoire that makes political identities intelligible, a repertoire that is often inherited from the very different realities of an earlier moment in history, frequently exercises its own powerful influence in the styles of doing politics that are sayable and thinkable.

This theoretical observation suggests some methodological principles for approaching the history of vernacular narrative. At the same time that the semantic content of terms like "culture" is flexible and subject to a range of tactical manipulations, the mechanisms that produce regularities in form can be found in concrete social behaviors, for example, the different sites where letters are composed, read out loud, and translated. Following Greg Urban and Michael Silverstein as well as other students of speech genre, we can see these sites as spaces of "entextualization" (Sherzer 1987; Silverstein and Urban 1996; see also Briggs and Bauman 1992). This term refers to the real-world contexts in which the socially regimented interaction of different individuals influences the ways in which they speak and write, creating regularities that turn specific utterances into examples of recognizable textual genres. In the case of letters written to different government agencies in the early twentieth century and the present day, this site of entextualization includes the various public settings in which letters are composed and performed. Continuities in the formal textual elements of letters—the fact that older and younger people are familiar with these political rituals, and so forth—suggest certain kinds of ethnographic analogy that can be used to flesh out the kinds of social contexts that contemporary multicultural politics shares with the corporatist agrarian politics of the past.

2

"How It Happened That We Fomented This Town"

Tensions between Family Autonomy and Community Solidarity during the Agrarian Reform

The story of twentieth-century identity politics in Oriente begins with the redistribution of land. In the 1920s a mixed state and federal bureaucracy instituted procedures through which communities could gain legal recognition and protection of the lands on which they lived and raised crops. This reform established a series of formally recognized, bounded territories referred to as *ejidos*, which were controlled collectively by communities of peasants. The peasants' previous means of claiming these lands had ranged from colonial-era documents to the simple act of occupying tracts that had been abandoned by the previous occupants. These claims were subsumed into a new system of titling that privileged claims based on usufruct, or on the current productive use of a given stretch of territory. Just as important, the agrarian reform of the 1920s fostered a series of vernacular ideas about citizenship and political

23

DOI: 10.5876/9781607322399.c02

participation in which self-identifying with the collective demands of a specific community became a crucial dimension of political participation.

That said, this reform brought about a tension between solidarity and factionalism that emerged consistently in different mobilizations of state-sanctioned identity. The realities of community membership and territoriality in Oriente were distinct from those in other parts of the state of Yucatán, and were often quite different from the image of the agrarian community that urban politicians had had in mind. The ambiguities that emerged between the state-sanctioned models of community membership and the realpolitik of agriculture and territoriality enabled many local factions to strike out on their own and fragment the territorial and demographic base of their home communities. In this sense, this key moment in the history of identity politics in Oriente was consistent with a pattern of tensions between solidarity and factionalism that would be a recurring theme in the region.

The ambivalence of the agrarian reform stems in part from the sometimes awkward relationship between notions of territoriality that were recognized by the Mexican state and traditional, Maya-language ways of naming and occupying places. Many of these tensions are still evident in the settlement patterns and collective memory of communities such as Xcalakdzonot, in the municipality of Chan Kom. A large village of around a thousand souls, Xcalakdzonot is both a discretely bounded political and territorial entity and a collection of named places that have existed more or less autonomously at different points in time. The community was first recognized as a bounded ejido in 1929, after the completion of an application by its residents. This act was quickly followed by the recognition of the village as a dependency (Sp. *comisaría*) of the municipal seat of Cuncunul.[1]

The village's name, which translates roughly as "Two Cenotes Next to Each Other," hints at a somewhat different dimension of local experiences with the landscape, one in which the ejido and other discretely bounded territorial entities play a less consistent role. The name refers to a geological feature several hundred meters from the church and municipal buildings that were constructed from the 1920s to 1950s. This place was settled in the beginning of the twentieth century by the grandparents and great-grandparents of those who live there today, the last in a series of populations that had settled and abandoned the site over several centuries. Their descendants, identified as "People from the Twin Cenotes" (Ma. *Xcalakdzonotilo'ob*), were not, however, the only "community" living within the boundaries of the ejido that was founded in 1929 and named after their settlement. Today, a series of winding bush trails links the core of the village to San Nicolás, Akula, Xtakejil, Siete Pilas, Chan Ichmul, and other more distant sites, each of which contains water sources and other necessities for human habitation. Each of these named places has also been home to human settlements in the past, some populated in recent decades. In the 1920s and 1930s, the residents of some of these other settlements considered themselves to be largely autonomous, not connected to the people settled at the Twin Cenotes, even if it was considered to be the residential and administrative seat of the ejido in which they grew crops. The residents of one of these settlements, known as San Nicolás (X-Lab Kaj), would later challenge the territorial integrity of the ejido of Xcalakdzonot in a conflict to which I will refer several times in this book.

The conflict that emerged at Xcalakdzonot, along with others like it, reflects a tension between two modes of understanding territory and landscape. One is an indigenous tradition of migration and settlement in which small and usually family-based factions can lay a more or less autonomous claim to places that have been abandoned and left fallow for generations. The residents of these small settlements were often bound to other agrarian communities through blood and friendship, but retained a strong sense of independence in their economic activities. In contrast, the agrarian reform constituted the ejido as a rationalizing process through which populations that met a minimum size requirement—usually thirty households—could stake claims on enough land to meet their subsistence needs. Implicit in this process was the creation of communities that would grow in population and that had a degree of long-term stability. This assumption was often difficult to reconcile with rural agriculturalists' desire to seek out better resources as families or smaller factional groups.

The encounter between these two territorial logics produced different effects in different communities. In some cases, it allowed factions within larger communities to carve out their own autonomous claims within a more expansive traditional territory. In other cases—those of Xcalakdzonot and San Nicolás, for instance—families that had settled in different named places forged pragmatic alliances, making a joint application as members of a single "community" that met the size criteria of the agrarian reform.

The complicated and often tense relationship between the desires of official agrarian institutions to incorporate rural populations and the periodic migrations that mark local forms of land use touches on some themes that have been prominent in the recent history and ethnography of Mesoamerica. Many of these studies have stressed how the ability of rural agriculturalists and urban officials to reconcile different modes of understanding space and territory has contributed to both the transformation of land-use regimes and the survival of forms of corporate identity in indigenous communities since the colonial period.[2] However, the cases that I will focus on here highlight an element of this process that is often downplayed in studies that emphasize the central role that collective decision-making and identity have for indigenous peoples. In my own examples, the dialogue between two different ways of approaching territoriality could also create the conditions in which factional conflicts and individual ambitions unraveled communities and larger coalitions.

For the sake of clarity, I will refer to several intertwined phenomena under the broad rubrics of political geography, vernacular forms of landscape use, and factional strategies. By "political geography," I am referring to the formal territorial divisions that were inherited from the colonial period and nineteenth century and that underpin the redefinition of political boundaries after the Mexican Revolution. These spatial hierarchies, like the bureaucratic protocols involved in asserting land title before urban authorities, were familiar to rural Maya speakers in Oriente at the time of the agrarian reform. But when I use the phrase "vernacular forms of landscape use," I will be referring to the somewhat different ways of interacting with the physical environment that were conditioned by Maya-language spatial categories and a collective memory of different places in the bush.[3] Transmitted primarily through oral narratives, this local knowledge often assumed a more fluid relationship between territory, history, and the connections between people and named places. It also enabled a process by which families and factions could seek greater autonomy in their means of subsistence by settling previously abandoned sites. Mediating between the state-sanctioned definition of territory and the desire for family-based autonomy involved a series of factional strategies that turned Oriente's agrarian reform into a paradoxical blend of collective mobilization and social fragmentation.

These developments in the 1920s and 1930s are especially important for later experiences of identity politics, given the degree to which the ejido committee was one of the most important political institutions of twentieth-century Oriente and continues to form the basic body politic of many small agrarian communities. The processes of land titling and settlement on which I focus here have been a factor in experiences of dozens of individual communities in the thirteen municipalities that make up Oriente, and thus provide a language for "doing politics" (Sp. *hacer política*) that is widely intelligible in the microregion. Though the examples that I will discuss most closely involve the experiences of fewer than a dozen communities, they reflect the potentials for solidarity and fission that were built into the local structure of the agrarian reform and that have important parallels in the development of ethnic identity politics generations later.

Oriente in the Political Geography of Yucatán

The ejidos and other territorial units established through the agrarian reform did not appear in a historical or social vacuum. The settlement patterns of rural agriculturalists, like the situation of these settlements in relation to the urban world, are consistent with a series of spatial hierarchies that developed through the colonial period and nineteenth century. One of the most distinctive features of the political geography of colonial and postcolonial Yucatán is decentralization or local autonomy. Compared with the better-known examples of the Aztec and Inca empires, the political landscape of Yucatán immediately before Spanish conquest (ca. 1441 to 1541) was fragmented into more than a dozen small polities that the Spanish referred to as "provinces." The conquest of this mosaic of autonomous statelets involved a long and drawn-out series of expeditions, and large areas in the south and east of the peninsula remained under only nominal Spanish control throughout the sixteenth and seventeenth centuries.[4] With few resources other than land and labor for maize and cattle agriculture, Yucatán remained a colonial backwater with a relatively weak infrastructure. Internal markets and political life were marked by the relative autonomy of the five "little fatherlands" (Sp. *patrias chicas*) of Campeche, Mérida, Valladolid, Bacalar, and the Sierra.

If the political geography of colonial Yucatán was marked by the relative autonomy of several microregions, it also involved a clear hierarchy between an "Indian" countryside and a "European" city. The Spanish conquerors wasted little time in formally titling strategic settlements as the "cities" of San Francisco de Campeche (1540), Mérida (1542), Valladolid (1543, relocated in 1545), and Salamanca de Bacalar (1545). Campeche, Mérida, Valladolid, and Bacalar would remain provincial and relatively sparse in population through much of the colonial period (Farriss 1984, 29–39). But as planned settlements modeled on the Renaissance ideal, they were imagined as a space in which the conquerors and their descendants could enjoy a civilized life, and from which spiritual and moral enlightenment could expand into the "Indian" periphery.[5]

A parallel series of processes took place in the countryside, as the forced resettlement of small agrarian hamlets into larger "reductions" (Sp. *reducciones*) facilitated religious conversion and the collection of tribute. The range of local ethnonyms that Yucatec Maya speakers had applied to themselves was subsumed under the ethnic and juridical category of "Indian" (Gabbert 2004). But in spite of these changes, Spanish colonial institutions also enabled the continuity of pre-Hispanic practices and social structures (Restall 1997). Though they were under the religious jurisdiction of Spanish priests and owed tribute to descendants of the original conquerors (Sp. *encomenderos*) until well into the eighteenth century, territories known as Indian republics (Sp. *Repúblicas de Indios*) were governed by local leaders. Many of these leaders were descended from the pre-Hispanic nobility (Ma. *almeheno'ob*). Spaniards, enslaved or free Africans, and people of all other "castes" were prohibited from settling within the Repúblicas, and certain legal protections of community lands were at least nominally observed by Spanish administrators and clergy (Restall 1997; see also Bracamonte y Sosa and Solís Robleda 1996).

Some traces of this colonial territorial and ethnic division played a significant role in the agrarian reform of Oriente. For example, the traditional land titles of the community of Ebtún, many of which refer to parts of the territory that the town had controlled as a colonial-era República de Indios, came into political play several times from the 1920s to 1940s. But by the beginning of the twentieth century, many of the central institutions that had maintained colonial land tenure had been undermined by liberal reforms.[6] One persistent theme in this liberal discourse on land was the assumption that Maya-speaking subsistence agriculturalists were inherently "idle" and made inefficient use of lands that could be put to more "rational" use if dedicated to commercial agriculture that would be directed by Hispanic landowners. Another assumption was that inducing "idle" rural people to work in commercial agriculture would provide much-needed moral uplift (Campos 2003; Guemez Piñeda 1994; Quezada and Yam 2003). Rural Maya speakers were not simply passive objects of this discourse, even though it tended to undermine forms of corporate land tenure that had been common for centuries. For example, Paul Eiss has documented cases in the mid-nineteenth century in which rural communities used a similar discourse on the moralizing effects of labor when advancing their own claims to collectively held lands (Eiss 2010, 34–36). As I will discuss further below, pragmatic appropriations of this liberal discourse form an important part of the vernacular ideas about territoriality that rural Maya speakers brought to their engagement with the agrarian reform in Oriente.

Even as Yucatecan liberals sought to undermine the collective landholdings that many indigenous communities had enjoyed since the sixteenth century,[7] regional elites had a more ambivalent relationship to the heritage of colonial ethnic categories. Whereas ideas of "rationalization" were applied to land tenure early on, policies that reinforced the second-class status of citizens labeled as Indians continued to have legal and political currency through much of the nineteenth century.[8] Not surprisingly, this process was experienced by rural Maya speakers as the loss of traditional privilege without a significant gain in citizenship rights. Tensions between liberal development and indigenous subsistence prompted a rise in the incidence of rural unrest beginning in the eighteenth century (Patch 2002; Reed 1962; Rugeley 1996; Sullivan 1989), a phenomenon that would come to a head in the massive 1847 uprising known as the Caste War.

Many of the distinctive notions of indigeneity that exist in contemporary Yucatán were shaped by the heritage of the Caste War (Gabbert 2004). Often referred to as "barbarian" (Sp. *bárbaros*) or "wild" (Sp. *bravos*), communities in eastern Yucatán and the territories that form the contemporary state of Quintana Roo maintained a great degree of political autonomy well into the twentieth century. The people of these autonomous zones tended to be identified with the pejorative label of Indian. Rural Maya speakers who lived closer to the core political and economic regions around Mérida were often referred to as *mestizos* (Gabbert 2004, 60–63). This particular distinction between Indian and mestizo also reflected a difference in the subsistence activities of different microregions. Whereas the east was a "maize zone" dominated by peasant cultivation of corn, beans, and squash (Warman 1985), the mestizos of the west became rural proletarians in the hacienda economy of the later nineteenth century.

The rise of a henequen monocrop industry in the later nineteenth century contributed to a deepening of these distinctions between the rural people of the west and east of the state. For centuries, henequen, an indigenous spiny agave, had been processed to make ropes and twine. The crop thrives in the rocky and dry soils of the north and west. There it became the basis of a massive industry, particularly after the invention of a class of popular wheat-harvesting machines in the United States generated a seemingly endless demand for vegetable-based binder twine (Cámara Zavala 1953; Joseph 1985). Peasants in the henequen zone were pulled into an economy that produced unprecedented levels of wealth and urban development for an elite based in the capital of Mérida. By the beginning of the Mexican Revolution, the majority of rural people in this part of the state were proletarians bound by contracts or debts to vast haciendas owned by absentee landlords (Joseph 1985, 26–32; Wells 1985). Things were very different in Oriente. Even though the military defeat of the autonomous Maya polity of Chan Santa Cruz in 1901 brought an effective end to the Caste War, the development of the hacienda economy in the south and east continued to lag far behind that of the henequen zone. This distinction implied that many rural communities still enjoyed relatively free access to land on which to practice subsistence agriculture.

The freer access to land in Oriente—like the tendency of families to preserve subsistence cultivation of maize, beans, and squash—shaped the relationship that these communities would develop with the post-Revolutionary government of Mexico. This relationship is particularly evident in how the 1917 constitutional article that instituted the ejido was applied there. In the henequen zone, resistance from landed interests hampered the redistribution of lands planted with the valuable cash crop, which did not take place on a significant scale until the later 1930s (Fallaw 2001). Even then, community management of these lands was limited by a dependence on government credits and a parastatal that managed exports (Baños Ramírez 1978; Benítez 1956; Fallaw 2004; Mattiace 2009). In maize zones such as Oriente, the relatively marginal role of landed estates meant that agrarian communities faced considerably less resistance to collective land claims. Most of the communities that figure in this study had formal title to their land by the late 1920s, and seem to have had relatively unhindered access to these lands even decades earlier.

Migration was another important factor in early twentieth-century Oriente. For many towns and villages, the official titling of their lands followed closely on the heels of the foundation of new settlements. In their classic ethnographic study of Chan Kom, Robert Redfield and Alfonso Villa Rojas (1934) observed that the village was founded as part of a general movement of peasants to the east and south of the peninsula (see also Alexander 2006). These agriculturalists were, in effect, repopulating areas that had been sparsely inhabited for generations after the Caste War.[9] Thus, by the 1920s the different communities that made up the society of Oriente had different degrees of time depth in their current territories. Some, such as the colonial town of Ebtún, had maintained substantial populations throughout the nineteenth century and laid claim to extensive traditional landholdings that were renegotiated through the agrarian reform (Alexander 2010). Others, such as Pisté, were largely abandoned amid the chaos of the Caste War, and were only gradually repopulated during the second half of the nineteenth century.[10] Others still, such as Chan Kom and dozens of similarly sized villages, experienced the agrarian reform as their first formal recognition by the federal and state governments. But in all of these cases, the formal protocols that were implemented through the agrarian reform entered into an often ambiguous dialogue with a body of vernacular landscape knowledge. More than a map of discretely bounded landholdings, this local knowledge reflected a shared heritage of ecological adaptations, the temporality of swidden agriculture, and a tendency of families or factions to explore sites for autonomous production.

Remembered Places and Dynamic Landscapes

The kinds of discrete boundaries that determined the extent of twentieth-century ejidos also figure in Maya-language narratives on territory, for example colonial land titles that describe the positioning of different tracts by narrating a walking tour of their borders (see Restall 1997; Roys 1983). However, particularly in the oral narratives that are told today, there are other dimensions of vernacular landscape perception that focus on the relative position of more vaguely bounded named places whose social and ecological statuses change over time. Like the landscape within the boundaries of the ejido of Xcalakdzonot, all of Oriente is dotted with toponyms that refer to wells or natural landscape features. After several cycles of abandonment and settlement, the exact boundaries of former territories faded from the collective memory.

What survives is knowledge of the name and location of the specific feature that gave the site its name, and stories about events that transpired there in the past.

Even the most basic Maya toponyms convey a considerable amount of information about the history and resources of a given place. Many sites that are currently populated or remembered by rural Yucatecans are named after a Catholic saint (e.g., San Rigoberto, to the east of Tinúm, or San Fabian, a settlement just outside of Xcalakoop). Traditionally, such names are chosen based on the patron saint of the day on which excavations for a well succeed in breaking through to water. Thus, places named for saints will contain at least one artificially excavated well. It is even more common for toponyms to be fairly matter-of-fact descriptions of some feature of the landscape (Xcalakdzonot, "two cenotes next to each other") or local flora and fauna (Xcocail, "firefly place"; Xtakejil, "deer dung place"). Some of these toponyms appear to have existed since the colonial period, or appear to refer to private properties that were abandoned or ceded to larger towns. Others toponyms could be of more recent origin, names that were given in the nineteenth or twentieth century to sites where a single peasant family farmed for a few seasons, or appear to promising-looking spots discovered while hunting.

Though toponyms tend to be preserved over time, the exact status of these places shifts across three broad Maya-language categories. At different points in its history, a named place can be a residential center (*kaj*), agricultural field (*kool*), or bush (*k'aax*) (Alexander 2006; Eiss 2010; Gabbert 2004; Hanks 1990; Quintal et al. 2003; Redfield and Villa Rojas 1934; Restall 1997). *Kaj* (pl. *kajo'ob*), a term often used as a literal translation of the Spanish *pueblo*, is a place where families are currently living, sleeping, and eating, and raising chickens, turkeys, pigs, and other small livestock. A related term, *kajtal* (pl. *kajtalo'ob*), refers to smaller settlements that tend to be satellites of a larger kaj, though they possess considerable autonomy in their production and use of land. The difference between a kajtal and a kaj is not simply one of size, but also one of permanence. Whereas kajtal usually refers to a household cluster that may be abandoned when its inhabitants move closer to new agricultural fields, a kaj community will have a central square (*k'iwik*) and usually additional kinds of public architecture.[11]

The colonial historian Matthew Restall has written at length about the central role that the kaj played in the lives of colonial Maya people, as both a unit of political administration and a source of collective identity (Restall 1997, 13–40). This role persisted through the nineteenth and twentieth centuries (Eiss 2010; Gabbert 2004), both through the role of kajo'ob in municipal government and in the tendency of people to identify primarily as residents of one kaj or another. Today, rural Maya speakers identify with the kaj in which they were born, appending the suffix *il* to the name of their native community. For example, someone might refer to a woman born and raised in Xcalakoop with the sentence "That woman is *xcalakoopil* [i.e., a native of Xcalakoop]" (*Xcalak'oopil le kolelo'*). Even if this woman moved to Xkatun, Pisté, or another neighboring community, she would always be considered xcalakoo-pil by her new neighbors. A range of popular metaphors for membership in a given kaj, including "having buried your umbilical cord" there (*Ts'o'ok a mukik a tuch*) or drunk the water of its wells, associate kaj membership with rituals accompanying childbirth and the basic life functions. Despite the fact that these metaphors—like the tendency of people to identify with the kaj of their birth throughout the course of their life—reflect the intense sentimentality and loyalty that are often associated with place, the examples that I will discuss below suggest some ways in which the association between individuals and specific kajo'ob could be surprisingly fragile and flexible in the territorial politics of Oriente.

If *kaj* and *kajtal* refer to settlements with varying degrees of public space, *kool* refers to swidden fields used for the production of the staples corn, beans and squash, and minor cultivations of tubers and vegetables. The activities and time investment vary depending on the time of year. The land is cleared in the winter in anticipation of a planned burn that takes place from March to May. The timing of this burn is crucial, as it must be completed and the seeds planted before the coming of seasonal rains, usually in late June or July. The summer rainy season is spent in weeding and cutting secondary growth. Different varieties of corn ripen at different times and are used at different stages of maturation, so harvesting tends to be a gradual process lasting from September into early winter. The number of years that corn, beans, squash, and other cultivars can be raised in a kool can vary depending on soil quality, but a given kool will generally produce one harvest a year for two or three successive years.

After the final harvest of a given kool, the land must be fallowed for extended peri-ods during which former agricultural fields revert to *k'aax*. K'aax is the territory that is least frequented by humans, but is still a source of economic utility and sentimental attachment. Women often venture into k'aax to gather firewood and wild herbs, and men go there to hunt and to gather construction material or sacred substances to be used in rituals. Up until the last third of the twentieth century, cattle were left to pasture in stretches of k'aax that had been fenced off.

The shifting transformation of places from k'aax to kool was one of the primary motivators for the patterns of movement that were common at the time of the agrar-ian reform. In the past, when population numbers were lower, the movement of whole communities in search of better agricultural land helped the long-term sus-tainability of swidden agriculture (Warman 1985). After many cycles of cultivation and fallowing, when the most viable agricultural lands are farther and farther from the residential core of the kaj, families and factions within the community might begin to contemplate the possibility of striking out to found a new kajtal settlement. If these places are populated for multiple generations, the residents are likely to identify them as their native kaj.

These small-scale migrations did not take place into *terra nullius;* the spaces that were resettled were almost always associated with some historical memory of previous occupancy. Though many kajo'ob and kajtalo'ob that had been abandoned in the nineteenth century had reverted to k'aax by the 1920s, knowledge of the names, locations, and general features of these places was preserved through oral narrative. In this regard, the territorial identity of rural Maya speakers in contemporary Oriente is closely associated with knowledge of the landscape and its history of human habitation, but is not necessarily tied to multigenerational residence in a single place. This presents an important contrast to the identity of other Mayan peoples, such as the Tzotzil-speaking Zinacantecos and Chamulas of highland Chiapas, whose mythological and ritual cycles link the souls of community members, elements of the regional landscape, and municipal shrines to events that took place at the time of creation (Gossen 1998; Vogt 1974). Tales about supernatural forces in the bush are common in Yucatán as well, but oral narratives about the foundation of the communities where I have conducted research tend to be fairly secular affairs. Rather than referring to events at the time of creation, the rural Maya speakers whom I have asked about the foundation of their community almost inevitably refer to the creation of new settlements in the early twentieth century, the granting of collective title to ejido lands, and the foundation of schools.

The centrality of ejido foundation in rural people's sense of territoriality is important in a number of ways. Even if rural Yucatecans used and perceived the landscape in some ways that complicated the process of creating stable ejidos, they also tended to invoke a series of concepts that resonated with the modernizing project of Revolutionary Mexico. As early as the mid-nineteenth century, rural people in Yucatán were making explicit invocations of liberal discourse to characterize work on their traditional lands as a means of promoting industry and other modern virtues among their population (Eiss 2010, 45–76). Similar claims became especially important in the legal procedures that were instituted through the agrarian reform in the 1920s. While some colonial and nineteenth-century titles were brought into play during the agrarian reform in Oriente, usufruct claim to a given stretch of farmland was one of the most clear-cut routes to establishing a valid claim. Whether they are narrated in Spanish or Maya, stories about the foundation of communities tend to hinge on the idea of "fomenting" (Sp. *fomentar*; Ma. *póomentar*), a term that has powerful resonance in the discourse of economic development. Today, these terms are still used when members of a community plan to make kool or herd cattle in stretches of their collective landholdings that have reverted to k'aax. For example, when a man from Xcalakdzonot was speaking about making use of Siete Pilas, a site in the ejido that had not been used extensively in several decades, he observed, "I want to refoment Siete Pilas" (Ma. *Tak in ka'a poomentar le siete piilaso*).

It is likely that this idea of "rehabilitating" a previously occupied area of k'aax figured in the experiences of many of the agriculturalists who settled new ejidos in the first decades of the twentieth century. This is evident in the documentary and oral history of Xcalakdzonot and other communities. Documents in the National Agrarian Registry (Registro Agrario Nacional, RAN) include censuses taken at the time of the foundation of different ejidos. These censuses include a list of residents, their ages, and the number of years that each has resided in the specific locality (Sp. *localidad*). Those for Xcalakdzonot show that the current community was settled by people from Kaua and several other kajo'ob around 1910, received a sizable influx of population from 1920 to 1925, and was confirmed as an ejido in 1929.[12] Like many of the other named places that would eventually be incorporated into the ejido of Xcalakdzonot, the area in the periphery of the twin cenotes had been inhabited intermittently in the past. Some of the oldest people in the community remember stories told by their parents, the original settlers, who recalled finding remains of houses complete with grindstones and pottery that had been left by the previous inhabitants. These vanished inhabitants were probably peasants associated with Ebtún, who had lived in the area at different points in the eighteenth and nineteenth centuries.[13]

Although knowledge of places in the landscape is a shared heritage of rural people in Oriente, the actual use of different sites could entail a degree of conflict. There are many cases in which groups of settlers who banded together to apply for ejidos did not necessarily think of themselves as an organic "community." This is particularly evident in the stories that document how some families moved to several different places throughout the 1920s to 1940s before establishing lasting roots. I asked a sixty-year-old woman from Popolá, a kaj of 200 people in the municipality of Yaxcabá, if the people who lived there now were natives of the area. She replied:

> Those with the last name Cen came from Ebtún. From Ebtún they went to Chan Kom, from Chan Kom to Nicté Há—no, to Ticimul and then to Nicté Há. Then they came to foment the village here.
>
> The Puc were from Chan Kom. They had come from Uayma, Pixoy, when the people came down [south] because there was nothing to eat. They had to find how to make a living. (interview August 1, 2001)

The settlers whom she mentioned arrived in the 1930s at the site of the former Rancho Popolá, which had been abandoned decades earlier by its owners, a family from Yaxcabá.[14] This account is striking in the complex series of territorial identities that it implies. When settlers arrived at the site, they could have been identified as any of the following Maya terms: *uaymail, ebtunil, chankomil,* and *pixoyil.* A coherent identity as *popolail* would emerge only in later generations. The narrative of their arrival also hints at the relative instability of recently founded kajtalo'ob. Given that the migrations to which this story refers took place in the 1930s, some of the stopping points of different families—such as Chan Kom and Nicté Há—would barely have been founded before the Cen and Puc families moved on to greener pastures in the west.

When I mentioned this brief migration account to a friend from Xcalakoop, he observed that the people of Popolá must have many "problems" (Sp. *problemas*), a term that is a common euphemism for factional conflicts. He said that the memory of that kind of migration—particularly several generations after the fact—could be a sign of the conflicts that preceded the foundation of the community and of the continued identification of families with their nonlocal origins. These factional disputes rarely result in out-migration today, since population growth and the evolving nature of agrarian law made the political geography of Oriente stabilize a great deal by the 1950s (Warman 1985). However, families often have long memories, and the "problems" of the early twentieth century serve as precedent for more contemporary tensions among factionalism, unity, and identity politics. In effect, this intersection of landscape use, vernacular memory, and agrarian institutions complicates the image of the corporate rural community that, despite generations of critiques by anthropologists, still tends to inform different regimes of state-sanctioned identity politics. The details of some specific territorial dramas highlight how the frequent lack of intra-community consensus and identity has shaped many people's perceptions of what territorial politics can accomplish.

Violence, Fission, and Agrarian Reform

The "problems" that accompanied the settlement and dissolution of peasant communities in the 1920s and 1930s are intimately tied to a period of violence that many of my older informants refer to as the Age of Politics (Ma. *U epoca le políiticao'*). In the next chapter, I will show how the oral history and the collective memory of communities in Oriente tend to frame this period in ambivalent terms. By the 1920s, a new government had popularized a narrative of peasant and worker identity that promised new forms of social justice. At the same time, the disruption of older political structures resulted in more than a decade of factional strife that fragmented larger class-based coalitions. This ambivalence is also reflected in the foundation of ejidos. In many cases, the application for autonomous ejido lands was framed as "revenge" against communities that were abandoned by dissident factions. This problem became especially acute for older towns—such as Ebtún, Kaua, and Cuncunul—all of which had existed during the colonial period and accumulated their fair share of internal conflict by the 1920s. Given the relatively weak development of the hacienda economy in Oriente, they had retained some control over their ancestral lands during the century that preceded the Mexican Revolution. But after the agrarian reform, the granting of usufruct rights to small and relatively recent settlements often led to the fragmentation of traditional land bases and to the dispersal of the population of residents that could be drawn upon for collective labor (Sp. *fajina*; Ma. *fajina, muulmeyaj*).[15]

A good example of these conflicts between larger towns and newly settled villages is a series of struggles that developed over the course of the 1920s between the dominant factions of the town of Kaua and those who eventually founded the ejido of Ticimul, located several kilometers to the southwest.[16] Oral narratives I have recorded in Ticimul cite Kaua as the source of most of the people who founded the current ejido, an origin also supported by documentary sources, particularly the census of the local population recorded when the residents of Ticimul made an application for an ejido grant. This census documents that while some individuals claimed to be residents of the site for over fifty years, many adults had lived there for ten years or fewer. Many of the names on the list have marginal notes marking specific *ejidatarios* as residents of Kaua,[17] or as persons who were in the process of transferring their residency from that town. Letters included in the files of other communities explain that similar annotations on the agrarian census mean that an individual was registering as a member of the agrarian committee of a newly founded community,[18] but still currently enrolled in another and possibly still entitled to the harvest of crops that had been planted before the formal transfer of his or her ejido membership.

For many of the out-migrants, moving to Ticimul might simply have come from the desire to seek out better opportunities. Such a move also seems to be associated with the inter- and intracommunity violence that was common in the early 1920s. An interview that I conducted in 2002 with a ninety-four-year-old man from Kaua lists a series of especially shocking murders and gunfights that took place in the central plaza (Ma. *k'iwik*) of that town from 1917 to 1921 (interview August 7, 2002). Documentary evidence also suggests that at least some out-migration from Kaua was a direct consequence of factional violence. For example, a letter written to the state governor in September 1921 warned of potential conflict when forty-four residents

(Sp. *vecinos*) of Kaua sought refuge in the neighboring town of Cuncunul, after having been forced out of their own community by a "large party of armed men."[19] In several additional interviews I have conducted with elderly people at Ticimul and X-Katun (a neighboring village that drew most of its original population from Kaua), resettlement in the bush was also recalled as a safety measure precipitated by violence in town.

Redfield and Villa Rojas (1934) and Goldkind (1965, 1966) discussed a similar, if somewhat less violent, conflict between Ebtún and Chan Kom. The settlers who founded the ejido of Chan Kom and later promoted its designation as a municipality (Sp. *municipio*) had all been prominent families in Ebtún, and had moved south after conflicts with rival factions (see also Goldkind 1965). This conflict persisted even after their resettlement, as many people in Ebtún resented the loss of agricultural land when the settlers applied for an independent ejido. The leadership of Ebtún was especially angered when members of the offshoot community would no longer participate in collective fajina labor in the municipal core. These tensions escalated to the point at which parties of armed men besieged the villagers of Chan Kom for a week in the 1920s (Redfield and Villa Rojas 1934).

In spite of this violence, the fragmentation of the landscape of Oriente into a myriad of small communities with independent land titles continued through the 1920s and 1930s. Even if larger communities could muster armed parties to bully the residents of offshoot kajtalo'ob, documents at the RAN suggest that the creation of new titles through the agrarian reform was tilted in favor of recently settled villages. In September 1924, villagers of Chan Kom directed a letter to the Mixed (state and federal) Agrarian Commission (Comisión Agraria Mixta) complaining of Ebtún's claim of an enormous ejido. It encompassed more than forty named places in the bush,[20] many of which seemed to be populated by kajtalo'ob that were only marginally dependent on the larger town. Several of these—including Xkopteil, Xcocail, Santa María, Dzucmuc, Tzeal, and Chan Kom—would later become independent ejidos and autonomous municipal entities. Noting the relatively small population of Ebtún, the vecinos of Chan Kom thought it "undue that a town consider itself so important as to measure lands that reach an extension of seventy square leagues." They themselves provided a more modest list of sixteen toponyms that corresponded to Ebtún.[21] Due in large part to persistent conflicts between the usufruct claims of new kajtal settlements and the traditional territorial jurisdiction to which the municipal authorities of Ebtún felt entitled, Ebtún's application for a land grant began in 1923 but was not resolved definitively until 1930.[22] In contrast, more recently settled kajtalo'ob found that their applications enjoyed a much faster turnover. For example, the contemporary communities of Xkopteil and Chan Kom are both on sites that were on the original list of lands claimed by Ebtún. Chan Kom solicited a grant in June 1924 and received provisional possession in October of the same year. Xkopteil solicited an ejido in August 1927 and received provisional possession in December 1928.

This chipping away of lands claimed by the residents of Ebtún would continue for years. In some cases, it clearly illustrated the precedence that new usufruct claims had over nineteenth-century and colonial titles. In May 1940, a piece of land known as Bubul was claimed as part of the ejido of Cuncunul, a neighboring town that was also of colonial origin. In a letter to the agrarian commission, the Ebtún authorities complained that Bubul had been "bought many years ago by our ancestors" and rightfully corresponded to their ejido. They sent the agrarian authorities a painstakingly transcribed copy of a document written in Yucatec Maya in 1798, which documented the sale of Bubul to the municipal authorities of Ebtún.[23] This colonial title was initially recognized, and prevented the concession of Bubul to Cuncunul. However, other letters filed in the RAN suggest that this colonial claim became largely irrelevant when a group of settlers claimed Bubul as an ejido that existed independently from Ebtún for several years.[24] While "traditional" claims may have been recognized when land allocation was debated between two communities whose territories had been defined during the colonial period, the new order established by the agrarian reform gave clear precedence to the kinds of usufruct rights that could be established by peasant settlers.

The most significant limit to the fragmentation of older kajo'ob was a requirement that a community meet a minimum population size in order to be eligible for an ejido. Joining with friends and allies to make a collective petition for independent ejido lands, one common strategy used by families, did not always result in the creation of functional communities. Over the course of the 1930s, these newer settlements also became sites of considerable conflict over land use. The internal pressures that led villages to fission—overpopulation, catastrophic crop failures, or interfamilial conflicts—were also common in newer communities. Another especially troublesome issue involved the municipal affiliation of these communities once they gained formal recognition as pueblos and ejidos. Even if the agrarian reform gave many formerly dependent kajtalo'ob a degree of autonomy in the use of their lands, these new communities were still under the executive jurisdiction of Tinúm, Kaua, Ebtún, Cuncunul, or other municipal seats (Sp. *cabeceras*). State and federal elections, criminal cases, and land issues that could not be resolved locally were all managed in the cabecera. As Goldkind noted in his restudy of Chan Kom during the 1960s, decisions made by rural municipal presidents could only be appealed in Valladolid or Mérida, urban contexts in which peasants from Oriente often found themselves without the necessary linguistic or cultural competency (see Goldkind 1965). Thus, for villages that faced potential conflicts over land use or collective labor, being aligned with sympathetic or more or less impartial municipal authorities was crucial.

A good example of conflicts that could arise over municipal affiliation occurred in Xcalakdzonot.[25] By the 1930s, conflicts had arisen between the families living near the twin cenotes and those who had settled several kilometers to the south in a kajtal called San Nicolás or X-Lab Cah. According to one septuagenarian from Xcalakdzonot whom I interviewed in 2004, the conflict stemmed from the unwillingness of the settlers of San Nicolás to come to the population core (Sp. *centro urbano*) to perform their weekly guard (*guardia*) or fajina service. A report from the municipal authorities in Valladolid written in 1932 refers to a conflict between "municipal commissar and schoolteacher" and several individuals who resided at San Nicolás.[26] In a letter dated February 1933, some vecinos of San Nicolás had contacted the Comisión Agraria Mixta to request division of the ejido. Xcalakdzonot had switched its municipal affiliation to Cuncunul, but the settlers of San Nicolás claimed membership in the old municipio of Valladolid, where their family had good connections among the municipal authorities.[27] As things stood, two mutually belligerent settlements within the same ejido claimed alignment to different municipalities, and the people living in Xcalakdzonot were blocking the residents of San Nicolás from access to the agricultural land.[28] The petitioned separation was denied by the Comisión Agraria Mixta. The conflict escalated until it reached a climax in a gunfight between village factions that left five villagers and the schoolteacher dead (see Chapter 4). In the end, the San Nicolás faction got the worse of the feud, and the former kajtal has long since been abandoned and reverted to k'aax.

A similar conflict arose in Tzeal, an ejido in the municipality of Cuncunul, which originally encompassed the smaller settlements of Bohom and Panbá. In 1935, when Chan Kom became the seat of its own municipality, the two smaller communities (being much closer to Chan Kom than to Cuncunul) fell under its jurisdiction. Though Bohom received its own ejido in 1940, the settlement of Panbá continued to be embedded (Sp. *enclavado*) within the ejido of Tzeal, which remained attached to the old municipality of Cuncunul. The few residents remaining in Tzeal claimed that those in the offshoot community of Panbá had abandoned their rights to use ejido lands when they became part of the municipio of Chan Kom. In September 1944, the *presidente municipal* of Chan Kom was forced to write to the state-level authorities concerning a series of incidents in which armed parties from Tzeal and their allies in Bohom had arrived in Panbá to collect exorbitant rents for the use of farmland to which the Panbá people claimed legal right.[29]

One final example of contention within newly founded ejidos is an especially rich testament to the fragility of community in the 1920s and 1930s, as it shows an evolving struggle between several families that ultimately encompassed a number of different formally recognized communities. It is also a struggle that has a special place in the history of Mexicanist ethnography because it involves Chan Kom, the field site of Redfield and Villa Rojas. In their classic 1934 ethnography, Redfield and Villa Rojas characterized the separation of Chan Kom from the parent kaj of Ebtún as a sign of the local leadership's tenacity and commitment to the opportunities for economic and cultural progress that were offered by the Mexican Revolution. In his restudy of Chan Kom, Victor Goldkind revised this somewhat idyllic vision. He noted how a number of prominent families—particularly the family of the charismatic political leader Eustaquio Cimé—secured political power and the best agricultural land for their own use. The Cimés promoted the illegal practice of cordoning off ejido land as private property, making milpas many times the size of those needed for subsistence and claiming ample pastureland for their livestock.[30] Goldkind argued that the designation of Chan Kom as an independent municipio in 1935, an act that Redfield considered to be a collective expression of autonomy, also aided the Cimé clan in consolidating its power. This act shifted the seat of municipal power away from Cuncunul, which had served as a means of appeal for villagers in local issues.[31]

My own oral history and documentary research show how these struggles for power extended well beyond the formally recognized boundaries of Chan Kom's ejido. These struggles contributed to a situation in which territory and membership in community have become especially fragile and contested. The machinations of the Cimé clan seem to have included a strategy that used the political geography that was embodied in the agrarian reform to effectively expand the territory that their own faction controlled. This process is well illustrated in documents from the ejido application of Xtojil, a kaj about twenty miles to the southwest of Chan Kom. In 1934, José Tun and three other peasants who had been making kool at Xtojil wrote to the governor of the state, noting that they had been unfairly excluded from the list of ejidatarios. While they and four other families had resided there for decades, a group of families from Chan Kom "headed by Eustaquio Cimé" sought to take over the land by the same means that they "took over Nicté Há."[32] The petitioners complained that the Chan Kom people had "exploited the ignorance of Martiniano Cen, José [Concepción?] Kuyoc, Álvaro Hau, Damasio Canul" to take the lands as their own ejido. The census that was recorded at the time of the ejido application seems to support this claim.[33] While the families of Cen, Kuyoc, Hau, and Canul had been living on the site for two to five years, the majority of the settlers had arrived no more than a year earlier. They included twelve bachelors in their late teens and early twenties who, in spite of being of legal age to be ejidatarios, were in all likelihood still socially bound to the paternal households in Chan Kom. Of these, six bore the last name Cimé, and were relatives of Don Eustaquio.

The practice of welcoming new settlers immediately before filing an ejido application was a common means of expanding the local population to or beyond the thirty heads of household needed to justify an independent land grant. But the rub in this case was that the inflated census of Xtojil excluded a number of families who were also long-term residents, and who would now be charged illegal rents on the use of lands that they had long worked once these were titled to their neighbors and the Chan Kom people. José Tun claimed that the audacity of the Chan Kom people was such that they proceeded to measure the boundaries of the ejido on their own and without the state's agronomist.[34]

This same strategy seems to have backfired on Don Eustaquio in the case of Nicté Há, which was founded amid a conflict between the wealthiest families in Chan Kom. Religion played a significant role,[35] as a number of families who had converted to Presbyterianism rose up in opposition to the Cimés.[36] Agrarian records suggest that the foundation of the ejido of Nicté Há began as a process similar to that of Xtojil. Nicté Há also received its ejido grant in 1934, and the agrarian census included in the file demonstrates a similar demographic: a small original resident population and new settlers from Chan Kom. Only six household heads had been living there for more than fifteen years. The remaining seven married household heads and more than twenty bachelors on the census had arrived only six months to a year before the ejido application.[37]

This pattern is consistent with the oral accounts that I have recorded, which reflect the distinct experiences of two separate waves of migrants. When I interviewed Don Adalberto Mex, the grandson of one of the brothers who had first settled Nicté Há around 1914, he made no mention of religious conflict, though he recalled that a number of Chan Kom families had collaborated with his uncles in making the first significant improvements (Sp. *mejoras*) to the village. It is unlikely that Don Adalberto would have observed the conflict between the families in Chan Kom. His family lived year-round in Nicté Há, whereas many of the newer settlers seemed to spend their free time in the centro urbano of Chan Kom. Furthermore, Don Adalberto does not link the original settlers of Nicté Há with Chan Kom, stressing that his own family had migrated there from the kaj of Cuncunul (interview June 24, 2004).

Speaking with the descendants of the Protestant families who moved to Nicté Há from Chan Kom in the 1930s—most of whom now live in Pisté—one hears a different story. They all identify as having been from Chan Kom and been forced to leave because of the other families' "hatred" of the Presbyterian faith. One recollection by a sixty-seven-year-old man is fairly typical:

I was very small when we left Chan Kom. I was born in Chan Kom, but when my father lived there, there were problems with the other people there, who didn't like our religion. Some were Evangelicals, and others were Catholics. There were problems because of this, and the people began to fight. Since my relatives, my grandparents, my uncles all left Chan Kom and passed to the little village of Nicté Há, we left too. They passed there. They were all cattle herders. They solicited their ejido so they could get ahead, because they didn't like all the fighting. (interview July 5, 2002)

Another member of the Chan Kom families, whose father left for Nicté Há, has similar recollections:

Nicté Ha was founded in 1932 [sic]. All of the people who went to Nicté Há were from Chan Kom. There was a problem with the authorities in Chan Kom, because the evangelism had arrived and they would even hold services in the municipal hall. The *comisario* was Don Eustaquio Cimé, my father's brother-in-law. I was a kid, around eight years old, but I was a boy that took notice of everything. There was a problem, and they went to Nicté Há. Venancio, Carmen and Pablo Mex, and Samuel Mex lived there, and they received us.

What they did to Chan Kom then was revenge. They decided to solicit an ejido, even though the land was marked off to be for Chan Kom. This caused a problem; the people of Chan Kom came after the ones who had left [Chan Kom]. There was a knife fight . . . it was a serious problem. Five *federales* [federal officers] came. We told them we wanted to start an ejido, and the government said we would have to go and live there. The government itself said that there should be a secretary, a comisario, and they donated the ejido. (interview July 8, 2002)

Although the ejido donation established the formal existence of Nicté Há as a political entity, the Cimé family and their allies seem to have employed a range of additional tools to put pressure on the settlers. Not least of these was calling attention to the fact that Nicté Há was still under the municipal jurisdiction of Chan Kom. There seems to have been significant social and economic interaction between the two communities, religious and factional tension notwithstanding. Doña Petrona Chan, who was a child when the last Presbyterians abandoned Chan Kom, notes that the settlers of Nicté Há continued to visit their former home to worship at the Presbyterian temple there, to shop for groceries, and to visit relatives who had stayed behind. Primitivo Pat, the prominent Presbyterian leader, still lived and operated a store in Chan Kom. Goldkind (1966) noted that the Pats lost their final foothold in the 1950s, when Don Primitivo was badly wounded and his family driven out after a long gunfight. Doña Petrona witnessed the event and recalled:

On one occasion, Primitivo's sons were taking their cattle to drink water by the cenote, and came across the cattle of Don Anacleto Cimé. The bulls started fighting, and they [the Pat boys] began to cheer, because their bull won the fight and Don Anacleto's fell in the cenote.

Then a [Cimé] boy ran to tell his relatives what had happened. There was a drunk outside who was a brother-in-law of Don Anacleto's, and he went to get his gun. Primitivo was a tailor; he was inside sewing when his little daughter said "Dad! Come out, my brothers are fighting!" When Primitivo came out, he whistled to the brothers, but they wouldn't come back. Don Anacleto's brother-in-law saw him, and shot him. One of Primitivo's sons saw this and ran to get his gun, he had a little carbine. His older daughter—she acts just like a man, and she had a gun. She put down the gun that she was carrying, and pulled Primitivo into the house.

Then the bullets started! I was hiding by the door of my house. All night, they were shooting. Some of the Pats were able to escape, and Primitivo's brother communicated with Mérida, and they came to get him and take him to the O'Horan Hospital. (interview July 24, 2002)

Primitivo and his closest kin left Chan Kom for good. Although some members of the Pat family settled in Nicté Há, the wealthiest members fanned out to nearby Pisté, to Mérida, and to Tizimín, where they founded prosperous businesses (see also Castañeda 2003, 629–31). In a crowning act of vengeance, Eustaquio Cimé is said to have razed the Presbyterian temple. Some of the descendants of Presbyterian *chankomil*, families who now live in Pisté, claim that the destruction of the temple triggered divine retribution. Weeks after the demolition, Don Eustaquio came down with a mysterious illness from which he would die a painful and lingering death a few months later. The old leader had died, but, as I will show in Chapter 6, the old conflict still plays a role in the tense relationship between the leadership of Chan Kom and the small population that clings to life in Nicté Há.

Conclusions

The evolving multisited struggle among Chan Kom families can seem like just another example of the discord that has been cited by critics of Robert Redfield's harmonious portrait of the "folk." But these incidents do more than just illustrate the impossibility of the gemeinschaft[38] imagined by the founding figures of peasant studies. They are a testament to the paradoxes that emerge within different regimes of state-sanctioned corporatism and identity politics in Oriente. The prominence that the agrarian reform gave to usufruct rights enabled families to seek formal title to lands of which they were de facto occupants, and to assert a degree of territorial autonomy from larger and older kajo'ob such as Ebtún or Kaua. In some places, this contributed to the decentralization of authority that had been more firmly established in these colonial-era communities. At the same time, the requirement that ejido applicants meet a minimum population in order to be eligible for a grant reasserted the importance of corporate management at the suprafamilial scale. In the cases of Chan Kom, Tzeal, Xcalakdzonot, and the like this requirement simply set the stage for the resurgence of older factional conflicts, albeit on a somewhat smaller scale.

This scenario suggests that the territoriality that emerges at the interstices of state-sanctioned agrarian politics and vernacular forms of landscape use is not necessarily the result of community-based identity or the long-term roots of individual families in specific places. Recall the narrative that the woman from Popolá provided for the origins of different families in the village: "The Puc were from Chan Kom. They had come from Uayma, Pixoy, when the people came down [south] because there was nothing to eat." At some point in the last seventy years, when enough generations had "buried their umbilical cord" in Popolá, the Puc family began to identify as popolail. But what were they considered at the time of the village's foundation in 1939: uaymail or pixoyil? Had their neighbors, the Cen family from Ebtún, resided in Chan Kom long enough to ever think of themselves as chankomil? The same question could be posed of the feuding families from Chan Kom. None of these people had resided there for more than a few decades before engaging in a struggle for land and autonomy that eventually encompassed the places that became the ejidos of Xtojil and Nicté Há.

This ambiguity suggests some ways in which we can rethink the relationship between the collective identities of rural communities and institutions such as the agrarian reform. In a detailed analysis of a 1993 case from a single village in Oriente, Bianet Castellanos shows how the juridical frameworks associated with the ejido can provide a tool with which rural people can reassert the values of collective labor and land management. She asserts that this allows people to protect traditional "Mayan" values from capitalist influences that lead to the disaggregation of the community (Castellanos 2010a). Cases like this *do* happen fairly often today, but the experience of Oriente in the 1920s and 1930s suggests that preserving the integrity of kajo'ob was not an inherent dimension of the ejido from the time of its inception. The fact that families pursued so many different strategies to carve out their own spaces of autonomy also suggests that there is not a universal cultural consensus on the value of community-based decision-making. This other side of the realpolitik of territory and community is an important starting point for thinking about later permutations of narratives that posit class- or ethnic-based solidarities as the basis for political action.

That said, some of the ways in which rural Maya speakers talk about the nature of their communities do justify the fact that Castellanos, Redfield, Villa Rojas, and other ethnographers have historically stressed the values of egalitarian cooperation. The factional discord that I have stressed above remains a part of the collective memory of these communities and an important historical caveat against some of the dangers of rallying to a collective cause. But many of the stories that I have encountered in the field seem to conjure more utopian fantasies of unity and social justice. It is this very ambivalence that has made different forms of state-sanctioned identity politics attractive to local people in spite of the "problems" that always seem to crop up in such mobilizations. In the next chapter, I will look more closely at oral narratives to highlight how people reconcile the myth of collective "redemption" with the realities of local factionalism. The narrative strategies that are applied to the collective memory of the Age of Politics have important parallels in the political imaginary that people bring to their engagement with contemporary multiculturalism.

Notes

1. It was later transferred to Chan Kom, its current municipal seat.

2. See Castellanos 2010b; Lockhart 1999; Restall 1997. For discussions of how this relationship between different forms of territoriality has been incorporated into discussions of indigenous rights, see Díaz Polanco 1991; López Bárcenas 2005; Yashar 2005. Important comparative materials include Povinelli 2002.

3. See Hanks 1990. The intimate relationship between space and memory has been a recurrent theme in anthropological discussions about the preservation of historical consciousness through oral narrative (Basso 1996; Rosaldo 1980), and is also an important element of the shared repertoire of narratives with which rural people in Oriente make sense of their own social and political history.

4. See Bracamonte y Sosa 2001; Clendinnen 1987. Major autonomous polities of Yucatec Maya-speaking people survived in what is now the Guatemalan department of Petén until the 1690s (Jones 1989, 1998).

5. See Clendinnen 1987, 39–41. The formal foundation of cities, complete with charters and lists of governing officials, was one of the central rituals of possession practiced by the Spanish in the new world (Greenblatt 1992). For a general humanistic treatment of the place of "city" in Latin American cultural history, see Rama 1996.

6. For the sake of readability, I have truncated my discussion of the literature through which self-consciously "enlightened" identity developed among certain elements of the colonial Hispanophone urban elite. In Spain and its colonies, scholars such as Benito de Feijoo (1676–1764), Francisco Xavier Clavigero (1731–87), and Gaspar Melchor de Jovellanos (1744–1811) developed a range of strategies for reconciling the "enlightened" letters of French and English philosophers with the requirements of Hispanic custom and Catholic religious

orthodoxy. For detailed discussions, see Beuchot 1998, 138–83; Bravo Lira 1985; Moreno 1975. See also Connaughton 2003; Hale 1968; Rodríguez O 2007.

7. During the decades that followed independence, the eastern districts of Yucatán—an area that encompassed the contemporary microregion of Oriente—seemed to have a promising economic future as producers of sugarcane, a cash crop that became significant when independence limited access to major sources of it in Caribbean colonies that were still under Spanish control (see Guemez Piñeda 1994; Rugeley 1996; Strickon 1965). The years following the crisis of the "Colonial pact" in the late eighteenth century saw an acceleration of reforms, such as the centralization of communal treasuries, the banning of several forms of collective property, and policies that facilitated the private purchase of "idle" lands (Sp. *terrenos baldíos*) within the traditional territories of different Repúblicas de Indios (Bracamonte y Sosa and Solís Robleda 1996, 50–61; Farriss 1984, 355–88; Guemez Piñeda 1994).

8. In the years leading to Yucatán's independence from Spain in 1821 (and its initial integration into the Mexican republic in 1823), a series of constitutional decrees ended the official recognition of the Repúblicas de Indios, effectively terminating the existence of so-called Indians as a legally distinct group. However, the Repúblicas were reinstated in 1824 to prevent the dispersal of the native population into smaller settlements and to facilitate the collection of taxes and incorporation of new municipal entities. Throughout this process, some members of the colonial-era indigenous elite were able to participate in municipal politics in such a way as to maintain the fundamentally "Indian" character of many municipalities, even as people who were not identified as indigenous gained increasing access to political power in the countryside (Guemez Piñeda 2005; Rugeley 1996). For an archaeological perspective on these processes, see Alexander 2005.

9. Though agrarian censuses establish the families that were present at a given ejido during its foundation, tracing the exact trajectory of individuals and families through census data is difficult and often impossible. Factors include the repetition of baptismal names in large families and the fact that individuals tend to drop or add names over the course of their lifetimes (so that a man baptized as Victor Manuel Tun might identify as Manuel Tun as an adult). Still, a comparison of archival records can be used to make broad inferences or confirm narratives from oral history. For example, the 1890 census, representing a period just before the settlement of the villages Chan Kom, Ticimul, and other similar ones shows that certain surnames were exceedingly common in some communities, and far less so in others. Tun, which appears in the 1890 census and continues to be an extremely common name in Pisté, is rare or nonexistent in the 1890 censuses of Kaua, Ebtún, Cuncunul, and other communities to the east. Camaal, an extremely common name in Ebtún's census but rare in neighboring kajo'ob, is associated in oral history narratives with the families that settled Ticimul and other communities in what is now the municipality of Chan Kom. In this chapter, I will refer to several other specific parallels between this early census and later agrarian headcounts. Archivo General del Estado de Yucatán (hereafter, AGEY), Poder Ejecutivo (hereafter, PE), Libros Complementarios, Población, Censo y Padrón del Municipio de Valladolid, 1890 Libro Número 48. Many thanks to Rani Alexander for sharing PDFs of the original documents.

10. For an account of the repopulation of Pisté written in the 1930s, see Steggerda 1932. The resettlement of Pisté in the late nineteenth century is evident in the 1890 census. Only a quarter of Pisté's hundred-plus residents are listed as having been born in the *kaj* (community). Compare this with the 1890 census records of Ebtún, Cuncunul, Kaua, and Tekom, all of which list the vast majority of the population as having been born there. AGEY, PE, Libros Complementarios, Población, Censo y Padrón del Municipio de Valladolid, 1890 Libro Número 48.

11. From the 1500s to early 1900s, kajo'ob that developed from colonial-era Repúblicas de Indios included churches, municipal buildings, and schools, as well as residential structures. By the mid-twentieth century, even many former kajtalo'ob that had gained greater political autonomy after the Mexican Revolution had begun programs of civic construction, instituting a new kind of public architecture that gave a prominent place to a secular municipal and ejidal structure (Alexander 2010).

12. Registro Agrario Nacional (hereafter, RAN), Xcalakdzonot, expediente (file; hereafter, exp.) 214, Censo de ejidatarios.

13. In eighteenth- and nineteenth-century documents associated with the colonial kaj of Ebtún, the Yucatecan historian Julio Hoil Gutiérrez (2010) has found mention of Akulá, a cenote that is currently in the ejido of Xcalakdzonot, approximately five kilometers from the core of the community. The fact that this old name was preserved by the ancestors of the current community—the vast majority of whom at the beginning of the twentieth century were monolingual in Maya and illiterate—hints at how local knowledge of landscape and territoriality preserved the memory of older communities through the generations. These continuities, like stories about discovering the remains of abandoned settlements, reflect how the landscape knowledge that guided the settlement and foundation of ejidos in the early twentieth century included the assumption that different named places in the k'aax were once kajo'ob or kajtalo'ob that had been abandoned in earlier generations.

14. In an interesting twist, none of the current residents of the community are certain of the etymology of the Maya name. The toponym that was familiar through oral descriptions of the landscape was composed of terms that had long since become obsolete in everyday speech.

15. *Fajina* refers to collective labor that could be coerced from community members. The Spanish term is often used in Maya. However, I have heard many accounts refer to *muulmeyaj*, a term that means simply "work in a group" in contexts that would be referred to as *fajina* in Spanish or that implied that participation was far from voluntary.

16. This conflict is mentioned in passing by Redfield and Villa Rojas (1934).

17. See RAN, Ticimul, exp. 205. "Kaua" is penciled in near the names of many of the ejidatarios of Ticimul. Other people in the ejido were most likely from Ebtún, given that the surname Dzul, which is closely associated with Ticimul today, is present there only in the 1890 census. However, oral narrative overwhelmingly states Kaua as the home of most of the population.

18. This situation is stated explicitly in several cases in the documents from the ejido foundation of Nicté Há (RAN, exp. Nicté Há), several of whose residents were entitled to milpa

harvests from the parent community of Chan Kom. Though I did not find similar statements in the documents from the Ticimul file, the fact that these are both cases of conflicts between kajtalo'ob and parent communities makes double enrollments in that community likely as well.

19. Alejandro Chan, Presidente municipal de Cuncunul to Governor of State, September 19, 1921. AGEY, PE, caja (box) 733.

20. Tzeal, Chebalam, Xiat, Bojom, Yokdzonot Aban, Chichan Tzucmuc, Sn. Prudencio, Sta. Rosa, Chacte, Sn. Pedro, Nocac, Sn. Isidro, Kopchen (Komchen? These are both viable phonetic variants of "rejollada-well"), Chan Kom, Tomtizmilu (?), Sta. María, Cosil, Panba (Panaba?), Sisal, Kancabchen, Cocula, Tikincaba, Cocay (present-day Xcocail), Santana, Yula, Uymichen, Sacbalcucan (?), Kulchechen, Mistunbalam, Sn. Andrés, Yokdzonot, Cancepchen (Kancabchen?), Xkopteil, Yohchenbak, Sahcabchen, Xtamil, Chunyaxcheil, Oxola (Oxila?), Chan Sn. Pedro. For a discussion of the eventual municipal affiliation of these sites, see Rodríguez Llosa 1991.

21. September 9, 1924, Vecinos de Chan Kom a Comisión Agraria Local, RAN, Chan Kom, Cuncunul, exp. 149.

22. See RAN, Ebtún, exp. 155.

23. May 5, 1940, Vecinos de Ebtún a Comisión Agraria Mixta, RAN, Ebtún, exp. 155.

24. September 16, 1940, Ing. Edelmiro Conde to Adán Cárdenas, RAN, Ebtún, exp. 155. Other documents in the file refer to a private property called "Bubul," but this appears to be different from the ejido referred to by the same name.

25. RAN, Xcalakdzonot, exp. 214.

26. J. Cruz Centano to Gobernador del Estado, June 26, 1932, AGEY, PE, caja 945.

27. Alberto Arjona Novelo and Vecinos de Xcalakdzonot to SEP DER, June 4, 1933, in Archivo Histórico de la Secretaría de Educación Pública (Historical Archive of the Secretariat of Public Education; hereafter, AHSEP), Dirección de Educación Primaria en los Estados y Territorios, 8966234, Referencia IV/161 (IV-14)/22908.

28. Vecinos de San Nicolás a CAM, RAN, Xcalakdzonot, dotación, exp. 214.

29. Presidente municipal de Chan Kom to CAM, September 19, 1944, RAN, Chan Kom, dotación, exp. 149.

30. Interestingly, Goldkind records that Don Eustaquio Cimé claimed that his land had been ceded to him directly by President Avila Camacho, consistent with the logic of contemporary narratives that legitimate land claims are made through imagined discourse with the president of the Mexican Federation.

31. Later discussions of Chan Kom have taken up this ambivalent image of Cimé, as when Castañeda characterizes the famous (mis)representation of life in Chan Kom as a process of transculturative dialogue in which the self-image crafted by Eustaquio Cimé plays a central role (see Castañeda 1996). Cimé is rehabilitated somewhat in a recent discussion by historian Ben Fallaw (2004).

32. José Tun, Gerónimo Nahuat, Severino Nahuat, and Anatolio Cen to Governor of Yucatán, October 9, 1934, RAN, Xtojil, dotación, exp. 246.

33. RAN, Xtojil, dotación, exp. 246.

34. José Tun, Gerónimo Nahuat, Severino Nahuat, and Anatolio Cen to Governor of Yucatán, October 9, 1934, RAN, Xtojil, dotación, exp. 246.

35. These conflicts are also treated in passing by Redfield in his *A Village That Chose Progress: Chan Kom Re-visited* (Redfield 1950), and discussed in more detail by Goldkind 1965.

36. Don Eus himself had converted briefly to Presbyterianism before returning to the Catholic faith. For Goldkind, the Protestant/Catholic conflict was a front for a struggle over control of local land, retail sales, and cattle production. The Presbyterian families exiled from Chan Kom, several of whom I've interviewed in Pisté, tend to emphasize the religious dimension of the conflict. At the same time, many of them do draw parallels between religious schism in Chan Kom and other social and economic conflicts within the kaj. Like Goldkind, some of the exiles have told me that their unwillingness to spend money in public saint worship initially singled them out for aggression. Likewise, their strict abstinence from alcohol consumption placed them at odds with the purveyors of bootleg liquor, the chief of whom were the Cimés. In many of the Presbyterian exiles' accounts of the Chan Kom conflict, rejection of both vice and "backward" religious practices is consistent with some of the explicit rationalizing aims of the Revolution and the agrarian reform. In many cases Protestantism is framed as a belief system synonymous with the "progress" being hindered by the Catholic leadership of Chan Kom. Several families who were exiled from Chan Kom are prominent amongst the old-money class of Pisté, and many Presbyterian brethren (Sp. *hermanos*) cite abstention from alcohol and strict moral discipline as one of the sources of their relative prosperity. See Goldkind 1965.

37. See RAN, Nicté Há, dotación, exp. 243. However, though it does appear that a second wave of migrants from Chan Kom was taking over Nicté Há, it seems unlikely that this was the same faction headed by Eustaquio Cimé. For one thing, the surname Pat—one of the Cimé clan's greatest rivals—is far more prominent in the census that lists the ejidatarios of Nicté Há.

38. This term is associated with Ferdinand Tönnies, and was used extensively by Redfield (see Redfield 1940).

3

"Back Then, There Was No Order"

THE EARLY TWENTIETH CENTURY IN COLLECTIVE MEMORY

The agrarian reform, a process that played a central role in the ideology of post-Revolutionary Mexico, was experienced in rural Oriente as an often incongruous mix of unity and discord. That is, the same juridical frameworks that promoted unity through the shared investment in *ejido* lands also enabled dissident factions to strike out and solicit their own autonomous grants. This ambivalence permeated local ways of making sense of the class-based identities that played a prominent role in post-Revolutionary Mexican politics. If the Revolution had "redeemed" rural agriculturalists from the "slavery" of the ancien régime and distributed land to those who would foment it through hard work and solidarity, why did these same agriculturalists fight so much among themselves?

These tensions between the heroic narratives of official history and the unruly realpolitik of rural Oriente are

51

DOI: 10.5876/9781607322399.c03

evident in the oral accounts in which members of these communities reflect on their ancestors' experience of the 1920s and 1930s. In this chapter, I will focus on stories that are told about two very different phenomena: paramilitary violence and the distribution of ejido lands. I approach these stories as an expression of a living collective memory. That is, my own analysis will be consistent with a longer anthropological tradition that critiqued an earlier paradigm of oral history studies that sought to distill concrete historical events from the more "mythical" narrative contexts in which they were presented. In critiquing this paradigm, authors articulated a vision of "collective memory" as an active process through which societies transform disparate events from their past into narratives that have some ideological coherence within their quotidian experience.[1] In my own work, such an emphasis is useful in making sense of the inconsistencies that occur between oral accounts that I recorded in the 1990s and 2000s and documentary sources written almost a century earlier. As I will argue, these inconsistencies give important insight into the political imaginings that allowed local people to reconcile their own experience with the mythical canons of Revolutionary nationalism.[2] As elements of a vernacular culture that has been transmitted through the generations, these political imaginings are currently coming into play in the politics of ethnic identity.

Another sense in which my analysis in this chapter is consistent with the tradition of anthropological history is in my focus on the often complicated relationship between documentary and oral history sources. Consistencies and inconsistencies between documentary sources and oral history can demonstrate what kinds of events had a lasting resonance within local conceptions of politics and social justice. For example, my investigation of paramilitary violence began with a series of brief oral narratives of a dramatic battle in 1921 that I refer to as the Burning of Yaxcabá. I was later able to document this battle in the archives, but many important details have virtually faded from living memory. In contrast, narratives about the foundations of the ejido have a far more prominent place in the oral history of these communities. I will focus on one long account of the foundation of a specific ejido, a virtuoso telling of a kind of story that I have heard repeated in at least half a dozen communities. The different imprint that the Burning of Yaxcabá and the formation of ejidos has left in the collective memory of these communities reflects important differences in the kind of historical events that could be made consistent with post-Revolutionary political ideals and those that proved impossible to reconcile with the idea of heroic collective struggle.

Despite these differences, some common themes in both sets of narratives provide important insight into the experiences and ideals of politics in rural Oriente. Stories about the violence of the early 1920s and about the foundation of ejidos both invoke a vision of justice in which "redemption" and the righting of wrongs tend to arrive from without. The motivations and ethics of local leaders are almost always suspect, and coalitions based on a shared identity or political affiliation tend to be quite fragile. But formal legal principles and ideals that can be brought to bear on local injustice exist in bureaucratic and political institutions that are distant from the "folk state" of rural Oriente. Thus one of the central dramas of these stories involves the arrival of different figures and the performance of certain specialized rituals that temporarily instantiate the Revolutionary state in the intimate space of rural communities. The dialectic between the ambivalence of local leadership and coalitions and the good faith of nonlocal characters has important parallels in contemporary narratives of what it means to "do politics" as self-identified Maya.

Felipe Carrillo Puerto, Socialism, and the Burning of Yaxcabá

The legendary Socialist governor Felipe Carrillo Puerto (1922–24) looms large in the historiography of the 1920s, a period during which the state of Yucatán had its most direct experience of the violence associated with the Mexican Revolution. Stories about him are a good point of entry into how the collective memory deals with a series of key ideological contradictions. Carrillo Puerto's assassination in 1924 granted him status as a "martyr" within the state-sponsored cult of Revolutionary heroes. This is very much the role that he plays in the oral narratives told in Pisté and other communities. But as a leader of the Socialist Party of Yucatán, he empowered a series of local leaders that contemporary stories represent as villains, indirectly contributing to a series of events that culminated in the Burning of Yaxcabá.

Though the hero cult of Felipe Carrillo Puerto has clearly been influenced by the histories diffused through schoolbooks—discussed in greater detail in Chapter 5— it also hinges on a series of more intimate recollections about specific visits that he made to rural communities. Advised by Mérida intellectuals such as Antonio Mediz Bolio, he drew deeply from romantic *indigenismo* in crafting his public persona, going so far as to publicly claim that he was a lineal descendant of the rebellious sixteenth-century Mayan monarch Nachi Cocom (Joseph 1985; Mediz Bolio 1951; Urias Horcasitas 2008). Contemporary oral narratives about Carrillo Puerto suggest that this performance of indigeneity was successful, turning the future "martyr" into an embodiment of the pact between rural communities and the state that was promised by the Revolution. Don Aurelio Uc, born in 1903 and a teenager at the time of Carrillo Puerto's governorship, recalled a visit that the governor made to several towns in Oriente:

> Don Felipe Carrillo was the governor from Mérida. He has come to visit here. So then
> [when] Don Felipe Carrillo comes visiting, he gives guns to each town; he gives out

guns like that. He leaves the guns so they can defend themselves, because there are those who go about killing people. I think it's what they call the politics. [They kill people] frequently, frequently. It's true what he [Carrillo] said. . . .

Carrillo Puerto is [like a] poor man. He goes about on a horse. When it gets tired, he comes down to walk, he goes walking. But he has no boots—he just has rope sandals on his feet! (interview August 12, 2002)[3]

The physical description of Carrillo, a powerful urban leader dressed in peasant garb and walking alongside a tired horse, reflects the degree to which his skillful performance resonated for rural people. A similar visit was recalled in even greater detail in the account that Don Carlin Chan, a sixty-five-year-old restaurant owner, heard from his grandfather:

When they made the plaza in Pisté, it was made by Felipe Carrillo Puerto. Then, it was Don Felipe who made the first road in Yucatán, which went from Dzitas to Chichén Itzá. Where that big tree that they call the *dormilona* is, that's where they got together with Don Felipe. He was a person . . . he was very handsome. He was the governor. . . . That man has green eyes, he's light skinned, and he says, "Let's drink *posole*." Because even he drinks posole, with chile, salt, everything. He really gets into the posole! That was in 1923. That is when the road was inaugurated by Don FCP. And in 1924 they killed him. January 3, 1924, amongst all his relatives. This was told to me by my grandfather and my uncle, Estanislao Chan. They met him. (interview August 31, 2002)[4]

Symbolically participating in physical labor and the consumption of peasant food played on two especially valorized markers of masculine solidarity in rural communities. Posole (see Figure 3.1) has traditionally been a food that peasant men take into the fields for lunch, and sharing it in a shady spot during breaks from intense labor—an act punctuated by extravagant comments as to the deliciousness of the meal—is a profoundly resonant social ritual. Several years ago, I participated in one such break after a morning hewing trees in the bush in order to make an open-walled building (*palapa*). One friend affectionately slapped my aching back after finishing his posole, shouting, "How delicious is a meal in the bush, boy!" (Ma. *Ki u janlil k'aax, xiipal!*). In the amused comments being made around me, my own famished gulping of a salted cup of posole was observed with the same approval as my previous willingness to participate in several hours of hard labor at which I was obviously incompetent. In the 1920s, a far more dignified version of this same ritual was performed by a statuesque, green-eyed *ts'ul* with real political power, embodying new kinds of solidarity between rural people and the agents of Revolutionary progress.

Some elements of these oral narratives show how the official history promoted by the Mexican state can permeate the more intimate snapshots of local memory. In

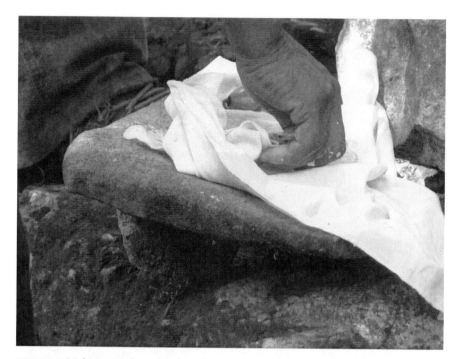

FIGURE 3.1. Making posole with salt and chile after a long hike through the bush in Xcalakdzonot, 2009. Photo by author.

many stories I have heard, Carrillo's rural followers are referred to as *indios*. Though this term is a very derogatory way to refer to someone—evoking a constellation of negative stereotypes about poverty, poor education, and vulgarity—it seems to lose its negative connotations in the presence of the "martyr." It reflects, among other things, the heritage of different state-sponsored rituals that commemorated the words that Carrillo Puerto is said to have shouted as he was dragged before a firing squad in 1924: "Forget not my Indians! (Sp. *¡No olvidéis a mis indios!*). This epitaph is inscribed on a number of public monuments in rural communities, and is hinted at in many phrases within oral narrative (see Figure 3.2). For example, Rubén Dzul, a forty-year-old butcher from Pisté, recalled his grandfather's stories:

> There is an old *pich* tree in Chichén [Itzá] where Carrillo Puerto read an act of liberty. They wanted to kill him, but the Indians saved him and took him to Motul, where he was very much loved. He had much love for the Indians, which is why they killed him. (interview November 11, 2003)

FIGURE 3.2. Felipe Carrillo Puerto and the Indians. Public monument on the Paseo Montejo of Mérida, Yucatán. Photo by author.

The fragment cited above is taken from a longer set of recollections about the hacienda Chichén Itzá, purchased in the early twentieth century by the Anglo-American adventurer Edward Thompson. Much of the hacienda was burned to the ground under mysterious circumstances in 1921, but in this story it becomes a symbol of how "Indians" resisted "enslavers." Rubén recalled his grandfather's words: "'I worked for a man in the rancho Chichén who was sort of Spanish. He treated me like a slave.'" Rubén continued: "My grandfather built the church at the hacienda. He would put up a course of stones; the man would knock them down so that he [my grandfather] would have to do it again" (interview November 11, 2003).[5]

Though this particular narrative sounds more allegorical than realistic, other accounts from this period also suggest that Thompson had a poor relationship with people in Pisté. This is due both to the belief (largely substantiated) that he had looted golden treasures from the cenote of Chichén Itzá and to disputes over the rent that he charged for the use of agricultural land on the fringes of the hacienda. Thompson himself was certain that the arson on his property was the work of "Socialist agitators" in the community (see Brunhouse 1973). The culprits were never found, but the report written by a police agent sent from Mérida to investigate noted that the people of Pisté were markedly hostile to his inquiries.[6] When I asked Rubén if his grandfather had ever told him anything about the burning of the hacienda, he replied: "The Indians themselves burned it, because they became frustrated that he was messing with them" (interview November 11, 2003).[7]

The labeling of the "Socialist agitators"—and by extension, the narrator's own grandfather—as "Indians" contributes to the overall ideological coherence of this account. As a rich person who charged rent on lands that would ultimately be claimed as ejidos by Pisté and surrounding communities, Thompson is easy to cast as an "enslaver" in a Revolutionary narrative of class and exploitation. As a foreigner who exploited the riches of the builders of Chichén Itzá and the labor of their descendants, he also plays the role of "Spaniard" within a narrative of "racial" war.

This kind of story highlights why incidents such as the Burning of Yaxcabá are difficult to reconcile with official narratives of collective class struggle. In the mytho-historical memories of the age of Carrillo Puerto, Edward Thompson is easily turned into the villain of a story about struggles between "Indians" and outsiders. But few of the rural *políticos* who took up arms for or against the Socialist Party in the countryside were as wealthy as Thompson or as easy to distinguish from the peasantry in terms of "race" or class. Nor did the rank and file of Socialist leaders who were known personally by the residents of rural *kajo'ob* manage to accrue the aura of heroism that is generally attributed to the green-eyed martyr. This ambivalence is especially evident in the sporadic narrative snapshots that constitute a collective memory of the period from 1917 to 1922, which was marked by a struggle between rural associates of Carrillo Puerto's Yucatecan Socialist Party (Partido Socialista de Yucatán, PSY) and the Yucatecan Liberal Party (Partido Liberal Yucateco, PLY).

The Burning of Yaxcabá seems to have been the Socialists' most significant military victory in Oriente during this period. In this battle, a coalition of several hundred men from more than a dozen Socialist-identified communities in Oriente successfully attacked the Liberal bastion of Yaxcabá. For some participants in the raid, this event seems to have had the potential to accumulate some trace of the aura that clings to memories of Carrillo Puerto. However, ambiguities that persist in the fading collective memory of this incident also reflect the difficulty of reconciling many local experiences of early twentieth-century violence with the hero narratives of official historiography.

I first became aware of the Burning of Yaxcabá through the autobiography of Eustaquio Cimé, included as an appendix in *Chan Kom* by Redfield and Villa Rojas. Don Eustaquio recalled having joined peasants from communities throughout Oriente in attacking Yaxcabá, a town affiliated with the Liberal Party of Yucatán. The leadership of Yaxcabá had sent armed men to assault villages throughout Oriente. Cimé's account gives the reader the sense that there was a strong collective class identity among the Socialist raiders. He states that he and his men charged into Yaxcabá with a shout of

> Long live the Supreme Socialist Government of the Nation and of the State! Long
> live liberty of the downtrodden workers and death to the Liberal assassins who do not
> want to work! Now, with plenty of noise, down with them! Let them die!" (Cimé, in
> Redfield and Villa Rojas 1934, 222)

But who were the "Liberal assassins who do not want to work"? Although it is almost certain that Liberal leaders in Yaxcabá *had* been orchestrating attacks and murders in communities to the north and east, the Liberals were mostly agriculturalists who had far more in common with their enemies than with Edward Thompson. Accounts of this time also cast doubt on the image of solidarity among "downtrodden workers" in Cimé's autobiography. Later in 1921, several nominally Socialist communities had taken to fighting among themselves (see below).

The moral and ideological ambiguity of party affiliation is a persistent theme in the oral narratives that I have heard about this event. Don Aurelio Uc, born in 1903, was eighteen when the raid took place. I asked him what he recalled of the Socialists and Liberals. He replied:

> The Liberals and the Socialists? Two parties. Their leader [the Socialists] was in Tinúm.
> San[tiago] Beana. San Beana was a Big Man [Ma. *nojoch maak*]. A politician [Ma.

póolitiko]. But he really threw himself into the politics! It tasted good to him . . . politics tasted good to him. [And so] they'd go around killing people. (interview August 12, 2001)[8]

Santiago Beana is one of the leaders whom Eustaquio Cimé listed as participating in the raid. He was allied with Lorenzo Barrera, the municipal commissar of Pisté, who will play an important role later in this chapter. Like most of the "big men" or "politicians" of the 1920s, he is not remembered with particular fondness by people living today, but as a potentially violent man distinguished only by his "taste" for politics.

Ultimately, the Burning of Yaxcabá owed less to clear-cut class conflict than to a more complicated series of processes that were altering the political geography of Yucatán and that allowed ambitious Socialist "big men" like Beana to cement their local bases of power. The Socialists' adversary, the PLY, had been founded by recalcitrant members of the old landed oligarchy as a response to a program of reforms initiated by the Revolutionary government in 1915 (see Domínguez 1979; Joseph 1985). This party managed to incorporate a number of key clients among rural political leaders.[9] Thus party divisions that had emerged in Mérida served as a broader rubric for the playing out of more local feuds, as dissident factions identified as "Liberal" in resistance to the Socialist peasant organizations that had been established from 1915 to 1919. Violent encounters between the two parties peaked from 1919 to 1921, a period when the relatively fluid nature of power at the state and federal levels reverberated in the countryside.[10]

The first phases of violence between Yaxcabá and its neighbors also reflect some of the patterns of fission and migration that would come into play a few years later with acceleration of the agrarian reform. In 1919, Liberals had emerged as the dominant faction in Yaxcabá. Socialist-identified families fled to outlying *kajtalo'ob* under threats of violence from their neighbors, much as some of the settlers I described in the previous chapter were forced from their home communities at gunpoint. The harassment of satellite kajtalo'ob by their parent kajo'ob—a phenomenon that figured prominently in the histories of Chan Kom, Ticimul, and Nicté Há (see Chapter 2)—was also an issue on the periphery of Yaxcabá. By 1920, numerous complaints that were sent to the governor of the state show that the Liberals had harassed Yaxuná and Kancabdzonot, nearby hamlets that had been settled by Socialists who fled from the municipal seat. The timing of these initial attacks seems to have been calculated to keep the exiled Socialists from effectively voting in state elections.[11]

By late spring 1921, after a series of further political convulsions within Yaxcabá,[12] this intimidation expanded to communities in Oriente where the exiled Socialists sought refuge and alliances. Men armed with military-issue Winchester rifles and dressed as federal troops made their presence known from Pisté and Dzitas in the north to Kaua and Cuncunul in the east. Their attacks ranged from taking potshots at travelers and merchants[13] to aggressive raids in which they murdered villagers, burned houses and fields, and carried off prisoners to be dispatched in the bush and thrown into cenotes.[14] Threats and the persistent fear of attacks by Yaxcabá led to the depopulation of Socialist communities. Pisté, for example, was reduced from several hundred in 1920 to sixty inhabitants by 1921.[15] By spring 1921, complaints surfaced that Lt. José Angel López, the commander of the *federales* stationed in Yaxcabá, was "interfering" in local politics on behalf of the Liberals.[16] This was an especially dangerous development given that the federales were generally called in to restore "tranquility" after incidents of violence perpetrated by local paramilitary factions.

In late June 1921, a party of between 200 and 300 villagers from Pisté, Tinúm, Cuncunul, Tekom, and a number of smaller communities in Oriente entered Yaxcabá around two in the morning and burned and looted the town for several hours. Newspapers and the official crime reports state that more than forty houses were burned, many cornfields destroyed, and from four to ten people killed. Oral accounts of this incident that I have heard in Pisté and elsewhere suggest that the death toll was quite a bit higher. Perhaps ironically, the official crime reports and newspapers note that López and the other federales who had reportedly been siding with the Liberals were conspicuously absent during the attack.[17]

How the raid on Yaxcabá was organized is a complicated question, and one that has a direct bearing on the credibility of Eustaquio Cimé's heroic account. In his autobiography, Cimé recalls a meeting sponsored by José María Iturralde Traconis, an associate of Carrillo Puerto's from Valladolid who would be interim governor after the "martyr's" death. He claims that it was in that meeting that Socialist leaders from across the microregion plotted their revenge on Yaxcabá (Cimé, in Redfield and Villa Rojas 1934, 220–25). While plausible, Cimé's account of events is somewhat suspect. Though high-ranking Socialist officials did little to discourage paramilitary violence, this kind of meeting would have been a political liability that they could scarcely afford (Joseph 1985). The conservative press hinted at the complicity of high-ranking Socialist officials, but stopped short of accusing the government of staging the raid. The daily *El Correo* referred to the raiders, several of whom are listed by name, as "savages," "cowards," and "bandits" who "threaten to attack any community that does not agree with their Bolshevik ideas." But even as it referred to the "impunity" that these raiders had before the Socialist government, the report also suggested that the raiders were in some way affiliated with "barbarian" groups from the autonomous territories of what is now Quintana Roo (*El Correo* 1921, 891).

Oral accounts have not given me the sense that people in Pisté or other rural kajo'ob associate the Burning of Yaxcabá with a visitation from Carrillo Puerto or other well-known Socialist leaders. I have, on different occasions, pressed informants to try to determine if they perceive any ideological motivation or deeper class conflict as having been behind the raid. The most common reply is that it was simply "because of *la política*." A pithy response from the son of one participant suggests that the Socialist government's role was peripheral at best:

> They [the Yaxcabá raiders] assaulted people on the road, and took away their goods. The people would complain to the government [Sp. *el gobierno*]. The government just got frustrated, and said, "Well, why don't *you* just screw *them*!" (interview August 31, 2002)[18]

Don Aurelio Uc, the only person I know with firsthand memories of 1921, does not seem to recall any intervention from urban politicians. In fact, except in response to my specific question about the two political parties, he made little mention of "Socialists" at all. He simply recalled a pact among people exiled from Yaxcabá, Santiago Beana's people in Tinúm, and Pisté's *comisario*, Lorenzo Barrera:

> Well suddenly they said to the people from here [Pisté] . . . Well, people from Tinúm [Ma. Tinumil] came, they had formed a group with people from Yaxcabá [Ma. Yaxcabailo'ob], [and asked] that we take a trip over to Yaxcabá. It was agreed, a group from Tinúm, a group from Yaxcabá, [we agreed] as well. So they started to get people together [to go to Yaxcabá]. (interview August 12, 2001)[19]

It is possible that Eustaquio Cimé invented the meeting with Iturralde Traconis.[20] Whatever the case, the few traces of the raid on Yaxcabá that I have been able to find in local oral history tend to treat this as a fight between communities, not parties or social classes. As such, memories of it are imbued with much of the ambivalence that tends to be applied to local leaders. Two incidents, the fracturing of the Socialist coalition in late 1921 and the expulsion of Pisté's comisario Lorenzo Barrera some years later, hint further at why the Burning of Yaxcabá failed to accrue the political resonance that Eustaquio Cimé seemed to attribute to it and that today is applied to the memory of Felipe Carrillo Puerto.

The Socialist coalition that attacked Yaxcabá crumbled fairly quickly. In the days immediately following the raid, several of the Yaxcabá exiles sent the state government a long letter with a litany of complaints against the Liberals in their home community. At the time, they were under the protection of Lorenzo Barrera, and most likely trying to justify their own actions before returning home.[21] Some of the Yaxcabá exiles never returned home, and seemed able to integrate into the community life of Pisté (see Domínguez 1979).

But not all of the transplants seem to have been so successful.[22] In September 1921, a group of men from Yaxcabá were arrested by Lorenzo Barrera on suspicion of planning an attack on Pisté in cooperation with relatives of theirs living in the village of Tacchibichen. Perhaps ironically, several of these men appear as signers of the letter justifying the actions of the Yaxcabá Socialists, suggesting that they had all been refugees from that community living peacefully in Pisté.[23] The desperate letter written by Lorenzo Barrera to the governor's office does not detail what prompted this latest conflict, but it is clear that the honeymoon for Socialists from different communities was over. Fearing that la política would soon turn against his own *kaj*, Barrera warned the governor of Yucatán to advise the authorities of Tacchibichen "not to be deceived by others, the people of this town [Pisté] are all Socialists."[24] I was not able to find anyone in Pisté who remembered this particular incident. But it is a good documentary example of the persistent factional conflicts that fractured the class-based umbrella imagined by the Socialist Party, and that make the violence of the Age of Politics difficult to reconcile with narratives about heroic collective struggle.

Something that I *did* manage to learn when asking about this incident involved Lorenzo Barrera's own fate. When I mentioned the name to Rubén Dzul, he thought for a moment, then his eyes widened and he said excitedly:

> I know that name. Lorenzo Barrera . . . Lol Barrera! He was my grandfather's enemy. Xi Lol Barrera [roughly, "damned Lol Barrera"], I remember that that's what he'd call him. That man [Barrera] was very bad. He killed many people here.

I heard the full story while butchering a pig with Rubén and his brothers a few days later. From what I have found in the archives, it seems that the events that they narrated occurred sometime between 1926 and 1939, when Barrera disappears from the archival records of Pisté.[25] Rubén's grandfather Lauro Dzul was a well-to-do peasant and one of the first residents of Pisté (*pisteil*) to adopt the Presbyterian faith. Like Eustaquio Cimé, Barrera had little love for Protestants, a fact that generated a deep hatred between himself and the well-liked Dzul. After one especially nasty confrontation, it was made clear that only one of the two men would walk away from their next meeting. Rather than wait in his home for Lol and his henchmen, Lauro went to complain of the comisario's excesses at the municipal seat in Tinúm. He was told that a delegation would come the following day and that if he proved that he had more support, he would replace his rival as comisario.

The following morning, Lol Barrera and Lauro Dzul waited in the *k'iwik* of Pisté. Dzul stood at one end, alone with a few friends, while Barrera stood at the other at the head of a sizable crowd. When the *presidente municipal* of Tinúm finally arrived, Lauro Dzul pleaded to the crowd to come together once and for all and replace the cruel Barrera. Suddenly, almost miraculously, the crowd that had gathered behind Lol walked across the k'iwik to endorse their new comisario. The victorious Lauro Dzul shouted to his rival, "There are no people behind that fool" (Ma. *Mina'an maak tu pach le péendejo*). Barrera replied, "They went with their co-fools" (Ma. *Bino'ob yeetel u yeet péendejoilo'ob*). By the following morning, Lol Barrera and his family were gone, never to be seen or heard from in Pisté again.

My reconstruction of the averted burning of Pisté, like the Dzul brothers' account of the fall of Lol Barrera, is consistent with the negative view that most people in rural kajo'ob seem to have toward the "politics" of the 1920s. It is possible that Eustaquio Cimé took advantage of Redfield's limited knowledge of local politics and the supposed naiveté of his foreign readers to compose an account of the Burning of Yaxcabá that would have been far less credible to his own neighbors. Especially significant in all of these cases are the reasons why certain incidents are so difficult to reconcile with the aura of sanctity that accrues to the image of Carrillo Puerto. Had it not been for events that transpired after summer 1921, San Beana and Lol Barrera might have been remembered as heroes of the crowning moment of solidarity among "downtrodden workers" faced with "Liberal assassins." But where the "martyr" Carrillo descended into the local landscape in a few carefully orchestrated performances of solidarity, local leaders were ever present in all of their power-hungry venality. Lol Barrera may have fought for Socialist Oriente late one night in June 1921, but in the years that followed, he also seems to have thrown his share of dead bodies into Pisté's cenote.

The Dzul brothers' story highlights the most common recourse against the violence of local leaders: appeal to higher-order political officials who bear witness to the needs of the people and reimpose the law.[26] Like visits from Felipe Carrillo Puerto, these interventions appear as moments of redemption and ideological clarity amid the discord that characterizes la política. This plot device becomes even more important in memories of the agrarian reform.

The Travels and Ejidos of Tranquilino Díaz

While incidents from the rural violence of 1921 have emerged only sporadically in my oral history interviews, detailed accounts of the foundation of ejidos are far more common. At first, I assumed that this was simply due to the positive valorization of land reform. But as I recorded more stories and read more archival documents, I realized that this difference also reflected the relative consistency of the ejido-soliciting experience across communities. Receiving a land grant involved a series of protocols—gathering a sufficient number of heads of household, measuring land with a government topographer, filing the necessary paperwork—that standardized the application process. Thus, a certain event in any kaj's application for an ejido was likely to be familiar to rural people throughout the region. Given that these consistencies arose from bureaucratic rituals that brought villagers into contact with urban politicians and technicians, interventions from without tended to represent pivotal moments in the plots of these accounts.

All of these elements play a prominent role in a long narrative that I recorded in the village of Popolá, a community of 200 on the northern extreme of the municipality of Yaxcabá. As I noted in the previous chapter, Popolá was founded in the 1930s by a number of families who had already meandered through a number of established kajo'ob and recently settled kajtalo'ob before laying down lasting roots. In terms of style and the sequence of events, this story is very similar to far more truncated accounts of ejido foundation that I recorded in Popolá, X-Katun, Ticimul, Xcalakdzonot, and Nicté Há. Several similar narratives from the village of Chan Kom have also been published as parts of the autobiography of Eustaquio Cimé and in Alicia Re Cruz's *Two Milpas of Chan Kom* (1996).

The narrator of this particular "Bestowal Account," whom I will refer to as Don Francisco Tec, is a man in his early eighties and one of three or four of the original founders of the village who were still alive in 2000/2001. He is a noted storyteller, and I have heard him perform narratives ranging from fables and fairy tales to discussions of biblical or apocryphal prophecy. Don Francisco refers to all of these narratives as "examples" (Sp. *ejemplos*), a term that suggests that they carry a moral lesson.[27] He referred to the following accounts as the "Example of the Founding of Popolá" (interview August 11, 2001), indicating that this is as much a moral fable as a commemoration of specific bureaucratic procedures of the agrarian reform.

Don Francisco's story chronicles the travels by which a local leader named Don Tranquilino Díaz meandered from an hacienda to the north of Tinúm to Ticimul, Nicté Há, and ultimately Popolá. The tale begins with the liberation of Don Tranquilino and his family from debt peonage:

> Well, what date could it have been? 1910, 19 . . . 1915. Something like that. I think I was born in 1915—it doesn't make much difference, since I can't remember. But let's get started, so I can tell you a little bit about those days.
>
> I was about six months old, when we left the *finca* [farm] of that man, Don Daniel Traconis. He was a general, and owner of the finca. It was called x-Muchukux, near Kaua. My grandfather told me about when they left. They had already given [us] liberty, but the General [Traconis] did not tell the people who were working [for him], the slaves. He did not tell them.
>
> One day, the government learned that Don Daniel Traconis had not released his children—the people who worked for him—that he was still enslaving. They sent a bat-

talion to free them. If he [Traconis] did not free them, he would be brought to Mérida. They sent *federales* to see.

They [the federales] ask, "Are you Daniel Traconis?"

"Yes. Why?"

"Look at this [written] order [to free the slaves]. If you comply right now, it's fine. If not, you come with us."

"Why?"

"Because these poor boys keep working! You have not freed them! You continue to exploit [them]! Summon them together here."

"Why?"

"*Summon* them together!"

And someone made all of them [the slaves] come together in order. They came together quickly. There were fifty, fifty people he had enslaved. The *federal* says: "Well listen, Daniel. All these poor people that have presented themselves here—you didn't tell them there was liberty even though you knew it for a year! Now, everything in your storeroom is theirs. Give each of them three changes of clothes—the women, the children, the old people, the men. That's good. And give them each 500 pesos. Afterwards, each of them has the right to work another month here on this land, and then see where they are going to live."

Now the *señor* has nothing to say. [The worker] is not a slave any more. Now there is liberty. "It's good, sir, it's good sir [say the workers]. Thank you very much."

"Now," says Daniel, "you will work on this land for another four weeks, and then look where to live, find some bush in which to work." Liberty. He left them *happy.*

Before four weeks, there are those who left for Chikidzonot, those who went to Ekpedz, those who went to Suchilá, those who went to Smulká. All the people were divided.

Muchukux was an hacienda to the north of the town of Kaua, near Pixoy. Several persons to whom I have spoken in Popolá corroborate Pixoy as the ancestral home of the Díaz family. Other elements of this account, however, are the product of literary license. The Traconis are a large and wealthy clan with many properties around Valladolid. General Daniel Traconis was a historically prominent native son of Oriente, famous as a fighter during the Caste War and as governor of Yucatán from 1892 to 1896 (Eiss 2010, 45–76). He had been dead some years before the events described by Don Francisco took place, but as a representative of the microregional elite and a political faction that represented the extreme Right during the rule of Porfirio Díaz (the *porfiriato*) and early Revolutionary period, he is an ideal figure for the reactionary landowner that this story demands.

The date of the events in the story—or at least the presence of the narrator— also seems to have been fudged. The year 1915 is well-known locally as the year that

General Salvador Alvarado arrived in Yucatán and enforced the ban on debt peonage, and is a good moment in which to situate the drama of the liberation of *peones*. On other occasions, however, Don Francisco placed his own birth around 1920. It is probable that the exodus from Muchukux was a less dramatic event taking place when the narrator was a small child in the 1920s, or that the narrator pushed back the date of his own birth to place himself within the narrative of his parents' liberation from debt peonage.

Whatever the facts behind the account of events at Muchukux, the role of the *federales* in this part of the story reflects a common device in narratives in which government officials "bring" justice. In this account, in contrast to Eustaquio Cimé's version of the Burning of Yaxcabá or stories told in Pisté about the destruction of the hacienda Chichén, there is no direct struggle between the peones and their former master. The representatives of the ancien régime were already defeated through some process that occurred far away from the isolated world of Muchukux. The Revolution is repeated at a smaller scale when Traconis is humiliated in front of his workers by a soldier bearing an order from the supreme government. As he told the story, Don Francisco emphasized the power of the written order by poking at an imaginary document in his left hand, then thrusting it in my face as the federal would have done to Traconis. This "imaginary document" gesture is common today in the performance of stories about legal disputes, in which producing an incontrovertible legal document is often associated with ultimate victory and "screwing" (Sp. *chingar*; Ma. *top*) an opponent. This function of documents recurs in other parts of Don Francisco's story.

His story continues with the departure of the Díaz family from Muchukux and their movement south to what is today the *municipio* of Kaua.

> And then, for the first time, they left x-Muchukux and passed for a time to Ticimul. In Ticimul, I grew up, seven, eight years.
>
> Then one day, the Comisario Ejidal Mr. Juan Chan says, "Since there are plenty of us, why don't we call the president of the republic and see if he will give us this bit of bush."
>
> And the President said, "Why not? Now you have a way to make a living. This is liberty." They measured the land of Ticimul, assured everything, turned in the plan . . . it was a little place, but it was beautiful.

Several other informants have confirmed that the Díaz family settled in the bush of what would become the municipio of Chan Kom from the 1920s to 1930s, where they made milpa at the places already known as Ticimul and Nicté Há.[28] Don Tranquilino's name also appears on the census of *ejidatarios* who solicited the lands of Ticimul in 1927.[29] Though settlements at both places seem to have existed before the 1920s, Ticimul was not constituted as an ejido until 1928, and Nicté Há until 1934. At several points in the narrative, Don Francisco seemed unsure in which of the two communities certain events take place. This probably reflects the degree of permeability that then existed in the boundaries between places in the bush that were only later transformed into formal political entities. It is also likely that agriculturalists making milpa in one location simultaneously advanced their claims on other sites through the agrarian office. The toponym "Nicté Há" is penciled in alongside Tranquilino Díaz's name on a 1928 census. Several other ejidatarios' names are also marked with the names of other communities, including Cuncunul, Kaua, Tinúm, and Muchukux-caj,[30] suggesting that they were or had been making *kool* somewhere outside of the surveyed boundaries of where they solicited their ejido.[31]

That the process of soliciting an ejido is represented through an imagined conversation between the peasants and the president of the republic points to a symbolically rich intersection between an actual bureaucratic process and the creative elaboration of a culturally comprehensible account. The "call" to the president of the republic refers to a stage in the ejido application process in which the final confirmation of the land grant was, in fact, established by presidential decree. Here, the president as a character in the narrative anthropomorphizes the state, momentarily transforming the association between "liberty" and federal intervention into the kind of face-to-face encounter that punctuates memories of Carrillo Puerto. It also mirrors a common device in a narrative tradition in which many stories hinge on the honoring or breaking of contracts made with wealthy *patrones*, the spirit-owners of the bush, or saints. For example, in Don Francisco's version of several popular fairy tales, "living happily ever after" comes about as a reward for honoring an oral contract between the hero and a magical animal or angel who is trapped by a villain (interviews August 17, 2001; August 24, 2001).

But whereas the contracts in Don Francisco's fairy tales are honored by a lone hero, the agreement here is between the president of the republic and a group of ejidatarios (as the comisario Juan Chan notes, "There are plenty of us"). This feature of the narrative alludes to the collectivity of the ejido association or committee that was the basic masculine body politic of the agrarian reform and a twentieth-century incarnation of the corporate bodies that had existed since the Repúblicas de Indios of the colonial period (see Castellanos 2010b). Don Francisco's narrative is unusual in that it lists only the ejido commissar Juan Chan by name. Other accounts I have heard of the founding of ejidos, including one told by Don Francisco's younger brother (interview July 22, 2001), carefully list the names of the members of the ejido, often with the various titles (president, vice president, secretary) that they assumed within the agrarian committee. The emphasis on commemorating individual participants is probably an artifact of the oral readings of the lists of signatures that are appended to letters written by local agrarian committees, a ritual that I've witnessed many times during formal meetings with the ejidatarios of Xcalakdzonot.[32]

The presidential telephone call that gave legal title to the ejido of Ticimul is not the only conversation with urban political leaders that is commemorated in this story. After describing the foundation of Ticimul, Don Francisco recounted how the pact between the ejidatarios and the state came into play in the long-standing feud between offshoot kajtalo'ob and their parent community. He made specific reference to the conflict that I discussed in Chapter 2 between the villages of Ticimul, Chan Kom, and Nicté Há and the municipal presidents of the older municipalities of Cuncunul and Kaua.[33] The grudge with the people of Kaua—a kaj from which many of the settlers had originated—came to a head when Ticimul built its own school.

> Then there was the time they sent the furniture for the school to Ticimul—now you'll hear about another mean bastard [the *comisario* municipal of Kaua]. Everything was assured, the school opens on Monday, and the furniture is nice. It was all sent by the government. Who knows how the president of Kaua knew? He sent men who took the furniture.
>
> But you'll see how they brought it back. They [people from Ticimul] went to Mérida. "Mr. Governor, the president of Kaua sent soldiers to take the furniture."
>
> "Oh, they took it?" he said.
>
> Well, they sent two federal officers and one police agent to tell the [municipal] president, "Well president, we have [written] orders, and if you comply now, it will be fine."
>
> The president can't find what to say. They are telling him to immediately send the furniture to Ticimul. He starts to look for someone who will take it. See, the furniture had an owner when it comes to taking it, but none [when it's time] to take it back! He takes out his money, so that he can pay the ones who are to take it. They found who would take it back, paying twenty pesos per person. That was a lot of money then! They found twenty people, who brought the twelve pieces of furniture.
>
> "Well," says the *federal*. "Because the government said you come with us unless you comply with the paper, we're going to spend the night here and stay until you send the furniture." Around midnight the furniture was back in Ticimul.

Like Lorenzo Barrera in the k'iwik of Pisté and Daniel Traconis on the doorstep of his hacienda, the municipal president of Kaua was left "with nothing to say" when faced by written orders and political superiors. In this vision of justice, nonlocal officials have no need to resort to violence in order to neutralize the power of local exploiters like Traconis, Barrera, and the municipal president of Kaua. They embody the more inexorable power of a bureaucracy and a state that is committed to holding up its end of a pact with ejidos and kajo'ob such as Ticimul.

The return of the furniture, like the donation of the ejido and the humiliation of Traconis, is an element of this narrative in which the experience of rural Yucatecans seems consistent with the idea of a Revolutionary "redemption" of the peasant masses. But even though these kinds of incidents are more common in stories about the foundation of an ejido than in recollections of the Burning of Yaxcabá, narratives about the foundation of community also record elements of discord. At one point in his story, Don Francisco notes how Tranquilino Díaz entered into an ugly feud with a neighbor whose son had accidentally wounded one of Díaz's children, and who later failed to hold up his end of a pact to collaborate in planting an unusually large stretch of kool. Rather than allow the dispute to escalate, Díaz struck out with his closest friend to Popolá, an abandoned hacienda far to the west on the borders with the municipality of Yaxcabá.

As he did in the case of the donation (Sp. *dotación*) of Ticimul, Don Francisco narrated the process of soliciting ejido rights to Popolá as a conversation between the villagers and different government officials, from the surveyor to the president of the republic, who approves the final donation. This time, however, there is a hitch. Don Francisco recalled that just before sending the final application for approval:

> The topographer said: "Well, it's all done. Let them secure it, and prepare the plan for the names of all the men, that they may know that the bush is of sixty people.
>
> But then [he said], "This land corresponds to Sotuta and Yaxcabá. Not Oriente. It is of Sotuta and Yaxcabá. All who came from Oriente, have to pass to Yaxcabá and Sotuta. So, you need to get everyone together and see if they agree."
>
> "That's fine." So, they got everyone together and said, "All of us were from Oriente, but not now. Now we are from Sotuta and Yaxcabá, and we must pass, because the land is Sotuta's." Then, they changed the list [of ejidatarios], because thirty men did not want to leave their towns. They changed the list like that, because they said, "I won't go. I will not pass over there."

On the southern and western fringes of the "folk state" within which Redfield and Villa define the life-world of the peasants of Chan Kom (see Alexander 2005), the new ejido of Popolá was in unfamiliar and somewhat hostile territory for settlers from Oriente. Even in 1939, when Díaz and his collaborators began their application for an ejido, the memory of the deadly summer of 1921 would have been fresh for some of the settlers. Furthermore, "passing over" to a new municipio would have spelled a definitive severance of formal ties to their former homes, subjecting them to unknown municipal authorities and distancing them from existing networks of political and economic alliances. In some cases, these fears may have been justified. As I will discuss in far more detail in Chapter 6, Popolá never prospered economically until it was incorporated into the tourist circuit of Chichén Itzá in the 1990s. Many locals to whom I've spoken feel that this was due to neglect by the municipal authorities in Yaxcabá, who showed a preference for helping Yaxuná, Kancabdzonot, and other communities to the south, whose populations have deeper roots in local soil.

Conclusions

Stories about the foundation of ejidos, like the memories of Carrillo Puerto and the violence of the Age of Politics, reflect the persistence of tensions between the populist mythology of Revolutionary Mexico and the lived experience of rural people in Oriente. I've stressed two themes within this mythology that were particularly difficult to reconcile with the realpolitik of the 1920s. The rhetoric of the PSY and a range of later populist institutions posited a class-based solidarity that is hard to locate amid factional conflicts that pitted peasant against peasant and in which allies could quickly turn into enemies. A similar tendency toward factionalism problematizes the very question of "community." The tenets of the agrarian reform, like many anthropological definitions of indigenous and peasant communities, assume an organic bond between a "traditional" community and the lands that they inhabited. But for Tranquilino Díaz, like the residents of the communities that I discussed in the previous chapter, the ties between a group of families and a given territory could be far more flexible. Be that as it may, the histories that I described in this chapter reflect some of the strategies that rural people in Oriente have used to reconcile their own experiences with a mythology that empowers them as Mexican citizens.

This empowerment stems from the ability of individuals, factions, and communities to assume a collective voice that compels translocal authorities to intervene in local matters. In the story of Tranquilino Díaz, a series of wrongs—the enslavement of peones by Daniel Traconis, the lack of land for rural agriculturalists, and the theft of school furniture—is righted through intervention from nonlocal leaders who range from federal police officers to the president of the republic himself. In stories about the characters and events that surrounded the Burning of Yaxcabá, similar interventions seem to distinguish the good collective memories from the bad. Acts perpetrated by Lol Barrera, San Beana, and other local leaders tend to be characterized, at best, with a degree of moral ambiguity. But stories about Carrillo Puerto and his "love" of Yucatán's "Indians" conjure a history in which there is a unity based on class and ethnicity, and in which the subaltern heroes of the Revolution are unambiguously distinguished from "enslavers."

Seen against the realities of ejido foundation and rural violence, these stories seem like utopian fantasies of social justice and local redemption. But they are also examples of rural people in Oriente reflecting on a way of relating to the state that embodies their status as citizens and that permeates many types of "doing politics." As I will discuss later in this book, this dialectic between distrust of local leadership and the desire for outside intervention complicates contemporary attempts to imagine multiculturalism as a bottom-up definition of identity. In many cases, narratives about "protecting" and "representing" the Maya culture today are consistent with an older tradition in which "culture" arrived through the intervention of urban teachers. There are important parallels between the experience these teachers had with rural communities and the experiences of factionalism and unity that I have described above. In the next two chapters, I will look more closely at the emergence of "culture" and other intangible goods as a key element of the pact between rural people in Oriente and the Mexican state.

Notes

1. The idea that oral history analysis consisted of separating objectively documentable facts from the meaningful narrative contexts in which they were embedded is often associated with the Africanist Jan Vansina (1942, 1985). Several works that are representative of more contemporary approaches to collective memory include Rosaldo 1980, on the Philippine Ilongot; Sahlins 1981, on the Pacific; Rappaport 1993, on the Columbian Andes; Slyomovics 1998, on the Middle East; Cole 2001, on Madagascar; Trouillot 1995, on the Caribbean. For a more general theoretical discussion of the role of narrative in historical memory, see Cohen 1987; Darnton 1984; Fabian 1983; LaCapra 1984, 1988; Norá 1996; Ricoeur 1990; White 1990; Tonkin 1992.

2. Donald Donham (1999) provides an excellent comparative example in his analysis of how people in southern Ethiopia framed their own experience in terms of the international discourse of revolution diffused from the north in the 1970s.

3. Original Maya: *Don Felipe Carrillo, gobernador Jo, Ts'o'ok u maan u xiimbatee waya', Ku maan u xiimbate Don Felipe Carrillo tune', ku ts'ail ts'oon ti kada kaaj beya', ts'aik ts'oon beya'. P'atik ts'oono'ob u deefendertikuba maak, tumen yaan u maan kinso'ob maak. Min ku ya'ak le poolitikao', seeguidokij, seeguidokij. Jaaj u t'aan . . . Carrillo Puerto, otsile', yo' tsiimin ku bin, ku ka'anal beyo' ku yeemel xiimbal, xiimbalil u bin. Pero mina'an u bootas ti, chen taabi xanab yan to yook beya'.*

4. Original Spanish: *Cuando se hizo la plaza en Pisté, lo Hizo FCP. Luego, fue don Felipe que hizo la primera carretera de Yucatán, que es la de Dzitas a Chichén Itzá. Donde está la mata esa grande que dicen dormilona, allí se juntaban cuando llegaba don Felipe, que era una persona*

así, como, una persona bien presentada. Es el gobernador. Que así se juntaban, y ese señor tiene los ojos bien verdes, es un guero, dice a ellos Vamos a tomar posole. Porque hasta él toma posole, con su chile, sal y todo. Le mete al posole. Creo que fue el 1923. Sí. Es cuando se inauguró esa carretera que puso don FCP. Y el 1924 es cuando lo mataron. 3 de enero de 1924 que lo mataron entre varios. Todos sus parientes. Nos contaba mi abuelo, mi tío, ellos lo conocieron. Don Estanislao Pech.

5. Original Spanish: *Trabajaba por un señor en el rancho Chichén que era medio Español. Me trataba como un esclavo. Mi abuelo construyó la iglesia. Ponía un curso de piedras, el señor las tiraba para que lo haga otra vez.*

6. Agente del Ministerio Público al Gobierno del Estado, June 11, 1921, AGEY, PE, caja 745.

7. Original Spanish: *Los mismos indios lo quemaron, porque se fastidiaron que les estaba fregando.*

8. Original Maya: *Le líiberales yeetel le soosialistaso, ka p'e páartidos. Tinumó, yan u nojocho'ob. San[tiago] Beana. San Beana jun p'el* [sic] *nojoch maak. Politiko. Pero ku yee u meetertikuba te poolitika. Uts tu t'aan, uts tu t'aan le poolitikao. Ku maan u kinso'ob maak.*

9. This party managed to cultivate a fairly broad rural constituency. As Wells and Joseph (1996) have shown, the *camarilla* or patron-client system of Yucatán in the nineteenth and early twentieth centuries extended webs of power with roots in factions based in Mexico City and Mérida into the municipal governments of rural districts.

10. When the Socialist Party fell out of favor with national president Venustiano Carranza in 1919, its repression by the *carrancista* General Jesús Zamarripa (a campaign popularly known as the *zamarripazo*) allowed the PLY to take control of many municipalities in the state. With the fall of President Carranza in 1920, the remaining members of the Socialist Party aligned themselves with President Álvaro Obregón and the Sonoran Dynasty, and gradually recovered regional control under the directorship of Carrillo Puerto, who became governor of Yucatán in 1922. As I noted earlier, Carrillo Puerto would be assassinated in 1924, but the consolidation of power by Obregón and Calles at the national level established the hegemony of the PSY as a regional force in the countryside (see Joseph 1985).

11. Vecinos de Yaxunah al Gobierno del Estado, July 31, 1920; Comisario Municipal de Yaxcabá al Gobierno del Estado, August 8, 1920; Comisario Municipal de Yaxcabá al Gobierno del Estado, August 27, 1920. All in AGEY, PE, caja 717.

12. This portion of the conflict is documented in a *licenciatura* thesis written in 1979 by the Yucatecan anthropologist José Domínguez. Drawing on eyewitness testimony from survivors, he described how Socialist leaders had been driven out of town during the statewide suppression of their party in 1919 and gradually returned home after their party's return to power on the state level. The return of the Yaxcabá Socialists was short-lived, as they were driven out yet again when die-hard Liberals seeking to control local politics murdered the Socialist leader Maximiliano Tolosa in 1921. Domínguez notes that it was at this point that the Yaxcabá Socialists forged alliances with the leaders of several communities in Oriente, who joined forces to wrest control from the Liberals in the dramatic 1921 attack (see Domínguez 1979, 156–220).

13. Eusebio Gutiérrez, Alcalde Municipal de Cuncunul al Gobernador del Estado, May 28, 1921, AGEY, PE, caja 735.

14. Raids of this sort are reported in Chan Kom, Ticimul, and Ebtún. See Santiago Beana, Delegado de la Liga Central de Tinúm al Gobierno del Estado, June 18, 1921, AGEY, PE, caja 747. Especially destructive were the raids at Xkatun and Sacbaquen, each of which led to at least five deaths. See Alcalde de Valladolid al Gobierno del Estado, June 17, 1921, AGEY, PE, caja 727; Comisario Municipal de Ebtún al Gobierno del Estado, June 13, 1921, AGEY, PE, caja 748B; Alcalde de Valladolid al Gobierno del Estado, June 15, 1921, AGEY, PE, caja 748B; J. A. López, Comandante del Destacamento de Yaxcabá al Gobierno del Estado, June 20, 1921, AGEY, PE, caja 748B.

15. It should be noted that though Pisté was Socialist by 1921, this was after its own internal struggle with Liberal militias organized in 1918 (see Castañeda 2003, 628; Steggerda 1941). Comisario Municipal de Pisté al Gobierno del Estado, June 27, 1921, AGEY, PE, caja 727; Lorenzo Barrera al Gobierno del Estado, June 7, 1921, AGEY, PE, caja 735. The authorities of Dzitas, though less directly affected, likewise reported widespread fear. See José M. Rejón, Diputado de Departamento de Espita al Gobierno del Estado, May 28, 1921, AGEY, PE, caja 747 (for figure on reduction to sixty inhabitants).

16. Nicanor Padilla, Presidente de la Liga de Resistencia de Sotuta a la Liga Central, April 21, 1921, AGEY, PE, caja 747; Vecinos de Tacchibichen a la Liga Central, AGEY, PE, caja 747; Nicanor Padilla Presidente de la Liga de Resistencia de Sotuta a la Liga, August 7, 1921, AGEY, PE, caja 748B; Lt. José Angel López al Gobierno del Estado, May 6, 1921, AGEY, PE, caja 748B.

17. AGEY, PE, caja 748B. See also *El Correo* 1921.

18. Original Spanish: *Ellos asaltaban a la gente en la carretera, se llevaba sus mercancías. La gente se quejaba al gobierno, pero el gobierno se fastidió y dijo "¡Pero ustedes, porque ustedes no los chingan a ellos!"*

19. Original Maya: *Pues de repente ku yaik ti le wayeiloba . . . Pues le maakoba', Tinumil u talo'ob yeetel Yaxcabailo'ob, ku agruparuba yeetel le yaxcabailo'oba', entonces mika'ajo'on ts'aik un p'e vuelta ti Yaxcaba'. De acuerdo u gruupo le Tinumila', u gruupol Yaxcabail, de acuerdo xan. Ko'one'ex. Tu juntaruba geente.*

20. Such an invention would not be the only time that Cimé justified a less than legal act by invoking a deal made with a high-ranking politician. Goldkind (1966) notes that Cimé had argued that ejido lands that he had illegally cordoned off for personal use had been a personal grant made to him by President Lázaro Cárdenas.

21. Vecinos de Yaxcabá al Gobierno del Estado, June 28, 1921, AGEY, PE, caja 721.

22. In a study of Pisté that he published in 1941, the American anthropologist Morris Steggerda noted that some of the exiles from Yaxcabá were later accused of theft by their new neighbors in Pisté and forced to leave the town (Steggerda 1941). Today, such accusations of theft are associated with a broader context of malicious gossip (Sp. *chisme*) and "hatred" among neighbors (Sp. *odio*; Ma. *p'ek*). This accusatory gossip is always experienced by newcomers who, accustomed as they might become to a life in a new community, are never quite as

"local" as those who were born there. However much the Yaxcabá exiles integrated themselves into the life of Pisté, they would forever be yaxcabail and viewed with some degree of reserve or outright derision by pisteil families who had lived in the kaj since its refounding at the turn of the century.

23. Lorenzo Barrera al Gobierno del Estado, September 24, 1921, AGEY, PE, caja 745. In this letter, Delfín Díaz, Federico Díaz, and Eustaquio Díaz are mentioned as participants in the plot. All three appear in the letter signed by *vecinos* from Yaxcaba on June 28, 1921, cited in note 21. It is telling that these are the three names listed by Barrera in the arrest letter that also appear in the June 28, 1921, letter and that all three are mentioned in succession.

24. Lorenzo Barrera al Gobierno del Estado, June 24, 1921, AGEY, PE, caja 745.

25. Here I am referring to censuses in the RAN file for Pisté, exp. 172. The 1926 census at the time of the initial application lists Barrera as having lived in town since 1910 or 1911. Along with the fact that Barrera does not appear as a resident of Pisté in the 1890 census, this confirms Rubén's assertion that he "was not from around here." Poder Ejecutivo, Libros Complementarios, Población, Censo y Padrón del Municipio de Valladolid, 1890, libro número 48. In the census recorded in 1939, when the ejidatarios of Pisté requested an extension to their lands, he is not listed.

26. There are interesting parallels between this theme in vernacular narratives about politics in Oriente and in discourses on corruption in India discussed by Gupta (1995).

27. To better understand the social and cultural relevance of the narratives that I will draw upon here, I should note how Don Francisco's own categorization of these stories contradicts a generic distinction made by many students of Yucatec Maya oral literature. There is a tendency to distinguish among narratives told with an explicit moralizing or didactic goal (*ejemplos*), accounts of true events (*historias*), and fictional or fantastical tales told purely for entertainment (*cuentos*) (see Burns 1983; Redfield 1935).

28. Interview August 1, 2001, and field notes.

29. RAN, Ticimul, exp. 205.

30. A kaj community not to be confused with the hacienda Muchukux. Many thanks to Rani Alexander for clearing up this point.

31. RAN, Ticimul, exp. 205.

32. Parallels between these features of oral narrative and the political rituals of the ejido committee are also evident in the fact that very few women seem to recall the foundation of ejidos in these terms. With few exceptions, women are excluded from participation as *ejidatarias*. When I asked Don Francisco's daughter Doña Simeona about the foundation of the village (interview August 1, 2001), or when I interviewed one of the women who helped to found the village of X-Katun, they emphasized the day-to-day living in the "early days" over the process of soliciting ejido lands. Even more telling was the fact that both narrated their memories to me in a series of loosely connected snapshots without the sequential description of the foundation process.

33. On one occasion, amid a village fiesta, the municipal president of Cuncunul and his men attempted to ambush the villagers in Nicté Há. They fumbled the attack, and the presi-

dent himself was captured and tossed into a cenote. He emerged soaked but none the worse for wear, and promised to return in a few days and burn Nicté Há to the ground. The attack never came, though all the men of the three smaller villages spent days in the bush waiting for the raiders.

4

"Now There Is More Culture"

The same ambivalence that inheres in the memory of
Socialist militancy and the agrarian reform also permeates
the experience of "culture" in rural Oriente. As I hinted
in Chapter 1, many people in these communities refer to
"culture" as something that individuals have more or less
of, depending on their degree of assimilation into ethnically unmarked Hispanic society. This element of vernacular speech reflects both the deep-seated heritage of ethnic
hierarchy and a more specific set of narratives that emerged
tangentially with the foundation of rural schools in the
1920s and 1930s. As I will discuss in greater detail later in
this book, the characterization of public education as the
"bringing of culture" by the Mexican state continues to
play an important role in vernacular narratives in an age
of multiculturalism. And just as the titling of *ejido* lands
enabled both factionalism and solidarity, the negotiations

77

DOI: 10.5876/9781607322399.c04

between local players and urban officials during the foundation of rural schools imbued this "cultural" project with a great deal of political ambivalence.

The history of rural schools has been one of the flash points of contemporary debates about the cultural politics of modern Mexico. Mexico's official historiography generally characterizes rural education as a project through which the state democratized knowledge and laid the groundwork for a population better equipped for industry and civic participation (Gallo Martínez 1966; Gamio 1916; Montroy Huitron 1975; Uc Dzib 1987). Revisionist and critical histories have focused on the fundamentally assimilationist nature of post-Revolutionary schools, which stressed the use of Spanish-language training and courses in national history as a means of incorporating members of diverse rural indigenous groups into a homogeneous Hispanic national culture (Bonfil-Batalla 1987; Dawson 1998; Vaughan and Quintanilla 1997). The critical historiography of rural education in states such as Yucatán has tended to focus on how indigenous communities acquiesced to or resisted this assimilationist project (Castellanos 2010b; Dawson 1998, 2001; Loyo 2003; Manzanilla 2004). For example, in a study of historical documents from the municipalities of Chan Kom and Chemax, the historian Ben Fallaw (2004) argues that the degree of acceptance of or resistance to public education in the 1930s reflected the diverse ways in which communities managed the relationship between traditional "Mayan" culture and the ideas of "civilization" and national identity that were imposed by the Mexican state.

Though some elements of Revolutionary-era education did challenge traditional values in rural Oriente, the local politics of school foundation tended to be somewhat more complicated than this dichotomy between the imposition of Western culture and indigenous acceptance or resistance. As the example of the agrarian reform demonstrated, the idea that "peasant" or "Indian" communities were organic corporate groups with close ties to a specific territory was difficult to reconcile with the relatively fragile integration of *kajo'ob* or *kajtalo'ob* in the 1920s and 1930s. Something similar occurred during the foundation of schools. Stating that Maya-speaking communities exercised different forms of self-conscious *cultural* resistance to assimilation implies that there was some degree of social consensus on the core values and customs that could be threatened by public education. But there is not always clear evidence for this kind of self-conscious consensus on "indigenous" identity in either the oral history or documentary sources. The labeling of some individuals as having "resisted" the implementation of schools often reflects a very different kind of conflict *within* rural communities. There is a similar ambiguity behind many rural Yucatecans' assertions that education is a right of all Mexican citizens. Before the expansion of the tourist industry in the 1970s—and even today for many people who work in unskilled labor or agriculture—schooling often seemed to be more self-referential cultural capital than an immediately exploitable good. In many cases (and as Fallaw himself observes), a community's receptiveness to the foundation of a school was often figured in negotiating a broader series of concessions from the Mexican state.

Though I look more closely at the effects of pedagogy in the next chapter, this chapter focuses on those elements of public schooling that had an immediate, tangible, and relatively unambiguous presence in the quotidian space of communities in Oriente. Even before the first generations of students set foot in the classroom, "culture" took on a physical presence through the distribution of books, the construction of schoolhouses, and the persona of the rural teacher. Each of these elements plays a powerful symbolic role in the political rituals of modern Mexico. Schools in contemporary Mexico are sites of commemoration, from the different historical heroes for which they are named to the pageants that are performed by students to celebrate Mexico's independence from Spain, the Revolution, and other major historical incidents (Rockwell 1994; Stephen 2002, 39–54). In the 1930s, schools were already a tangible manifestation of an institutional pact that translated the social contract embodied in the foundation of ejidos into a commitment to "cultural" progress. And like the rituals and physical texts associated with the agrarian reform, the material culture of education played an important role in a range of different expressions of solidarity and factionalism in rural communities. Before turning to two very different case studies in which the establishment of these institutions prompted collective mobilizations and family disputes, I look more closely at the material and social assemblages that give culture a tangible form in the quotidian politics of rural kajo'ob.

Schools and Tangible Culture

The movement of books, pedagogical materials, and teachers from urban areas to rural communities was the most immediately tangible manifestation of the post-Revolutionary educational project. Schools had existed in the eastern city of Valladolid and larger towns such as Tinúm and Dzitas since the nineteenth century, and were founded sporadically in smaller communities in the years after the Revolution. But public education expanded dramatically in more isolated kajo'ob in Oriente in the 1930s.[1] By then, public education was well established in the Revolutionary lexicon of Yucatán.[2] When Salvador Alvarado took control of the state government in 1915, one of his first prominent acts was to found a series of public schools and libraries in rural communities, primarily in the henequen zone. Yucatán's schools were administered at the state level throughout the 1920s, before their operation was gradually handed over to the federal Secretariat of Public Education (Secretaría de Educación Pública, or SEP; Alvarado 1994; Alvarez Barret 1972; Betancourt Pérez 1969; Echeverría 1996; Eiss 2004; Fallaw 2004; Paoli 1984; Trejo Lizama 1988).

One thing that stands out in the communications between rural communities and urban officials is the degree to which these educational projects took on a tangible form through the transmission of physical things. Recall, for example, the drama over the school furniture in Don Francisco Tec's story of the foundation of Ticimul, Nicté Há, and Popolá (see Chapter 3). Like the bureaucratic protocols of the agrarian reform, the process of soliciting and receiving didactic materials became a ritual through which specific objects and performative acts instantiated the commitments of the state in the everyday lives of rural citizens. Note, for example, this section of a petition for a public library written in 1917 by the municipal president of Temax, a town in the henequen zone:

> The Revolution brought to fruition by you in Yucatán has as one of its principal
> goals the culture of the inhabitants, and thus libraries have been established in the
> cities, towns and villages under the care of the [local] authorities ... we ask you
> very respectfully to send the respective volumes for the formation of the library of
> this town as soon as possible, so that the inhabitants may enjoy the benefits that the
> Constitutionalist Revolution brings to Yucatán.[3]

"Culture" in this statement is a project that will eventually be evident in the minds of individual citizens, but that is currently situated in the specific books— "volumes"—that could be physically distributed by representatives of Alvarado's Department of Education. The library books are as much a token of the state's commitment to its citizens as they are a tool for the intellectual development of the people of Temax. This kind of bestowal ritual was repeated, often on a minuscule scale, in communities across the state, where it served to embody a number of different ties between citizens, political leaders, and collective identities. For example, Santiago Beana, the political leader from Tinúm who had participated in the Burning of Yaxcabá alongside Lol Barrera and Eustaquio Cimé, brokered the delivery of books and other pedagogical materials to short-lived schools that were founded in some of the smaller communities under his control in the early 1920s. In 1921, residents from the *kajtal* of San Francisco wrote to the leadership of the PLY in Mérida to request books and writing implements for "the children of the workers, who are Socialists like us."[4] Less than a month later they were able to report that the materials had personally been delivered by the "compañero" Santiago Beana.[5]

These early examples provide a precedent for what would become a durable rhetorical device: representing the delivery of educational material as a tangible example of the social "vindication" of rural people by the Mexican Revolution. Urban political leaders who succeeded Alvarado and Carrillo Puerto continued to give education a prominent place in their propaganda. Residents of rural communities, in turn, often made explicit references to campaign promises in their request for these materials. In 1935, the residents of Haimil, a hamlet (*ranchería*) outside of Tinúm, addressed a request for supplies with which to build a new schoolhouse directly to the Mexican president Lázaro Cárdenas. They cited his campaign promises in "[the] Sexennial Plan and the labor of improvement that this will develop in favor of the working and peasant masses of all our country."[6]

A more elaborate reference to Cardenas's campaign promises occurred in 1939 in the kajtal of Xalau, near the far eastern town of Kanxoc. It refers to the rural school as a fulfillment of the Revolutionary state's "redemption" of the "peasant masses":

> We solicit your help or economic cooperation, so that when we finish this work posterity can observe that in the lapse of your time in government the saving revolution of our times arrived even to this isolated place of our Fatherland. Alphabetizing the peasant masses as the maximum redemption of its revindication, so that they may incorporate themselves to the civilized social world, finding their economic, social and moral well-being.[7]

Given that the 1930s offered few alternatives to subsistence agriculture, it's difficult to see exactly how the adult residents of rural communities of Oriente thought that knowledge of reading and writing would bring "economic, social and moral well-being." Still, the desired school would survive into "posterity" as a monument to the president's commitment to Revolutionary ideals and rural citizens.

The ideological charge of this act of donating pedagogical materials is evident in the ways that physical objects in the schoolhouse figure in the oral narratives with which people commemorate the 1920s and 1930s. In Don Francisco's story about the foundation of Ticimul (Chapter 3), an intervention by federal troops led to the return of the furniture that had been stolen from the schoolhouse by the municipal president of Kaua. This act of restitution turned school supplies into another token of the pact that had been established between the president of the republic and the *ejidatarios* through the donation of agricultural land.

The presence of a rural teacher was another embodiment of the pact between rural Maya speakers and the post-Revolutionary urban world. For one, it implied the long-term residence of an individual who was decidedly an "outsider" to the community. Although peasants relied on surveyors and other government experts to determine and record the boundaries of their ejidos, the day-to-day development and administration of these landholdings were entirely in the hands of the local agrarian committee. In contrast, the operation of a school required that a teacher educated in an urban setting establish a permanent presence in a rural community, from which he or she would serve as a conduit for the curricula articulated by state educational institutions and the broader administrative and material framework of public education.

The prominent place that the first generation of rural teachers has in the oral histories that are told today gives us a sense of the political symbolism that was imbued in this role (Brito Sansores 1987).[8] Housed and fed by their host community, the ideal schoolteacher (*maestra* or *maestro*) got involved in local social life in ways that went far beyond teaching in the classroom. Teachers were also expected to disseminate modern notions of communication, hygiene, and work ethic to the adult population. As culture brokers, rural teachers were often charged with mediating in such bureaucratic transactions as applications for ejido grants and extensions, and in many cases gave literacy training to the adults who would serve as community officers. For example, I interviewed the elderly town clerk of the village of Xcalakoop (interview July 29, 2003) who recalled how the teacher José Cruz—who will figure in later sections of this chapter—had taught him how to read, write, and type as a teenager so that he could begin his clerical duties. Just as Xcalakoop's first public school was providing mass literacy education to a generation of local schoolchildren, the maestro Cruz was preparing the adults who would conduct the modern administration of the community.

The collective memory of legendary teachers such as maestro Cruz is consistent with a rhetoric of the "good" teacher that seems to have been well established in correspondence between rural communities and the SEP. Many of the themes that emerge in letters written during the first decades of public education are still common in oral narratives that extol the virtue of dedicated rural teachers. For example, a 1945 request written by community leaders of Tekom, near Valladolid, asks that a new post be created for the maestra Consuelo Osorio, who

> knew how to capture the sympathies of the people in general and the parents of families in particular, given the dedication she always put in the education of the children that were entrusted to her and her enthusiasm in procuring the cultural advancement of the people in general through any means available.[9]

The maestra Osorio's success in gaining the "sympathy" of local families hints at a kind of rapport that is still seen to be at the heart of the relationship between teachers and communities. In oral narratives told today, this rapport is generally articulated in terms of the willingness on the part of the maestra or maestro to "live alongside" (Sp. *convivir con*) her or his respective community. Given the differences in social class between most teachers and the residents of the communities where they teach, this effort at "living alongside" is often characterized as a willingness to suffer the discomforts of a different lifestyle. Stories told by retired teachers, including those contained in a number of published autobiographies, almost always include details of the arduous journeys down bush trails that linked the nearest town to the most isolated villages and of "becoming accustomed" (Sp. *acostumbrarse*; Ma. *suktal/sukchaj*) to the simple food and rustic accommodations that their host communities could offer (see Brito Sansores 1987; Quintal Martín 2002; Uc Dzib 1987). Although infrastructure and public health in the countryside have improved a great deal since the 1920s and 1930s, this kind of "suffering" is still seen as a crucial element of the experience of newly graduated teachers who are posted to geographically isolated schools after years of life in Mérida and other cities.

The place of teachers in rural society was a recurring theme of my own experience as an ethnographer, since I myself was addressed and referred to as a maestro in many of the communities where I did research. This was due in large part to several English classes or archaeology and history workshops that I taught in these communities over the years.[10] My age, class, social background, and many of my activities while in the field also seemed to evoke the persona of a rural teacher. Friends and informants often referred to my "becoming accustomed" to local food, sleeping in a hammock, and traveling in the bush in terms reminiscent of similar narratives about rural teachers.[11] My own experience with the maestro persona also gave me some insight into the temporality of this rapport, the fact that the relationship between teachers and communities tended to be as fragile as it was intimate. This parallel became hauntingly clear during one particular conversation with Don Dagoberto Tec, a man in his seventies who had grown up in Chan Kom. Don Dagoberto had been a student of Alfonso Villa Rojas, the Yucatecan teacher at a primary school who was a coauthor with Robert Redfield and ultimately became a professional anthropologist. He remembered the day that Villa Rojas returned briefly from his studies in the United States before leaving Chan Kom forever (probably in the early 1950s):

> The maestro Villa said, "Well, I'm going. I got a job as an anthropologist in the United States. I won't return anymore."
>
> [We said] "That's *fine*! You did a good job here. You suffered here with us, and now you have a good job. You go well."
>
> Because that's how it is. That's how it will be with you too, [Fernando]. You suffer here with us now, but when you finish the work you are doing here, you will have your good job too. (interview July 31, 2002)

Though as anthropologists we tend to focus on how our personal and political commitments to the communities we study extend beyond the demands of pure research, elements of this analogy are quite accurate. For both myself and Villa Rojas, "becoming accustomed" to rural Yucatán entailed a relationship that was ultimately ruptured as the maestro left to occupy a potentially lucrative post in places where rural Yucatecans would probably find themselves uncomfortable or even unwelcome. In both cases, it was "work" defined by "bosses" in a distant city (be they the Secretaría de Educación Pública in Mexico or the anthropology department at Stanford) and not a direct organic connection that bound maestro or ethnographer to a local community.

The intimate but ultimately tenuous relationship between the maestra or maestro and "her" or "his" community alludes to the primary difference between the agents of public education and other figures who served as brokers between rural communities and the state: the local "big men" (Sp. *caciques*). Today, as it was a generation earlier, teachers are assigned postings based on the needs of the education system, and are rarely sent to teach in their home communities. Whereas people such as Lorenzo Barrera or Eustaquio Cimé were natives of their respective kajo'ob, an urban schoolteacher sent to teach in Pisté or Chan Kom is unlikely ever to be considered to be *pisteil* or *chankomil*. Whereas an assertive cacique could bring the demands of the community to urban representatives of the state, the role of the maestra or maestro tended to embody "cultural promotion" and other elements of modernity that radiate from the top down. This particular "positionality" was an ever-present element of the role of rural teachers in navigating forms of factionalism and solidarity in which school foundation played a crucial role.

Public Schools and Communities

Books, furniture, and other teaching materials, like the person of the maestro or maestra, represent the parts of the public education complex that arrived in rural communities from urban areas. Besides these supplies, a significant part of the work of school foundation still lay in the hands of community members. From the local men who would provide the labor to build the physical structure of the schoolhouse to the women who would cook and wash clothes for the teachers, the foundation and operation of early public schools would have been impossible without the collaboration of adults who were often not formal participants in the educational process. Through the participation of local civil society, teachers and other SEP officials also tended to inherit many of the same intracommunity conflicts that figured in the agrarian reform.

Whereas the teacher as pedagogue engaged local children in a clearly defined role, his or her relationship to the adult population was often marked by a more delicate process of persuasion and accountability. Given the exigencies of swidden agriculture and housekeeping, parents were often reluctant to sacrifice the labor of both female and male children.[12] The work of persuasion often persisted long after the initial acquiescence of parents to send their children to school. From the 1930s to the present day, different committees made up of the parents of school-age children have played an important role in the financial management of schools. Meetings between teachers and parents' committees were instituted as a space in which accountability for the management of school funds and the progress of children could be tested.[13] In many cases, these parents' committees were successful in exercising a great deal of oversight over the conduct of rural teachers. Documents from the 1930s to 1950s at the SEP archives show that complaints from the parents' committees were often channeled upward through the educational bureaucracy. These grievances include the denunciation of teachers who were less dedicated to their teaching duties than to setting up shops or raising livestock on ejido land, who became inappropriately entwined in local politics (see below), who failed to appear at work for weeks and months at a time,[14] and who drank in public.[15] Parents' committees continue to exercise a similar role today. In Xcalakdzonot and several other communities, I observed a number of meetings during which pointed questions from local families obliged teachers to make careful accounts of their expenditures to a large assembly of parents and local political officials.

Conflicts that emerged within this carefully managed relationship between urban or urban-educated teachers and rural families were not the only factors that could potentially undermine a rural school. Many schools seem to have collapsed under the same social pressures that led to the fragmentation of kajo'ob and kajtalo'ob throughout the 1920s and 1930s. The difficulties of instituting rural education in demographically unstable communities are evident in the history of a series of sixteen Federal Schools that opened in the *municipios* of Cuncunul (or Chan Kom) and Tinúm in the 1930s, nine of which were closed permanently or inoperative for extended periods of time by the 1940s.[16] Some—such as the schools in the settlements of Pom, Haimil, Xcocail, Yaxché, and San Rigoberto (all in the municipio Tinúm)[17]—closed within a few years of their foundation, after the depopulation of their host communities brought the school-age population below the required minimum of thirty students.

In summary, social conflicts, demographic instability, and economic pressures all conspired to turn the foundation of rural schools into a complex political drama. As such, it could contribute to either the emergence of broad coalitions within rural kajo'ob or the retrenchment of older factional divides. Two examples—the Escuela Felipe Alcocer Castillo in Xcalakdzonot and the predecessors of the Escuela Miguel Hidalgo y Costilla in Pisté—reflect two very different outcomes for this process.

In the case of Xcalakdzonot, the foundation of the school seemed to be the final straw that fractured a tenuous coalition between two factions occupying different sites within the ejido. This ejido was founded around a series of kajtalo'ob that had been settled by families from several communities to the north at the beginning of the twentieth century, and gained formal political recognition in 1926. As it was drawn and titled, the ejido of Xcalakdzonot encompassed both the eponymous settlement at "Twin Cenotes" and a more or less autonomous cluster of homes at a site called San Nicolás (X-Lab Cah).

The first public school in Xcalakdzonot was founded under SEP jurisdiction in the early 1930s under the directorship of José Cruz, the now-legendary teacher who would later serve in Xcalakoop and other communities. However, letters written in the 1930s suggest that his initial reception in the ejido of Xcalakdzonot was not unanimously friendly. The school foundation seems to have brought to the surface latent tensions between people at the core settlement and at San Nicolás. Letters written by the maestro Cruz in 1932 suggest that several members of the dissident San Nicolás faction were forced to abandon the ejido of Xcalakdzonot under pressure from the authorities in the main settlement and from the teachers at the school. The maestro alluded to the fact that these same dissidents had been raising obstacles to the construction of the school.[18]

Such conflicts between rural teachers and families or individuals in the villages that they served were fairly common, and were often framed by proponents of the SEP as resistance to progress and culture by "anti-Revolutionary" elements within the community.

Interviews with older people in Xcalakdzonot suggest a different and more strictly economic motive for this conflict. The residents of San Nicolás didn't feel that they needed to contribute labor and money for the maintenance of a school that had been solicited and built in the name of their neighbors from Xcalakdzonot. What's more, while the new school was being built at a site within easy walking distance of the settlement at the Twin Cenotes, it would have represented an additional six or seven kilometers of walking to students from San Nicolás.

The running feud between the residents of San Nicolás and the Xcalakdzonot faction was inherited by the maestro Cruz's successor, Felipe Alcocer Castillo. The feud reached a climax in a gunfight in which Alcocer Castillo and several villagers were killed. In 2004, I interviewed Don Miguel Uc (interview April 18, 2004), an octogenarian who had been a student in Alcocer's primary school. Don Miguel recalled that the gunfight was instigated when the maestro went off to gather some squash from a milpa that he maintained on ejido lands near San Nicolás. Knowing that the maestro was not liked by the dissident faction, some residents of the Xcalakdzonot core accompanied him down the narrow bush trail as an armed escort. En route to the milpa, they chanced upon one of the San Nicolás residents, who insulted the maestro before being chased off into the bush. Hours later, as the party returned warily from the milpa, they were ambushed by the San Nicolás people. Don Miguel recalled that various people from both factions were killed. Alcocer was carried from the bush with a head wound from which he died on the way to the hospital in Mérida. The perpetrators of this attack were prosecuted, but letters written by Alcocer Castillo's successor to the Mérida offices of the SEP noted that, along with other relatives who "enjoyed firm support in Valladolid," the killer had initiated a private campaign of intimidation against the residents of the core settlement of Xcalakdzonot. They were also said to be threatening the federal teachers of several communities who had collaborated in the apprehension of one of the shooters a year earlier.[19]

"Resistance" to education in this case reflected more than the simple choice of a community to accept or reject the modernizing cultural project embodied by the schoolteacher. Conflict over the foundation of the school was inseparable from a broader feud over land and municipal affiliation between two essentially autonomous settlements within the same ejido. The placement of the school was based on the assumption that the boundary of the ejido encompassed a single community, ignoring that this was not much more than a pragmatic boundary drawn around land whose stewardship was based on an informal and apparently tenuous understanding between the residents of San Nicolás and the Xcalakdzonot core. Thus the feud that ultimately cost Alcocer Castillo his life was not about education per se, but about a preexisting set of frictions between the claims of local factions and the officially recognized "community" into which public education had been thrust.

Alcocer Castillo's successors in the local school sought to subsume the complexities of local struggles over land and political patronage to a much simpler battle for the establishment of "Revolutionary culture." Commemorations affiliated with the primary school quickly transformed Alcocer Castillo and the dead villagers from the Xcalakdzonot settlement into "martyrs." In July 1933, the new director of the school and the municipal government of Xcalakdzonot wrote to the SEP seeking official recognition for their commemoration of the slain maestro and the villagers Doroteo Balam Uc and José Santos Uc Couoh as "Heroes of the Town" (Sp. *Beneméritos del Pueblo*). The letter quoted a declaration that had been made in honor of the "Martyrs of Xcalakdzonot" for

> having offered their glorious lives for this town of Xcalakd-dzonot [sic], for which they fought with exemplary dedication and valor, procuring its prosperity and beautification, with the sage direction of the citizens Director of Federal Education and the Federal School inspector. with eternal gratitude and remembrance, we inscribe your

immortal names in our consciousness with indelible characters!!! glory and honor to you, immortal teacher and compañeros!!![20]

The commemoration proposed to the SEP leadership in 1933 still occupies a solid place in the official history of the village and demonstrates how the narrative of "Revolutionary culture" embodied in rural schools can be used to overwrite the complexities of local experience. A monument to the "Martyrs of Xcalakdzonot" stood near the plaza of the village until the late 1990s, and the local primary school still bears the name Felipe Alcocer Castillo. Today, the old conflict over the ejido seems to be a story only vaguely known to all but the oldest living residents, whereas the "martyrs" of education are memorialized in the name of the institution visited daily by the community's children. But despite its gradual absorption into a much simpler narrative of Revolutionary-era struggles for "culture," the history of Xcalakdzonot's first school serves as a good example of how the "problems" associated with the imposition of rural education can have less to do with conflicts between indigenous and Western culture than with conflicts internal to Maya-speaking kajo'ob.

If the foundation of a school in Xcalakdzonot made SEP officials choose sides in an existing factional conflict, the creation of a new school in Pisté seems to have come in the wake of a period of relative tranquility and social cohesion. Pisté had seen its share of trouble in the 1920s and early 1930s. By then, the community had developed a reputation for lawlessness and antiprogressive properties. The American adventurer Edward Thompson cited it as the home of the "Socialist agitators" who had destroyed the majority of his archaeological collection when they burned down the Hacienda Chichén Itzá in 1921 (see Chapter 3). This negative portrayal of Pisté also pervades a study of the community published in 1941 by the physical anthropologist Morris Steggerda. In his own ethnography, Quetzil Castañeda (1996) has linked the contrast between Redfield and Villa Rojas's positive portrayal of the people of Chan Kom and Steggerda's negative characterization of the people of Pisté to the particular context of each author's work and personality. Be this as it may, a negative stereotype of Pisté also seems to have pervaded the SEP. In a report celebrating the inauguration of the new school in 1933, Pisté was characterized as having been "one of the communities that was most resistant to education" (Sp. *una comunidad que era una de las más refractorias a la educación*).[21]

It is possible that this so-called resistance to education was due to bad experiences with previous rural maestros. One of my older informants from Pisté recalled a maestro who had been murdered there in the late 1920s or early 1930s after "throwing himself into the politics" (Sp. *por meterse en la política*) during the dangerous reign of Lorenzo Barrera (interview July 15, 2002). In a 1932 report to the SEP, the residents of Pisté are quoted as requesting an instructor with a "nationalist and not localist" orientation (Sp. *criterio nacionalista y no localista*).[22] This statement might suggest that the previous maestro had become too entangled in local affairs for his own good.

Reputation notwithstanding, conditions within the community were clearly improving in the early 1930s. The population, which had dwindled to a few dozen families in the time of the Burning of Yaxcabá (see Chapter 3), had rebounded considerably (see Steggerda 1941). Lorenzo Barrera, the cacique who has a somewhat bloodthirsty fame in the stories told today, was no longer leading the community. The founding of Pisté's new school in 1933 also reflected that community's growing profile through its association with the ruins of Chichén Itzá. Letters archived in the SEP archives suggest that additional funding to complete the construction of the new school building came in part from the Carnegie Institute of Washington through the archaeologist Sylvanus Morley, who was then directing the restoration of the site. Morley also convinced many of his workers to make individual donations of five pesos toward the construction of the school.[23] Perhaps because of this association with high-profile international sponsors, the groundbreaking ceremony was deemed important enough to be coordinated with a visit by the interim president of Mexico, Abelardo Rodríguez, and the SEP director, Narciso Bassols.[24]

For the leadership of 1930s Pisté, the performances that developed around the foundation of the new school served as an important expression of a collective commitment to "progress" just over a decade after the violent summer of 1921. In this case, the request that pisteil made in 1932 for a teacher with a "nationalist and not localist" orientation might also be read as implying a shift toward a more general "nationalism" in keeping with the town's growing prominence through association with Chichén Itzá. It seems like no small coincidence that the primary school of Pisté—a direct institutional descendant of the school refounded in 1930s—is named after Miguel Hidalgo y Costilla, a figure from the 1810 War of Independence who is often referred to as the "father of Mexico." Whereas the school of Xcalakdzonot commemorates a "martyrdom" that took place in the community's own ejido, Pisté's makes a reference to the creation myths of the Mexican nation-state. Though the tourist boom that would transform Pisté into a bustling commercial town was still almost half a century away, the optimism fueled by Carnegie Institute money and the new SEP school seems to anticipate the wealth and cosmopolitanism that mark the *kaj*'s place in contemporary Oriente.

Conclusions

In the 1930s, the kajo'ob of Xcalakdzonot and Pisté shared a number of important features: populations dedicated to full-time maize agriculture who spoke the Yucatec

Maya language more than they spoke Spanish and had lived without formal educational institutions at the beginning of the twentieth century. They also shared a series of experiences with institutions of the post-Revolutionary state: participating in the bureaucratic protocols of the agrarian reform and interacting with the objects, rituals, and social relationships that were associated with school foundation. Still, the social realities of these two communities provided a very different valence for these shared experiences. The SEP school in Pisté was founded during a period of relative calm, economic prosperity, and apparent social cohesion. In contrast, the maestros Cruz and Alcocer Castillo became participants in a factional dispute that ultimately rent the fragile coalition between the settlers of the Twin Cenotes and those of San Nicolás.

The contrast between these two examples suggests some ways in which we should reframe discussions about the impact of public education on communities that spoke indigenous languages. Clearly, there were some parts of the SEP project that challenged values or ideals held by families in Xcalakdzonot and Pisté, such as the importance of children laboring alongside their parents in different domestic or agricultural pursuits. However, focusing on a Manichean clash between "Mayan" and Western culture shifts attention away from the more complex local politics that is often more important to residents in rural communities. In neither of these cases was accepting or rejecting the education being offered by the SEP schools simply a question of choosing local traditions over the prestige of a modernity being diffused by ts'ulo'ob from the city. Instead, these choices were made as members of different factions mediated their relationship to other families in their own kaj, whether this mediation took the form of conflicts over land or a collective desire to celebrate a shared prosperity.

The fact that rural people reacted to public education through a triadic relationship with both urban teachers and other local families is still an important element of the vernacular politics of culture in Oriente. In the 1920s and 1930s, the bestowal of books and other objects and the physical presence of the teacher became tangible markers of a relationship between communities and the Mexican state. Just as different factions sought to manipulate the protocols of the agrarian reform, groups such as the residents of the Xcalakdzonot core turned their close relationship to Cruz, Alcocer, and other "cultural promoters" into a political tool. Similar factional competition often takes place when groups in communities seek to position themselves advantageously in relation to the very different cultural institutions that are promoting ethnic rights and heritage today. As it was eighty years ago, rural people in Oriente make statements about their relationship to culture that are aimed as much at their neighbors as they are at the Hispanic outsider.

This chapter has focused on the elements of public education that were immediately tangible to adults who, in many cases, did not attend the schools themselves. This is not to say that the work of pedagogy and its effects on the subjective experience of students do not constitute a major dimension of the local politics of culture. What went on in the classroom certainly has influenced the repertoire of narratives with which people make sense of multicultural politics, though it did so in ways that do not necessarily conform to a simple tension between "Maya" and "non-Maya" culture. This phenomenon will be the focus of the next chapter.

Notes

1. A list of public education employees from 1922 (when public education in Yucatán was under state-level control) includes only twenty-six schools in the Departamento de Valladolid, all of them in the seats of municipalities (*cabeceras municipales*) or in communities well established by the nineteenth century. See AGEY, PE, caja 703, "Educación Pública, 1920."

2. Although it was associated with the earlier stage of school foundation, the expansion of school foundation in Oriente by the Secretariat of Public Education included some administrators who were versed in the anarchist-inspired "rationalist" pedagogies that were experimented with in the state-run schools of the 1920s (Betancourt Pérez 1969; Echeverria 1996; Mena 1919). Many younger educators in the 1930s also sought to implement different models of "Historical Materialist" and "Socialist" education during the presidency of Lázaro Cárdenas (1934–40; see Britton 1976; Boyer 2003; Fallaw 2004). Though the actual practices used in schools often differed considerably from the theory of radical pedagogical philosophy, the institutional commitment to populist politics in the classroom made the substance of public education compatible with the larger constellation of social identities that were popularized by the PSY.

3. AGEY, PE, Educación Pública, caja 606.

4. Eleuterio Balam to Presidente de la Liga Central de Resistencia, October 13, 1922, AGEY, PE, caja 755, "Educación Pública."

5. Eleuterio Balam to Presidente de la Liga Central de Resistencia, November 11, 1922, AGEY, PE, caja 755, "Educación Pública."

6. Junta de Educación de Haimil a Presidente Lázaro Cárdenas, March 20, 1935, AHSEP, Departamento de Escuelas Rurales, 257, exp. 3.

7. Vecinos de Xalau a Presidente Lázaro Cárdenas, October 18, 1939, in AHSEP, Dirección de Educación Primaria en los Estados y Territorios, Escuela Rural Federal, Xalau, Chemax, 9035142/23032.

8. Metaphors associated with rural teachers in the Revolutionary period allude to the broad appeal of this figure as a metonym for the process of "cultural" modernization, and hint at a dense series of associations with a relationship between the city and the country

that has deep roots in Yucatecan popular culture. One of the most common metaphors used for the work of the rural teacher is that of the *missionary*, an agent of the contemporary educational project who continued the task of uplifting the "Indian" peasantry that figured so centrally in the historical identity of the urban elite (see Dawson 1998). Perhaps less common, but just as evocative, is a military metaphor. In his inauguration of the 1915 pedagogical congress that would mark the beginning of his educational project in Yucatán, General Salvador Alvarado declared his desire to "command these soldiers of the pen as I did those of the sword on the battlefield" (Voz de la Revolución 1915). Alvarado's "soldiers of the pen" represent the birth of a new kind of intellectual—populist, self-sacrificing, and trained at the bosom of the Revolutionary state—who is quite distinct from the effete and parasitic *literatos* associated with Porfirian decadence (see Gamio 1916).

9. Ayuntamiento of Tekom to the Governor of Yucatán, March 23, 1945, AGEY, PE, caja 1045, "Educación Pública."

10. My introduction to ethnography was through a field school in Pisté where most students taught English, and where I conducted workshops on Maya epigraphy and iconography for local artisans. When I conducted my most intensive fieldwork in the village of Popolá in 2000, I taught a triweekly English class to the community's school-age children, who were eager to learn the language and sell their artisanry directly to tourists. I taught a similar class in Xcalakoop during the last phases of my fieldwork in 2005.

11. If becoming accustomed to local food and habits was read as a show of solidarity, other parallels that some local people drew between my seasonal visits to their communities and those of many maestros also underscored a more ambivalent side of this relationship. Many people whom I had limited contact with seemed to think that my ethnographic activities were all meant to facilitate my work in teaching, which they assumed was a form of obligatory "social service" (Sp. *servicio social*) performed toward the end of my university studies. This sort of service is still common among university students in Mexico, both as a requirement in public universities and through specialized programs, such as the National Council for Education Development (Consejo Nacional de Fomento Educativo, CONAFE), that allow students from rural communities in Yucatán to attend university in exchange for teaching in a rural kindergarten or "cultural mission."

12. One man in his nineties from the town of Kaua told me of the pithy phrasing of his father's initial refusal to send him to school: "How are you going to eat what you learn?" (Ma. *Bi'ix ka jaantik le ba'ax a kanik*; interview August 16, 2002).

13. I have observed these meetings in small villages several times over the years. Though rural teachers in Mexico still tend to be addressed and treated with a far greater degree of deference than their counterparts in the United States, these meetings can become fairly lively affairs, with the school staff having to answer to public questions about the need for upgrades to facilities and the price of individual contributions for textbooks, supplies, or uniforms.

14. AHSEP, Dirección General de Educación Primaria, Escuela Rural Federal, Estado de Yucatán, exp. Xcatun, Tiquimul [*sic*] 239045; AHSEP, Dirección General de Educación Primaria, Escuela Rural Federal, Estado de Yucatán, exp. Tzeal, Cuncunul 23033.

15. AHSEP, Dirección General de Educación Primaria, Escuela Rural Federal, Estado de Yucatán, exp. Xcatun, Tiquimul [*sic*] 239045; AHSEP, Dirección General de Educación Primaria, Escuela Rural Federal, Estado de Yucatán, exp. Tzeal, Cuncunul 23033. These abuses are still reported in smaller and more isolated communities, and parents' committees are just as successful in prosecuting complaints. From 2003 to 2007 in the municipalities of Tinúm, Chan Kom, and Yaxcabá, I learned of several cases of SEP representatives investigating what they considered to be credible accusations of wrongdoing that ranged from teachers selling school supplies to parents at inflated prices to a case of sexual abuse. In at least one case, local parents successfully petitioned for the firing of a teacher without having to pursue criminal proceedings beforehand.

16. AHSEP, Dirección General de Educación Primaria, Escuela Rural Federal. See later in this chapter.

17. AHSEP, Dirección General de Educación Primaria, Escuela Rural Federal, Estado de Yucatán, exp. Pom, Tinúm 23108; exp. Haimil, Tinúm 22921; exp. Xcocail, Chan Kom 23328; exp. Yaxché, Tinúm 23081; exp. San Rigoberto, Tinúm 22906.

18. J. Cruz Centano to Gobernador del Estado, June 26, 1932, AGEY, PE, caja 945.

19. Juan I. Flores (Inspector Escolar Federal) to Director de Educación Federal del Estado de Yucatán, May 3, 1934, AHSEP, Dirección de Educación Primaria en los Estados y Territorios, 8966/11, Referencia IV/161(IV-14)/22929.

20. Alberto Arjona Novelo and Vecinos de Xcalakdzonot to SEP DER, June 4, 1933. AHSEP, Dirección de Educación Primaria en los Estados y Territorios, 8966234, Referencia IV/161(IV-14)/22908.

21. Report November 29, 1933, AHSEP, Dirección de Educación Primaria en los Estados y Territorios, caja 9035, exp. 23036, "Pisté Tinúm Yucatán."

22. Vecinos de Pisté a la SEP, April 14, 1932, AHSEP, Dirección General de Educación Primaria en los Estados y Territorios, exp. IV/161 (IV-14)23026.

23. This philanthropy was praised by some representatives of the SEP, but seems to have been met with consternation by others who felt that a foreigner, no matter what his intellectual credentials, should not be intervening in the matter of Mexican education. See Ing Mariano Moctezuma to Sylvanus Morley, January 21, 1935; Luis G. Ramírez to Celso Flores Zamora, January 7, 1935; Rafael Ramírez to Dirección de Escuelas Rurales Federales de Yucatán, May 16, 1934; Dirección de Escuelas Rurales Federales de Yucatán to Rafael Ramírez, May 5, 1934, all in AHSEP, Dirección de Educación Primaria en los Estados y Territorios, 8966/11, Referencia IV/161(IV-14)/22929.

24. Report November 29, 1933, AHSEP, Dirección de Educación Primaria en los Estados y Territorios, caja 9035, exp. 23036, "Pisté Tinúm Yucatán."

5

"When I First Went to Study"

PEDAGOGY, NATIONAL HISTORY, AND BILINGUALISM

This chapter focuses on two contemporary oral traditions
that are intimately tied to the legacy of rural schools: narratives about national history and a language ideology that
distinguishes between "good" and "bad" Spanish. Though
the first generation of rural schools taught a range of subjects that included mathematics, natural science, and various
technical professions, Spanish and national history were at
the heart of the stated goals of post-Revolutionary education. The way in which these two subjects were taught played
a key role in shaping a series of oral narratives with which
rural Maya speakers today are making sense of the politics
of multiculturalism. These two subjects also figure in contemporary iterations of an older dialectic between solidarity and factionalism that is enabled by identity politics.

I am not claiming that the pedagogy of early rural
schools was the only source of the notions of national

DOI: 10.5876/9781607322399.c05

identity and language ideology that have filtered into the everyday speech of rural Oriente. However, there are important parallels between the texture of contemporary ideas about national and linguistic identity and attitudes that seem to have been pervasive in early classrooms. Eighty years after the foundation of the first rural schools in Oriente, characters from a nationalist pantheon that had been unknown to most rural Maya speakers at the beginning of the twentieth century are often invoked to frame contemporary political projects in the familiar terms of official historiography. There is a parallel continuity in the ideas about language use and "civilization" that figured in early rural schools. Today, most rural people in Oriente have at least a basic proficiency in Spanish. However, a prejudice against code switching and "bad" Spanish instituted by teachers in the 1930s and 1940s is still evident in the way people refer to their neighbors' speech habits as an index of their "level of culture." In one of the ironies of contemporary multiculturalism, these same purist ideals are being incorporated into everyday narratives that turn speaking "good" Maya into an important element of the identity of rural commercial elites.

Narratives of national history and language purism are more than just traces of early twentieth-century pedagogy that have survived in the everyday speech of living communities. They also represent opposite poles of the dichotomy between factionalism and solidarity that marks the politics of "culture," just as a dialectic between fusion and fission marked the territorial politics of the agrarian reform. Narratives of national history tend to subsume the experience of diverse sectors of Mexican society into a coherent portrait of struggle and redemption, and provide a series of models for representing the projects of larger political coalitions. In contrast, language ideologies (Woolard and Schieffelin 1994) that distinguish between good and bad Spanish tend to focus on habits that are cultivated—or neglected—by individuals. Though government institutions and some local movements have cited speaking Maya as the basis for a collective identity, many of the everyday conversations that I have observed over the years focus on the value of speaking good Maya. In many of the communities where I have conducted research, the critique of *bad* Maya is a technique with which some families highlight their own cultural credentials over those of their neighbors.

In discussing the heritage of schoolbook history and early Spanish classes, I will move among documentary sources, oral history, and ethnographic observations of how these discourses are used today. This movement reflects in part the processes through which I became aware of some consistencies in vernacular discourse on national and linguistic identity through simultaneous research with these diverse sources. It also illustrates how many of the shared experiences that shaped local oral traditions in the early twentieth century—the texts and pedagogical techniques that taught students how to speak and reflect upon the past, for instance—continue to influence more recent patterns of identity politics, solidarity, and factionalism.

Schoolbooks, Exams, and National History

For Maya speakers in the rural Oriente of the 1930s, classes in "national history" (Sp. *historia patria*) were an introduction to events that took place far away and in a mythohistorical past. The fact that educational planners in Mexico equated ignorance of this historical narrative with the lack of nationalist identity is evident in reports written in the 1930s. Guidelines distributed by SEP officials urged teachers just arriving in their host communities to make sure that their students had "an idea of what the Mexican republic is" (Sp. *una idea de lo que es la república mexicana*) by knowing "the lives of the greatest Mexicans" (Sp. *conoce[r] las vidas de los más grandes mexicanos*).[1] By the middle of the twentieth century, rural education had succeeded in turning a series of key names, dates, and events into a common currency for vernacular narratives about a national past. Certain ambiguities in the relationship between this national past and the intimate sphere of local memory played a central role in how stories of the "Great Mexicans" could be associated with local projects and experiences.

The impact of schoolbook history is not something that can be gauged simply by the fact that rural Maya speakers can name Miguel Hidalgo, Benito Juárez, and other nineteenth-century figures as "Great Mexicans." The work of rural teachers also contributed to the popularity of a series of narrative plots that are used to make sense of experiences and political projects. Like any historiographical tradition, schoolbook history tends to impose a limited series of narrative plots with which we pour the past into intelligible and ideologically consistent molds (see White 1975). In early school textbooks and other pedagogical materials, "Great Mexicans" and events from different periods become practically interchangeable incidents in an archnarrative that emphasizes how the consciousness and courage of masculine heroes drive collective struggles against foreign and local oppressors. The role of this populist narrative in legitimating the post-Revolutionary Mexican state has figured prominently in several generations of writing about Mexican nationalism.[2]

One element of the schoolbook history of post-1920 Mexico that had a particularly powerful resonance in Yucatán was the revisionist treatment of "Revolution" as the essence of national identity. Figures such as Miguel Hidalgo and Benito Juárez had been heroes in the schoolbook history of the nineteenth century (Benjamin and Ocasio-Meléndez 1984), but a range of new individuals and incidents were added to the nationalist mythos after the 1910 Revolution. A good example of this expansion of the patriotic canon is the popular writings of the Yucatecan poet Antonio Mediz Bolio, who composed an especially influential narrative of his native state's Revolutionary heritage by synthesizing the nationalist sensibilities of the 1920s with a regional tradition of writing about the ancient and living Maya. Mediz characterized a sixteenth-century rebellion of the Cocom Maya against the Spanish, a war that earlier Yucatecan historians had seen as pagan resistance to the Christian conquest, as an embryonic manifestation of twentieth-century anti-imperialist struggles. Even the Caste War, the conflict that was cited as the epitome of a war between "civilization and barbarism" by nineteenth-century Liberals, was revalorized as a "social struggle" against the oppression of a landed aristocracy that was finally defeated by the Revolution (Mediz Bolio, 1934, 1951; see also Chuchiak 1997; Joseph 1985; Peniche Vallado 1985).

This tradition of populist historiography enabled a model of nationalism that could incorporate a range of different interests into a widely intelligible narrative. Just as the "mestizophillic" ideology of Revolutionary Mexico stressed the blending of races and cultures (Miller 2004; see also Gamio 1916), schoolbook history assimilated conflicts that nineteenth-century authors had characterized as "race war" into a more homogeneous body of "popular" or "social" struggle. This conflation of indigenous rebellions with other struggles for "national" liberation reconstituted the "Indian" as a figure compatible with other heroic subjects, evident in the stories of Felipe Carrillo Puerto discussed in Chapter 3. But it also blurred the boundaries between struggles based on class and ethnicity to such a point that it becomes difficult to distinguish claims made for indigenous rights from those of a more general Mexican nation. This pervasive feature of vernacular narratives about history persists today, and complicates attempts by self-identified Maya to articulate narratives of struggle that distinguish their history from that of a more generalized Mexican population.

A second dimension of oral narratives about national history that has been influenced by the heritage of public schooling is an anthropomorphization of the past, a phenomenon that is well documented in schoolbook histories in the United States and elsewhere (Anderson 1983; Moreau 2004; Restall 2003; Trouillot 1995). This is evident in the emphasis on "Great Mexicans," a cast of almost exclusively male characters who served as metonyms for more complicated events or concepts. Just as the distinct social contexts of conflicts such as the Caste War and the War for Independence are effaced by the narrative that treats them all as examples of a generalized popular struggle, the complexity of each of these historical periods is often reduced to a date and an easily identifiable masculine figure. Thus, the War for Mexican Independence tends to be summarized by citing the popular mobilization that began in 1810 with Miguel Hidalgo's famous "shout of freedom." Similarly, many of the complexities of the wars between Liberals and Conservatives of the mid-nineteenth century are reduced to the figure of Benito Juárez, who fought against Conservatives and French invaders to defend the Constitution of 1857 (Benjamin 2002; Gilbert 2003; Lomnitz 2001).

Pedagogical materials provide useful insight into how the form and content of national historiography were transmitted into the vernacular consciousness and oral tradition of rural people. A number of studies of rural education have documented how textbooks contributed to the popularization of this historical ideology (Benjamin 2002; Dawson 1998; Gilbert 2003; Vaughan 1997). But more ephemeral sources provide even more specific insights into how the formal and conceptual elements of schoolbook history were converted into a kind of knowledge that could be reproduced in oral narratives by students. At the SEP archive I found a few surviving examples of school exams from the 1940s that reflect the state of rural education in a number of districts shortly after the building of the first schools. The correct answers to these exams represented the minimum knowledge required for students to successfully complete their course. That is, they provide a portrait of the specific narratives that successful students performed for their teachers. The examples cited below are taken from exams approved by the SEP for Yucatán's Ninth School Zone—which encompassed the city of Valladolid and the rural communities of Oriente—for the 1942–43 school year.[3]

Several reading comprehension samples in the Spanish grammar and writing section of these exams are truncated versions of standard official narratives about the lives of Miguel Hidalgo and Emiliano Zapata, the peasant leader who had played an important role in the Mexican Revolution from 1910 until his assassination in 1919. Students were expected to answer a series of questions about the characters in the reading that would demonstrate their comprehension of the passage. The reading for the first graders (eleven years old) concerned Zapata:

> The Supreme Chief of the Revolution in the south had been Emiliano Zapata.
>
> When he was a child, he perceived how the wealthy and powerful took the lands of the humble agriculturalists, since his father was one of the victims of this. It is remembered that, full of anger, he said, "Father, when I am big I will make them give us our lands back."
>
> Being convinced that only through the force of arms could he attain his hope for justice, he launched himself into the Revolution through the same southern mountains that saw the courage of Pedro Ascenso, of Morelos, of Galeana, of Guerrero, and so many other patriots.
>
> Zapata could have been rich, but he disdained wealth and always proclaimed that luxury corrupts men. He could have been president, governor, a congressman, he could

have dressed in fantastic dress clothes, but never abandoned his typical cowboy dress or his hardworking peasants.

Emiliano Zapata was born in Anenecuilco, Villa de Ayala, in the state of Morelos in 1879, and was assassinated in Chihuahua on the 10th of April 1919 as a consequence of an infamous treason.[4]

Compare this with the reading comprehension selection given to the second graders (fourteen years old), this one concerning Father Miguel Hidalgo:

He embodies the unrest of his time.

Of an exquisite sensibility and a boundless generosity, he knew how to feel the scourge of exploitation that opened painful wounds in the lacerated flesh of the people. Because of this, he always sought to help the victims of that situation, introducing new crops and industries.

He was a creole priest and, like all of his class, felt himself as being very close to the rough inequalities of that time. The Spanish enjoyed all prerogatives; the Indians lived marginally.

Tired of so much injustice, he congregated the people by the conjure of the bell of Dolores, gave the shout of independence and the beginnings of a War that, after eleven years of fighting, consummated our political emancipation and consolidated our nationality.[5]

Given the brevity of these two narratives, it is obvious that many historical details are not included. Still, the specific facts that have been selected in both cases produce a similar plot from the very different historical contexts of Zapata and Hidalgo. In all likelihood, familiarity with the stereotyped bildungsroman of a "Great Mexican" made it easier for students to decipher unfamiliar words and intentionally obscure phrasing. The plot structure at the heart of these short narratives turns the peasant leader of the early 1900s and the popular cleric of a century earlier into interchangeable examples of a particular kind of life, one in which the hero turns his personal experience of injustices suffered by the masses into a cause for action. In both cases, the narrative device also subsumes the history of the indigenous peasants who fought in both of these conflicts into the biographies of the creole Hidalgo and the mestizo Zapata.

This simplified biographical structure of history is even more evident in the history portion of the exams, which reflects a style of teaching and learning historical facts that I refer to as historical "name tagging." In exams, posters, and public commemorations, the names of individual heroes are almost always accompanied by a short description or appellative name tag. Just as the name of Emiliano Zapata is closely bound to phrases that allude to "struggling for peasants," Hidalgo's is bound to the "shout of independence," a reference to his 1810 declaration in the parish of Dolores. Given the relative interchangeability of the plot structure used for Revolutionary life stories, this name tag represents the minimum bit of historical information that defines the specific character of an individual "Great Mexican."

This name-tagging function is at the core of the history portion of the 1942–43 exam. This section of the test consisted primarily of "matching" and "fill in the blank" questions in which students were required to provide the appropriate name tag for several historical characters. A correct matching answer for Miguel Hidalgo was that he "gave the shout for independence." A fill-in-the-blank question about Zapata was correctly answered by completing the sentence "Emiliano Zapata's primary Revolutionary *activity was with the peasants.*" Matching and fill-in-the-blank questions make similar one-line associations between President Lázaro Cárdenas and "nationalizing petroleum" or Benito Juárez and "establishing the republican government."

When I first read these old exams in 2004, I was struck by how consistent the pedagogy of the 1940s seemed to be with the historical narratives spoken by people today. Early on in my ethnographic research, I had noticed that many people who had completed elementary school had a comprehensive knowledge of the specific activities and images associated with each of the "Great Mexicans," even though they seemed to have only a vague sense of the chronology of actual events. When most people referred to an incident as having taken place during the Caste War, they were referring to the violence of the 1920s rather than to the peasant uprising of 1847. Even though teachers place some emphasis on the memorization of key dates—for example, the 1810 "Shout of Liberty"—chronology seems to fall by the wayside in a more general tendency to assimilate events into a universal history of struggle.

In this sense, a schoolbook historiography that relied on stereotyped biographies and one-line name tags did not simply comprise a version of national history that was compatible with the objectives of the Revolutionary state; it reinforced a tradition of vernacular narrative and political rhetoric that could incorporate many different events into an ideologically consistent nationalist cosmology. This is especially evident in the rhetorical heritage of Felipe Carrillo Puerto. Recall how Carrillo Puerto drew intentional parallels between the rural mobilizations of the early Revolutionary period and Maya resistance to the conquest (see Chapter 3). The political statement that he made in the 1920s was reproduced decades later by the styles of teaching history in public schools.

What results is a body of narratives in which the national history of Mexico and the events that form a part of the collective memory of local communities become practically indistinguishable. This is nowhere more evident than in the way that many people in Oriente tend to conflate local events from the 1920s with the Caste War and with the independence of Mexico. Many people of all ages assert that the paramilitary violence of the 1920s took place during the "time of Father Hidalgo." Many others have referred to the banning of debt peonage in 1915 as "when they shouted liberty and ended the age of slavery" (Sp. *Cuando gritaron la libertad y terminó la época de esclavitud*), conflating the Revolutionary-era reform with the famous "Shout of Dolores" that initiated the Wars of Independence in 1810.

Over the years, I have attempted to flesh out the picture of vernacular knowledge of historical chronology that I gathered from spontaneous comments such as those quoted above. On a number of occasions, I directly asked people to tell me about the history of Mexico from the Spanish conquest to the present day. This almost always proved to be an awkward, even uncomfortable, line of questioning for both my informants and me. One woman in her fifties was particularly blunt in expressing her incredulity that I, someone "who knew all about these things," was interested in what someone "who had barely finished primary school" had to say about them.

One exception was a story I heard when I was conducting oral history research with a Yucatecan colleague named Julio Hoil. It was told by Don Rodrigo Nahuat, a ninety-four-year-old man who had been the dominant political leader of Kaua for many years, and who characterized his exposure to public education as a pivotal moment in his life. Unfortunately for Julio and me, the tape recorder that I had brought with me failed. The fragments of the narrative quoted below are gleaned from jottings that Julio and I compared afterward (interview August 7, 2002).

What is striking about Don Rodrigo's story is how the tendency to subsume different events and periods into manifestations of the same struggle constitutes an inclusive collective identity. After a description of how he first learned some Spanish and began to study history as an adult, Don Rodrigo opened his narrative of the history of Mexico with the miraculous birth of the Aztec god Huitzilopochtli. He characterized the deity as "a sort of saint" conceived when his mother discovered a small picture of Christ while sweeping. Time passed, and Huitzilopochtli grew to be a ruler who led his people across a "desert land called Mesoamerica" (Ma. *Jump'el lu'um, jach déesierto. Méesoamerika u k'aaba*). In a spot where they found a cactus upon which an eagle was devouring a serpent, they founded México.

It is significant that Don Rodrigo's origin myth opens in the distant land of "Mesoamerica" and the foundation of Mexico City, and not in the spaces of Yucatec Maya stories about the creation of Chichén Itzá that are still an important part of local oral traditions. This distinction underscores the nationalist versus regionalist tone of his own story. His conflation of the indigenous Aztecs with the origins of the Mexican state is just as important, since it reflects the degree to which this tradition of vernacular historiography blurs the lines between the history of indigenous ethnic minorities and that of the Mexican nation at large. Throughout his narrative, Don Rodrigo used the pronoun "we" to refer both to the Aztecs and to the colonial and postcolonial Mexican nation; he made no clear-cut distinction between people who were specifically marked as "Indian" or "Maya" and a more generalized Mexican identity.

Don Rodrigo followed his account of the foundation of Mexico by describing how the Spanish came, bringing slavery (Ma. *éesclabitud*). Mexicans were forced to work and given their clothes and tools each year from the *patrón*'s storehouse. The Spanish also brought smallpox, vomit, diarrhea, and fever, because "we did not have illness back then" (Ma. *tumen mina'an to'on k'ojanbil ka'ach uchi*). Don Rodrigo did concede that the foreigners also brought many improvements (Ma. *ya'ab méejoras*), building the great colonial churches and introducing cattle, pigs, and the means of cooking them. The conflation of colonial and postcolonial forms of exploitation in this story shows some important parallels with the narratives about Felipe Carrillo Puerto and the "Indians" discussed in Chapter 3. Don Rodrigo's account of the "age of slavery" collapses different periods (from sixteenth-century *encomiendas* to nineteenth-century debt peonage) and different forms of suffering (from forced labor to disease) into a generalized dystopia that preceded the coming of "liberty."

Don Rodrigo's account of the end of slavery further reflects the truncating of historical chronology. He recalls that Father Hidalgo, "the Father of México" (Ma. *Letí u padre méejiko*), brought liberty "in around 1903" (Ma. *min 1903 u áanyo*). He mentioned a number of skirmishes and raids that he had seen firsthand as a boy in Kaua, some of the same violent incidents that led families into more isolated bush settlements such as X-Katun and Ticimul in the 1920s (see Chapters 2 and 3). Don Rodrigo seemed convinced that Hidalgo was a protagonist in these events. He closed his narrative by recalling that "that man [Hidalgo] died long ago, but I have seen his picture" (Ma. *Uch kíimik le maako', pero tin wilaj u réetrato*). This is a reference to one of the portraits that are a common decoration of schools and municipal buildings, tangible images that add to the credibility of the narrator's situating this historical figure's death within his own lifetime.

This elaborate account of national history was a relatively rare moment in my experience with oral narrative in rural Yucatán. However, it showed an ordering of events broadly consistent with the archnarrative and name tagging embodied in the exams from the first half of the twentieth century. Similarly "flattened" accounts of national history appear in more spontaneous and fragmentary ways in everyday conversations, when people refer to events from the collective memory of the 1920s as happening when "liberty was shouted," or associate them with the activity of Hidalgo, Juárez, and other nineteenth-century figures.

As an element of oral narrative, these invocations of national history have shaped how generations of rural Yucatecans articulate the essence of Mexicanness through the idea of a permanent and unfolding struggle between oppressors and oppressed. What's more, this is a relatively inclusive identity in which different sources of inequality—the difference between indigenous and ethnically unmarked citizens, for example—tend to be effaced by the more generalized sense of subaltern struggle that characterizes the essence of being a "great Mexican." As will become clear in later chapters, this function of narratives of national history is still a common recourse of local mobilizations that seek to create larger coalitions around specific issues of justice.

Spanish-Language Education

If the heritage of national history classes is evident in stories that constitute spaces for unity, Spanish-language education has contributed to an oral tradition that highlights social and cultural hierarchies within society. Whereas stories about the national past are verbal representations of a specific historical subject, discourse on language can be as much about the formal performance of "good" Spanish or Maya as it is about the specific denotative content of a narrative statement. In early classrooms, this emphasis on proficiency and proper style emerges through an often tense interplay between pragmatic strategies that were employed during the early phases of language training and linguistic purism that sought to purge students' speech of code switching and other interlinguistic behaviors. This dimension of early education has important parallels in local language ideologies that figure in contemporary experiences of cultural politics.

In theory, language training was meant to complement the educational project of national history classes. Paralleling other nation-building projects in Europe and the Americas (Bauman and Briggs 2003), authors in early twentieth-century Mexico saw the "unification of language" as a fundamental step in fomenting a strong and basically homogeneous Hispanic nation by replacing the myriad indigenous languages that they felt fragmented national cultural life (Gamio 1916; see also Bonfil-Batalla 1987). In more practical terms, Spanish-language training laid the foundation for literacy and was thus the condition of possibility for all of the subsequent components of public education.

That said, the practicalities of Spanish-language training also involved a number of challenges that were not part of teaching national history. Whereas the students' assimilation of narratives about the "Great Mexicans" took place when they had already attained some degree of Spanish proficiency, "Castillianization" (Sp. *castellanización*) began when there was a fundamental linguistic gap between the oral vernacular of the students and the standard language of education. Many rural teachers in Yucatán were themselves native speakers of Maya, though quite a few found themselves developing a basic proficiency in Maya as they tried to teach their students. In predominantly Maya monolingual communities—which seems to have been the case in much of rural Oriente during the 1930s and 1940s—these linguistic and cultural gaps demanded a range of creative solutions.

In most cases, engagement with formal pedagogical materials was preceded by a period of oral interactions between the teacher and students. Some teachers seem to have drawn inspiration from a series of "Rationalist" and "Socialist" active learning pedagogies that gained greater popularity in the 1910s and 1920s (see Britton 1976; Betancourt Pérez 1951; Mena 1919; Vaughan and Quintanilla 1997). Though these experimental pedagogies have been celebrated in the historical literature on Mexican education (Betancourt Pérez 1965, 1969, 1983), the full implementation of the radical agendas that they embodied was always mitigated by local realities. For example, I interviewed a retired rural teacher who had interacted extensively with older *maestras* and *maestros* who had begun teaching during the heyday of Socialist education. He observed, "The Red teachers talked a lot about the Socialist school. But if the teacher was Red or not, it didn't matter. He couldn't be Red in the classroom" (interview February 5, 2004). Still, different ideas of active learning were part of the toolkit that many rural teachers carried with them into the field, and a pragmatic necessity of many classrooms.

In the SEP archives, I found a series of unique documents that provide a vivid portrait of the pedagogies developed by instructors "in the trenches" of early rural education. This was a 1935 survey used to poll teachers working in Yucatán about their preferred method of castellanización.[6] One common feature of these letters was the recognition that teaching Spanish to monolingual students should be based on the association of words and objects in the classroom, and a rejection of the repetitive grammatical exercises used for students who were native speakers of Spanish or in traditional foreign-language instruction. One maestra dismissed such methods as consisting of "artificial language exercises that do not have any utility."[7] More informal practices were also seen as a means of overcoming the cultural and social gulf between students and teachers. As one maestro, Álvaro Noh Pereira, noted:

> It is well known that the Indian is distrustful and bashful by nature, and given to speaking very little. Those defects impede him from speaking Spanish to strangers, particularly if these know more than him, thus he also does not learn for fear of being

made fun of. Therefore, the teacher must earn his trust, without losing his authority, to perform the work of *castellanización*.[8]

Noh proceeded to describe a method that seems to have been common among maestros/as of his generation. Low expectations of rural students' capacity to learn aside, this method reflects a combination of the "active learning" pedagogies with a series of more practical concerns:

> Taking advantage of the diverse activities of the school, one can begin teaching the names of the objects that the children see and manipulate, passing from these to their augmentative and diminutive varieties, until getting to form small phrases in which the diverse parts of the sentence intervene, simple associations of words in which adjectives, qualifiers, verbs, etc., intervene. These should be so simple that the child need not make a mental effort to retain them.[9]

A similar account of this method of Spanish teaching was described by the teacher Pedro Nah Santos:

> One looks for objects or animals of the same place and begins to form phrases or sentences of the same place which are easy to understand and pronounce, taking care to teach them word by word. Suppose that the teacher is standing before a table. He will then ask, "What is this?" asking that they reply "That is the table."[10]

Another respondent to the survey wrote with unusual candor about the primacy that such active learning of Spanish had over other dimensions of rural teaching. He distinguished between this approach and pedagogical styles in which teachers taught all topics in Spanish and students were "forced by necessity" to reach some understanding of the language. He considered a more active and dynamic approach to Spanish as preferable, noting that the teacher must "forget that he is going to teach reading and writing" (Sp. *olvidar que va enseñar a escribir y leer*) in the first months of instruction. Rather, he or she should teach spoken language through the names and actions of the parts of the body, of household objects, farm animals, and so on. Still, the respondent warned, "I announce at once that I know the Maya tongue well and that these methods can only be applied by teachers who know that language."[11]

That this form of language training was widely used by several generations of SEP teachers, and that it entailed a transitional use of Maya, were confirmed by the retired teacher I interviewed in 2004. He had employed this method in rural schools in Oriente and the state of Quintana Roo in the 1950s:

> You would speak to them in Maya, saying "lelá in k'ab" [Ma. *this is my hand/arm*]. Then you would say, also in Maya, "lelá in brazo" [Ma. *this is my* brazo] just changing the word for "arm" into Spanish. And from then on, they [the students] would say "brazo"

instead of "k'ab" and learn many words, and you already had something with which to work. (interview February 5, 2004)

All of these teachers seem to have employed a style of word substitution, in which the Spanish names for some objects are gradually substituted for the Maya, that mirrored and accelerated the processes of lexical borrowing by which certain Spanish words have become common in Maya since the colonial period (Lockhart 1999; Restall 1997). In this sense, rural schools did not initiate the process of lexical borrowing and transmission from Spanish to Maya. But by employing this systematically as part of a transitional bilingualism, they diffused the Spanish language into the vernacular speech of Oriente on an unprecedented scale.

In spite of drawing on practices of word substitution with a deeper local history, and in spite of the extensive use of Maya in many classrooms, this transitional bilingualism was a far cry from contemporary experiments in "bilingual and bicultural" education (Pfeiler and Zámišová 2006). I have spoken with many older Maya speakers, and some people in their thirties and late twenties, who even recall being subjected to corporal and other punishments for speaking Maya in school. In effect, the ultimate goal of castellanización for the respondents to the 1935 survey and later generations of teachers was to produce a standard-sounding Spanish.[12] A tension between the pragmatic necessities of bilingual classrooms and this desire for purism was already in evidence in 1935. A respondent named Martín Buenfil cautioned that though the "natural method" of instruction must always be employed, teachers should avoid using word substitutions and focus on teaching whole phrases and sentences:

> [Teaching should be through] simple phrases and never through [individual] words, because once the child learns these and wishing to express a thought solely through them, he inverts the order, or adds or removes words. This results in the language that is being taught being mangled (Sp. *se estropea*). Afterwards, it is difficult to teach them to speak correctly, because speaking in this way is almost a habit for them.[13]

What Buenfil cautioned against is a fairly common element of the vernacular Spanish spoken in Yucatán today. Many rural bilinguals employ nonstandard word order and constructions that are calques of Maya syntax (see Amaro Gamboa 1999). For example, Yucatec Maya expresses possession by adding a series of prefixes and suffixes to the object possessed; this form is often transposed to Spanish. Thus the common nonstandard Spanish phrase "Su sombrero de Juan" (His hat of Juan) is a word-for-word translation of the standard Maya phrase *u p'ok Juan*. As Buenfil noted, bilingual students could learn all of the correct lexica with which to translate this sentence through simple word substitution, but this is no guarantee that they would produce standard word order or grammar.

Another habit of local speech that probably did—and still seems to—irk many teachers is the fact that the same word substitution that was exploited in the schoolhouse also works in reverse, when bilingual speakers interject Maya terms into their Spanish. For example, the interjection of Maya terms such as *jach* (very) or *jan* (to do something quickly) is quite common, and strongly associated with the "bad" Spanish of rural people.[14] In many cases, these interjections are intentionally done for effect. The ability to improvise new words in the interstices of Spanish and Maya is a style of wit highly valued in rural Yucatán, and has figured in everyday practices with which native speakers assert different kinds of localist identities against speakers of the more prestigious Spanish language (Armstrong-Fumero 2009b). So just as rural teachers taught Spanish by interjecting words into their Maya-language dialogues with students, bilinguals today can achieve a range of effects by incorporating "new" Maya terms into their Spanish. In this sense, the forms of Spanish training that were used in early rural schools had an organic relationship to ways of thinking "between languages" that Mignolo (2000, 226) refers to as "languaging" and that tend to reproduce a distinctly local variety of nonstandard Spanish.

The Spanish that is spoken in the communities where I have conducted research is particularly rich in Maya word substitutions. Many of the specific substitutions that have been popularized in recent generations refer to contemporary habits associated with the tourist trade, and often seem like an ironic commentary on the quotidian side of the "Mayanness" that has become a valuable commodity (see Chapter 6). For example, a term that is common in communities that participate in the tourist industry at Chichén Itzá refers to the ambulant sale of wood carvings to tourists as *tich'ear* (Sp. to tich') or *hacer tich'* (to do tich'). This is derived from a Maya word that roughly translates to "raise an object over one's head," and has no clear analog in Spanish (see Figure 5.1). Most bilingual Yucatecans whom I know seem conscious of the fact that words like *tich'ear* are "bad Spanish," and use this kind of substitution as an intentional subversion of "good Spanish" for humorous effect. For example, it is common to hear sentences such as *"Está nojoch esa madera"* (That carving is *nojoch*! i.e., large) or *"¡Está ki esta salsa!"* (This sauce is ki! i.e., delicious) uttered by people who are perfectly capable of rendering the same sentence in standard Spanish. The diffusion of English in many communities has added a third dimension to this style of playful code switching. For example, it is popular among teenagers to refer to one's home with the phrase *tu jaus*, using the Spanish word for "your" and the English word "house." One of the most popular phrases that people mention as a humorous example of this "mixed" local language is the trilingual phrase *"ch'in e boolao' brooder!"* This is often shouted by catchers during baseball games, and is composed of the Maya word *ch'in* (roughly translat-

FIGURE 5.1. Doing tich' (Pisté 1999). Photo by author, negatives archived by Quetzil Castañeda.

able as "to throw with aim"), the Spanish word *bola* (ball), and the English word "brother."

As the teacher Martín Buenfil observed in 1935, the necessary complicity of pedagogy with these local styles of languaging has always been at odds with the purist aims of castellanización. Today, teachers in rural schools still struggle to promote standard Spanish among both Maya monolingual and Spanish/Maya bilingual students. Yet in many ways, public education has succeeded in validating the use of "good" Spanish, even if many bilinguals refuse to comply. Even in communities where certain kinds of code switching and interlinguistic play are considered humorous, people who are simply unable to speak standard Spanish are likely to be mocked by their better-educated peers and neighbors.

As I will discuss further in Chapter 7, this elitist discourse on "good" language use is not limited to how educators deal with Spanish; it has also become a common feature of discourse on the Maya language that has emerged as a part of Mexico's official multiculturalism. The same critique of speech habits that "mangle" the structure of Spanish, distressing a teacher in 1935, is increasingly applied by Maya-language activists who are critical of the use of common Spanish borrowings and sentence-level calques in Maya speech (Hoil Gutiérrez, May, and Martínez Huchim 2008). This kind of purism has also been assimilated into vernacular narratives about cultural hierarchy. Many people who are better off and better educated in the communities where I have conducted fieldwork perform what they often refer to as a "legitimate" Maya—a hyperpurist register purged of common Spanish borrowings—as a mark of distinction (Armstrong-Fumero 2009b; Berkeley 1998). I have even spoken to people who, in defense of this "legitimate" Maya, cite the catcher's call as a barbarous habit that needs to be eliminated if the Maya language is to be preserved. Thus, where heritage of national history classes tends to posit an inclusive collective identity, the heritage of linguistic purism often injects a divisive tone into narratives about Mayan linguistic identity.

Conclusions

Oral narratives about Mexican history and local language use, along with the collective memory of the rural violence of the 1920s and the agrarian reform, form part of the basic repertoire with which people in Oriente can make sense of the different collective labels that have been applied to them as rural citizens of the Mexican state. Just as the experience of the agrarian reform embodied a paradoxical series of centripetal and centrifugal social processes, these artifacts of public education are used to manifest different dimensions of solidarity and factionalism. Even as stories about the "Great Mexicans" provide some means of articulating fairly inclusive political coalitions, a metalinguistic discourse that values purism over other linguistic habits provides the tools for individuals to exalt their own cultural credentials at the expense of others.

Both of these dimensions come into play in everyday narratives about the nature and politics of Mayan identity. In the field of contemporary multiculturalism, the heritage of twentieth-century education forms the substrate for speaking about a range of new economic possibilities and political openings amid the decline of many older welfare institutions. This context of social, economic, and political change is generating some new configurations of local identity, even as it reproduces the dialectic between solidarity and factionalism that figured in the emergence of twentieth-century cultural politics. This context of change and continuity will be the focus of the next chapter.

Notes

1. Though such comments on inspection reports are common, the specific phrasing I use here comes from a report of the school of Xcan, Chemax, in 1932, AHSEP, Departamento de Escuelas Rurales, caja 9044, exp. 28647.

2. For general treatments, see Brading 1973; Benjamin 2002; García Canclini 1989; Keen 1971; Tenorio-Trillo 2009; see also Anderson 1983. Building on the work of Marxist scholars who criticized the "politics of the masses" in post-Revolutionary Mexico (Gilly 1979; Córdova 1986), Roger Bartra identified a wide-ranging literary and popular culture canon based on stock characters that ranged from the heroic warrior-peasants of the Revolution to their lumpen proletarian urban descendants, to whom he attributed an important role in maintaining PRI dominance (Bartra 1987, 1999). The agency and political subjectivity of citizens might not be as directly overdetermined by the ideological framework of post-Revolutionary Mexico as Bartra and other Marxist authors suggest (see Stephen 2002; Gutmann 2002), but the consistency with which a limited number of plots is used in everyday narratives about the past does reflect the success of educational institutions in shaping the formal and substantive elements that give a tangible and widely intelligible form to historical consciousness.

3. AHSEP, Departamento de Directores de Educación Federal e Inspecciones Docentes, Referencia R/100(04)(IF27604). Several sets of tests were filed here as a single *expediente*.

4. Original Spanish: *El Jefe Supremo de la Revolución del sur había sido el general Emiliano Zapata.*

Cuando fue niño aprendió a los acaudalados quienes arrebataban sus tierras a los humildes agricultores, ya que su padre era una de las víctimas de aquellos. Remuérdase que desde entonces, lleno de coraje, le dijo, "Padre, cuando yo sea grande haré que nos devuelvan nuestras tierras."

Por eso convencido de que solo por la fuerza podía conseguir su anhelo de justicia, se lanzó a la Revolución por las mismas montañas del sur que supieran la bizarría de Pedro Ascencio, de Morelos, de Galeana, de Guerrero, y de tantos otros patriotas.

Zapata pudo ser rico, pero desdeño la riqueza y siempre proclamó que el lujo corrompe a los hombres. Pudo ser presidente, gobernador, diputado, pudo lucir fantástico traje de gala y nunca abandonó su típico traje de charro ni a sus sufridos campesinos.

Emiliano Zapata nació en Anenecuilco, Villa de Ayala, Estado de Morelos en el año 1879 y murió asesinado en Chihuahua el 10 de abril de 1919 a consecuencia de una infame traición.

5. Original Spanish: *Encarna las inquietudes de su tiempo.*

De una sensibilidad exquisita y de una generosidad a toda prueba, supo sentir el flagelo de la explotación que habría heridas de dolor sobre las carnes laceradas de su pueblo. Por eso procuró siempre ayudar a las víctimas de esta situación, introduciendo nuevos cultivos y nuevas industrias.

Fue sacerdote y criollo y, como todos de su clase, sentía muy de cerca las ásperas desigualdades de la época. Los españoles gozaban de todas las prerrogativas; los indios vivían postergados.

Hastiado de tanta injusticia, congregó al pueblo y, al conjuro de la campana de Dolores, dio el grito de independencia e inició una Guerra que, al cabo de once años de lucha, consumó nuestra emancipación política y consolidó nuestra nacionalidad.

6. The responses to the survey are copied from the following file: AHSEP, Departamento de Escuela Rurales, Informe de Inspección, Yucatán, 1935, legajo (document) 9.

7. Original Spanish: *Artificiosos ejercicios de lenguaje que no tienen ninguna utilidad.* María A. Viuda de Reyes, April 28, 1935, AHSEP, Departamento de Escuelas Rurales, Yucatán.

8. Original Spanish: *Bien sabido es que el indio es desconfiado por naturaleza vergonzoso y de muy poco hablar. Esos defectos le impiden hablar el español ante persona extraña, principalmente si ésta sabe más que él, así también como no hace aprender por temor a ser burlado. Por tanto, el maestro debe otorgarle toda su confianza, sin perder su autoridad, para desarrollar su trabajo de castellanización.* Álvaro Noh Pereira, April 25, 1935, AHSEP, Departamento de Escuelas Rurales, Yucatán.

9. Original Spanish: *Aprovechando las diversas actividades de la escuela, se puede ir enseñando los nombres de los objetos que los niños ven y manejan, pasando de éstos, a sus variaciones en aumentativo y diminutivo, hasta llegar a formar frases pequeñas en que intervengan las diversas partes de la oración, asociaciones de palabras sencillas, en que intervengan adjetivos, calificativos, verbos etc., debiendo ser éstas tan sencillas que el niño no tenga que hacer esfuerzo mental para retenerlas.* Álvaro Noh Pereira, April 25, 1935, AHSEP, Departamento de Escuelas Rurales, Yucatán.

10. Original Spanish: *Se buscan objetos o animales del mismo lugar y se van formando frases u oraciones del mismo lugar fáciles de entender y pronunciar teniendo el cuidado antes de enseñar palabra por palabra. Supongamos que el maestro ésta delante de una mesa. Por consiguiente preguntará. ¿Qué es esto? Esa es la mesa dirá que le contesten.* Pedro Nah Santos, April 21, 1935, AHSEP, Departamento de Escuelas Rurales, Yucatán.

11. Original Spanish: *Advierto de una vez que conozco bien la lengua maya y estos métodos solo pueden aplicarlos maestros que conocen este idioma.* Pedro Nah Barón [n.d.] response to survey, AHSEP, Departamento de Escuelas Rurales, Yucatán.

12. Alfonso Novelo, April 25, 1935, AHSEP, Departamento de Escuelas Rurales, Yucatán.

13. Original Spanish: *El natural por medio de frases sencillas y nunca por palabras porque el niño al aprender éstas y querer por si solo expresar un pensamiento invierte el orden, pone o quita palabras resultando con esto que estropea el idioma que se trata de enseñar y después cuesta trabajo enseñarlos a hablar correctamente porque ya en ellos hablar de esa forma es casi un hábito.* Martín Buenfil, April 27, 1935, AHSEP, Departamento de Escuelas Rurales, Yucatán.

14. Urban Yucatecans use a number of Maya borrowings in their spoken Spanish, such as the standard use of *xik* for "armpit" or *wech* for "armadillo" (Amaro Gamboa 1999). But in over a decade of conversations with urban Yucatecans from a broad range of socioeconomic backgrounds, I have never heard Spanish-speaking city people interject *jach, jan,* and other adverbial terms in Spanish-language discourse the way that rural people do.

6

"That Time of Change"

THE LIMITS OF AGRICULTURE AND THE
RISE OF THE TOURIST INDUSTRY

The histories that I traced in Chapters 2 through 5 documented a series of parallels between local experiences of
early twentieth-century institutions and those of post–
Cold War multiculturalism. The legal protocols associated
with the *ejido*, objects such as books and schoolhouses, narratives about national history, and the concept of culture
all became part of a language for talking about the collective identity of rural communities and their relationship to
the Mexican state. This deep-seated discourse is still present in different iterations of local identity politics, even as
a series of economic and political transitions have altered
the social makeup of the region and shifted some of the
axes along which the dialectic between factionalism and
solidarity plays out.

In some cases, the development of new alternatives to
"peasant" identity and agrarian organizations seems to be

113

DOI: 10.5876/9781607322399.c06

defining new political possibilities. As I noted in Chapter 1, many students of post–Cold War indigenous politics associate the rise of multiculturalism in Mexico with new forms of neoliberal citizenship that have developed amidst the decline of older peasant institutions. However, the case of Oriente in the second half of the twentieth century complicates this picture on a number of levels. Although maize agriculture faced a series of crises (see esp. Warman 1985), there is a less clear-cut correspondence between the decline of the ejido and the rise of ethnic politics. A tourist industry that brought unprecedented wealth to many communities in Oriente played an important role in turning Maya culture into a valuable commodity decades before multiculturalism came into vogue as a mainstream political currency. The persistence of older agrarian institutions in the midst of a tourism boom, like the ambiguity that has always marked notions of ethnicity in Yucatán, influenced the particular texture of multicultural discourse in Oriente. These factors have also conditioned a new iteration of the dialectic between solidarity and factionalism in identity politics.

In the remaining chapters of this book, I will focus on how ambiguities regarding who exactly counts as an Indian or a Maya person in Yucatán have enabled the formation of a diverse and often contradictory series of multicultural identities. There is an especially important contrast between communities and families for whom engaging the Mexican state as "Mayas" is consistent with older agrarian institutions, and others for whom ethnicity figures in what I will refer to as "postpeasant" identities. The corporatist iteration of ethnic politics in predominantly agrarian communities and the postpeasant Mayan identities that are emerging in more urbanized *kajo'ob* involve different ways of reconciling narratives inherited from the early twentieth century with the realities of regional development in the past few decades. A closer look at the geography of modernization imagined by Robert Redfield and his Yucatecan collaborator Alfonso Villa Rojas in the 1930s, and at how the developments of the twentieth century were actually experienced by these communities, is a good point of entry into this question.

Geographies of Yucatecan Modernity

Chan Kom: A Maya Village by Redfield and Villa Rojas (1934) is a classic in two senses. First, it represents a defining argument about "folk" society in the canon of anthropological literature. Second, it provides a portrait of a place and time that became the definitive scholarly representation of rural Yucatecans as "Maya Indians." Central to both of these legacies is the authors' insistence on the "intermediate" nature of Chan Kom and other similar communities, which made them an ideal site from which to study the cultural processes associated with modernization. Though

Chan Kom was still peripheral to the urban world of Mérida, its residents' interaction with institutions such as the PSY, the agrarian reform, and rural schools had transformed them into "Indians" who were quite different from the descendants of Caste War rebels in Quintana Roo:

> The Quintana Roo Indians are still politically independent: their organization is local and tribal; and schools have only a recent and precarious foothold among them. The Indians of the Chan Kom area, however, are integral parts of the State of Yucatan. This is the outermost region in which governmental and educational controls function effectively. The interests of the villagers here are not wholly turned in upon themselves, but directed northward towards the towns from which come their school teachers and the orders of the state and federal governments. To these governments they are politically responsible. The villagers here are economically independent of the large landowner; the ways of life are primitive and largely Indian; but the people are voters and taxpayers. (Redfield and Villa Rojas 1934, 3–4)

For Redfield and Villa Rojas, the people of Chan Kom were still "Indians" in many respects, but a series of transformations over the previous decades had effectively turned them into self-conscious citizens of the Mexican state and participants in a translocal economy. In some of his later works, Redfield would elaborate on this characterization of the "intermediate" geographical and cultural place of Chan Kom, drawing a more comprehensive portrait of the west-to-east movement of modernization in Yucatán.[1] He maintained that through the expansion of public education and the cash economy, modernity flowed from the city of Mérida to the town of Dzitas, from whence it trickled to the "folk" village of Chan Kom and onward to the "tribal" village of Tuzik in the then-territory of Quintana Roo (Redfield 1941; see also Hawkins 1983).

As I noted in Chapter 1, several generations of scholars working on Mexican peasant studies have produced a number of important revisions to Redfield's "folk urban" continuum.[2] But even if these critiques have made important contributions to anthropological theories of the Yucatecan peasantry, revisions of Redfield's scholarship have done little to displace this spatialized model of modernity from the popular imaginary of Yucatán. During my own fieldwork, the narratives with which rural people commemorated the "coming" of culture in the 1920s, like their characterizations of more contemporary experiences with economic modernization, had more in common with Redfield's analysis than with those of any of his critics. This reflects the second "classic" dimension I ascribed to Redfield's work. That is, many of the same processes that were bringing about social and cultural change when he conducted his research from the 1920s to 1940s—from PSY militancy to the agrarian reform and the foundation of schools—have exercised a lasting impact on the ideas about citizenship, modernity, and culture that are still common among the descendants of the people whom he studied.

The persistence of certain elements of this "classic" narrative of modernization and culture is noteworthy, given that contemporary forms of multicultural politics emerged in the wake of significant political and social changes. In many ways, the development of the regional economy in the last third of the twentieth century has defied earlier expectations that economic prosperity diffused from well-established urban cores such as Mérida. A marked spatial reorientation was triggered by the tourist boom initiated by the creation of Cancún in the state of Quintana Roo in the 1970s (Kray 1997; Castañeda 1996; Castellanos 2010b; Re Cruz 1996; Ramírez Carrillo 2002; Warman 1985). In a relatively short span of time, labor migration and the flow of tourists westward from Cancún created new possibilities in an eastward-oriented tourist economy. For a generation of rural men and women, labor in construction, the hotel industry, and other tourism-related trades has provided unprecedented access to cash wages.[3]

By the 1980s, Oriente had emerged as an important core of the tourist economy in its own right. The archaeological zone of Chichén Itzá is the primary inland attraction of the contemporary tourist circuit. An influx of foreign cash gradually transformed the town of Pisté—just two kilometers from the ruins—into a source of economic opportunities that ranged from wage labor in construction and the hospitality industry to the production and sale of handicrafts (Castañeda 1996; Peraza López and Rejón Patrón 1989). Profits from the tourist industry enriched a native bourgeoisie, many of whom are children and grandchildren of wealthy peasants like those who had participated in agrarian wrangling at Nicté Há. Local-born businesspeople from Pisté continue to exercise considerable economic power in their own *kaj* and in a number of neighboring communities.

The effects of this tourist economy have expanded far beyond the immediate vicinity of Chichén Itzá and Pisté. The hotels, artisanry shops, and restaurants of Pisté employ labor from Xcalakoop, Nicté Há, Ticimul, San Felipe, and most other communities within twenty miles. Even individuals with only basic Spanish and literacy skills could find work as housekeepers, construction workers, teamsters, and artisans (Castellanos 2010b).

By the 1990s, migration was no longer a necessary element of participating in the tourist market, as residents of small agricultural communities could now participate in the tourist industry without leaving their own homes. Here, a cottage industry based on handicrafts production played a central role. In the 1970s, a few families from Pisté had developed a style of archaeologically inspired stone and wood carving

(Castañeda 2004). By the time I began my research, hundreds of individuals in the community were employed in the full-time creation of handicrafts that ranged from wood carvings to molded cement figurines and hand-painted batik. Like the market for tourist-sector labor, this cottage industry expanded beyond the boundaries of Pisté, further cementing the core-periphery relationship between the tourist hub and nearby agricultural communities through the production, wholesale, and retail of artisanry. By the mid-1990s, Yaxuná, Popolá, Kancabdzonot, and about a dozen other villages specialized in the production of inexpensive wood carvings that are shipped en masse to Pisté, where they are sold in lots to local merchants who sand and paint them for retail sale in local stores or in the archaeological zone of Chichén Itzá (see Armstrong-Fumero 2000). This kind of wholesaling has become increasingly important to well-established merchants—mostly from Pisté families who had been engaged in the tourist industry for decades—as sources of carveable wood in their own ejido became depleted. Artisans' production is now the dominant nonagricultural occupation in Popolá, Yaxuná, Kancabdzonot, and other villages. By 2008, this occupation was catching on as far to the southwest as Xcalakdzonot. In many of these places, wholesaling to merchants in Pisté has supplanted the reliance on more distant urban sources of cash income. Andrea Pat, the leader of an artisanry cooperative in Popolá, noted that one of the greatest benefits of the trade was that it eliminated the necessity for many young men to seek work in construction in Cancún (interview July 9, 2000).

To summarize, the rise of the tourist market transformed Quintana Roo from an eastern periphery to a new economic core, just as the communities closest to Chichén Itzá emerged as core communities in their own right. This shift has transformed the "classic" geography of modernity and prosperity that had been oriented westward toward the capital of Mérida. However, it has not displaced the conflation of time and space that figured in Robert Redfield's ethnography and in the oral narratives of many of the people whom he interviewed. Writing in the 1930s, Redfield (1941, 55) argued that the tribal village of Tuzik appeared like the Chan Kom of a few decades earlier, and he drew parallels between the social organization of the town of Dzitas and an older incarnation of Mérida's urban landscape. Today, people in larger and wealthier towns like Pisté characterize the lifestyle of peripheral agrarian villages as similar to the way of life in Pisté "a long time ago."

This vernacular equation of space and time was a recurrent theme in my own experience as an ethnographer. In 2000, when I first announced my plans to begin research in Popolá, one Pisté woman in her fifties warned me that people would be much less extroverted than I had become accustomed to in Pisté, and were likely to "just peek from between the wall posts" (Sp. *acechar desde los bajareques*) when I first arrived. She added that this was something that she recalled people in Pisté doing when she was a child. On a separate occasion, her husband warned me to be sure to pack enough food, because any outsider's request for goods in agricultural villages tended to be answered by a hostile shout of "There isn't any!" (Ma. *Mina'an!*), just as it had been in Pisté generations ago. Fortunately, neither of these warnings matched up to my actual experience in smaller agrarian kajo'ob.[4]

Not all characterizations of the habits of temporally and spatially distant communities are so negative. Just as they have warned me of stingy and suspicious peasants, many people in Pisté have also referred to the honesty and simplicity of people in smaller villages as "very noble" (Sp. *muy noble*). This character is also ascribed to people in their own community during simpler and poorer days. In Chapter 1, I mentioned a comment that Mario Mukul made regarding marriage customs in a conversation with me and his mother, Doña Petrona. The major points that he cited as signs of the "culture" of Pisté are worth quoting at length:

> Culture? Like the type of culture of the Mayas? There is no more, there isn't as much old culture as before. Before, you would hear every now and then that they were going to the *ch'a chaak* [shamanic rain ceremony] to make it rain. What is another thing they did before, of the Mayas? Before, when you asked for your bride, you had to look for someone who speaks prettily, who speaks sweetly. [*Speaking sweetly*] it's his job, because he would charge you. He arrived [at the bride's house], and had agreeable words for the father-in-law and mother-in-law before they become angry with you. And if you go and ask for your bride, you do it three times, four times, and not once. And you bring bread, soda, beer, chocolate. That's how it was before. Not now, the bride and groom just say "we're getting married tomorrow."[5]
>
> Here among the Mayas, we use the word "uncle" even if the person is not your uncle, out of respect. [You would greet them] "Good night, Uncle" or just " 'night Uncle" in Maya, it's a type of respect. The little grandparents, it's the type of respect that they were shown. Now, someone passes you, they'll push you or run you over. [Not like before,] people greeted and there was respect. Now I think that we have more, we have more ease to study, there are more modern schools, but we lost respect. Before, there were no colleges or universities, but there was respect.[6]

Mario Mukul conflated "modernity" and "education" with the loss of traditional behaviors, from shamanic religion to wedding ceremonies and respect for elders, a litany of loss cited by many of his contemporaries. This characterization of modernity as the "subtraction" (Taylor 2007) of specific traditional practices is one of the most common ways in which the idea of the "modern" is evoked in the most quotidian contexts. For example, when I asked thirty-three-year-old Mathilde Pech what was the best way to eat pumpkinseed dip (Ma. *siklip'ak*), she replied: "Well, the *modern* way to eat it is with tortilla chips [which are usually store-bought in Pisté]. Before, it was eaten with thick [handmade] tortillas [Ma. *Pimo'ob*]."[7]

Again and again, when I began to conduct research in Popolá, Xcalakdzonot, and other smaller and agrarian kajo'ob, people from Pisté assured me I would have the opportunity to observe customs they themselves had lost. The reality, however, often belied this faith in the correspondence between spatial and temporal distance. The practice of the *ch'a chaak* rain ceremony is an especially interesting example. In my experience, the number of people who practice the cha' chaak in any community is more proportional to the number of Roman Catholics engaged in agriculture than to the levels of education or economic differentiation of the village as a whole. Even the smallest communities where I have conducted research have significant numbers of Protestants who, in spite of being agriculturalists and often monolingual in Maya, have not taken part in syncretic religion since the 1920s and 1930s (see also Goldkind 1966). For example, in 2000, about a third of the 200 villagers of Popolá were Seventh-Day Adventists, and there was a growing Presbyterian congregation. Even there, a substantial local population of peasant agriculturalists no longer participate in the ch'a chaak. On the other hand, larger communities such as Pisté and Xcalakoop—with populations of 5,000 and around 1,500 respectively—are home to members of half a dozen different Protestant religions as well as to Catholics, and to significant populations of wage earners and capitalists who take no part in agriculture. But in both places, there are some Catholic agriculturalists who either visit ch'a chaak ceremonies in other villages or host their own ch'a chaak every year, often hiring the same well-known traditional ritual practitioners (Ma. *hmeeno'ob*) who are in demand in the smaller villages. In this case, narratives about the loss of the ch'a chaak seem to reflect a notion of modernity that expresses itself through subtraction at least as much as the empirical observations of the ritual life of different communities.

It is my experience that people in Popolá and other smaller agrarian communities, whose material wealth is meager compared with that of Pisté, are less likely to express this kind of nostalgia for the past. I have rarely heard people there or in other small kajo'ob refer to their own retention of peasant customs as making them "more" Maya, as Mario Mukul and many people in Pisté do. However, they are just as likely to equate "progress" with the diffusion of specific goods from spatial cores to peripheries. Especially after 2005, when the paving of the main road facilitated movement to and from the main tourist corridor, many of my friends and informants from Popolá have referred to their kaj "becoming large" (Ma. *nojochtal*). The prosperity gained from easy transportation to jobs and sites of sale in Chichén Itzá supported a vision of modernization in which the flow of "progress" was gradually allowing their small kaj to catch up with communities that had had more facile access to the archaeological zone (Figure 6.1).

The fact that people in communities as different as Pisté and Popolá often share the assumption that prosperity and modernization diffuse through space and time in more or less predictable ways belies some very real differences in the realities of these two kajo'ob. The tourist industry is just one of a series of factors that contributed to a growing socioeconomic gap between, on the one hand, families who rely on some combination of maize agriculture, manual labor, and handicraft production and, on the other hand, families who were better positioned to take advantage of the tourist boom. As I will show in the next chapter, this growing social hierarchy complicates the already ambiguous notion of "the Maya people" held by contemporary multicultural politics in Yucatán. The remaining sections of this chapter provide some examples of how the social and economic processes that transformed Oriente in the late twentieth century were experienced very differently by kajo'ob that remained dependent on maize agriculture and those that were better situated to take advantage of the tourist industry. By the time that I began my fieldwork, these two different experiences had produced some clear hierarchies in a regional community of rural Maya speakers that shared an investment in the market and politics of culture. These hierarchies play a central role in the forms of factionalism that are currently expressed through the idiom of Maya culture, even amid some experiments in using ethnic identity to generate broader forms of solidarity.

The Decline of the Settler Villages

In Oriente, the tribulations of peasant agriculture have been experienced far more keenly by some kajo'ob than by others. This difference plays a crucial role in the rise of contemporary hierarchies within the community of people who make political claims based on Maya identity. No single late twentieth-century crisis of agriculture contributed to the rise of indigenous identity politics in Oriente. In fact, the forms of land tenure that allowed rural agriculturalists to "foment" prosperous communities in the 1920s faced a series of economic and ecological problems well before the end of the millennium. The very structure of political power and municipal hierarchy in the countryside, like the relative fragility of the social bonds in many kajo'ob, contributed to the economic marginalization of many of the villages that received the first rounds of ejido donations. Redfield (1941, 1950) could argue that from the 1920s to 1950s, Chan Kom embodied the potential for new forms of economic and cultural progress. By the 1970s, the sleepy municipal seat, the kajo'ob that were politically dependent

FIGURE 6.1. The road to Popolá as it appeared in 2000 (*top*). The same stretch of road in 2012 (*bottom*). Photos by author.

on it, and most of the other villages that were founded in the 1920s were in a less than advantageous position to profit and prosper from the tourist boom.

Even in the 1930s and 1940s, the odds seemed to be stacked against the long-term continuity of many of the smaller communities. The case of Popolá is especially telling. As told by Don Francisco in the epic oral narrative from which I quoted extensively in Chapter 3, this was the final stop in the journeys of Tranquilino Díaz. There, he and his friends from Kaua and Ticimul founded an ejido in 1939, leaving behind some old conflicts in the municipality of Chan Kom. Droughts, crop failures, and locust plagues led to the abandonment of Popolá on several occasions. For example, documents from 1942 show that the only residents were the families of Don Tranquilino and one other *ejidatario*.[8] Several of his children and grandchildren whom I have interviewed stress that this was because of the old founder's foresight in planting *macal* (a root vegetable), manioc, and other root crops that survived infestations, which forced the planters of less diverse milpas to seek better opportunities elsewhere. Even though the village received several small influxes of population, most of the 200 individuals who live there today are descended from a tiny fraction of the original settlers of 1939, and nearly all of them are first cousins. Local teachers began a campaign against consanguineous marriage, and young people today tend to leave at an early age to seek wage work and spouses in Pisté and other nearby communities. Were it not for the collective claim to ejido lands from which they harvest carveable wood and grow crops, it is likely that the kaj of Popolá would be abandoned within a generation.

In the case of Nicté Há, the offshoot of Chan Kom (see Chapter 2), these natural factors seemed to conspire with a range of political conflicts to create a "perfect storm" of misfortune. The Presbyterian dissidents who settled the community may have scored a victory against their rivals in Chan Kom in 1932 by gaining title to a separate ejido, but when Chan Kom was promoted to a *cabecera municipal* in 1935, Nicté Há became part of the new municipality. Given that its residents could no longer rely on the mediation of municipal authorities in Cuncunul during conflicts with the parent community, representation by kinspeople or friendly parties in Chan Kom became essential. When Don Primitivo Pat was driven out of the municipal seat by the 1950s gunfight, this protection was lost. Today, the Cimé clan still controls the politics of Chan Kom, and what some villagers of Nicté Há refer to as the old "hatred" (Ma. *p'eek*) seems to continue unabated. The old religious and familial differences have now been redressed as a conflict between the PRI-dominated municipal seat and communities that have periodically been controlled by the National Action Party (Sp. Partido Acción Nacional, PAN). Don Adalberto Mex, the son of one of the first settlers of Nicté Há who is one of the few members of his family to still live in the village, observed:

The municipal president does not make a single improvement. We have no pump to draw water from the cenote. We have no electricity. The president hates us [Ma. *ku p'eeko'on*], so we are abandoned. He gets money from the government, but does not send it. Because the president is a PRIista, and he hates us because we are PANistas. (interview July 24, 2004)

Nearly everyone I have spoken to in Nicté Há says the village's biggest problem is a lack of electricity, which even the most marginal villages in Oriente seem to have had since the 1980s. In the mid-1990s, repeated requests to the state government produced some results, and cement posts were placed along the unpaved and poorly maintained road between Nicté Há and the nearest electrified village, Ticimul. Yet the funds to complete the task are channeled through the municipal government in Chan Kom, and the posts stood silently in the bush for nearly two decades before electrical cables were installed (Figure 6.2).

Even as political feuds with the municipal seat derailed a number of early development projects in Nicté Há, the collapse of cattle husbandry eliminated the kaj's only remaining source of economic prosperity and autonomy. From the time of its foundation as an ejido, the raising of cattle that pastured in the bush was one of the primary economic activities of the village. Some of the wealthier families had amassed herds of several hundred head of cattle by the 1950s. Unfortunately, this was always a contentious practice. Cattle that pasture in ejido lands have a tendency of, or at least a reputation for, entering and destroying milpas. Laws passed by the state government have often sought to limit large-scale cattle raising to individual tracts of fenced land. Still, a son of one of the *chankomil* settlers of Nicté Há who now lives in Pisté feels certain that the law had more to do with eliminating the competition that small herders posed to commercial ranchers in the northeast of the state (interview July 8, 2002). In the end, and in spite of these laws, the fate of cattle raising in Nicté Há was sealed by a plague in the 1960s,[9] which decimated local herds (Don Adalberto Mex, interview June 24, 2004).

The collapse of cattle husbandry in Nicté Há prompted the abandonment of the village by the families who had owned the most cattle. Many of them moved to Pisté, where they joined relatives who had fled from Chan Kom after the 1950s gunfight. This migration appears to have been a considerable drain of cultural as well as economic capital. When they took up permanent residence in Nicté Há in the early 1930s, the Chan Kom exiles were both wealthier and better educated than the families who had been living at the site since the early twentieth century. In a census completed before the first unsuccessful attempt to found a school in the village, all of the men and some of the women who had come from Chan Kom spoke Spanish and were literate, while few of those who had been living there since the 1920s even

FIGURE 6.2. The electrical cables leading to Nicté Há, finally installed by 2012. Photo by author.

spoke Spanish.[10] Don Adalberto Mex recalled that after these families left, the once prosperous village "became poor [Ma. *otsilchaj*], because it didn't have many owners [Ma. *yumilo'ob*]."

For many of the families who abandoned Nicté Há, life in larger towns brought much more success and economic stability. The descendants of Primitivo Pat, the families who abandoned Nicté Há in the 1960s, and other Protestant exiles from Chan Kom did very well by founding shops and mills in Pisté, Tizimín, and other large towns. With the advent of the tourist industry, many families within this emergent rural bourgeoisie were able to invest in profitable ventures in artisanry sales or in providing a range of goods and services to communities whose residents had a growing cash income. Speaking of a former neighbor he had known as a boy who now lives in Pisté, Don Adalberto noted, "He has a son who is a schoolteacher, a son who is a nurse, one who is a political leader. He even has one who traveled to the United States to do his studies."

Don Adalberto's own children grew up working the land, but have since left Nicté Há in search of wage labor. For many older agriculturalists such as Don Adalberto, the low status ascribed to maize agriculture is exacerbated by a generation gap that emerges when children and grandchildren leave to seek better opportunities elsewhere:

> I have one son who went to Pisté, and two who went to Xkopteil. Only I remain here by myself. But like I told you, I like it here. I have my beehives, I have my few cows. Who will watch them if I leave? I like to work the bush here. (interview June 24, 2004)

Of the communities that I have studied, Nicté Há presents the extreme case in which ecological factors, political conflicts, and the lure of wage labor are contributing to the gradual depopulation of a once prosperous kaj. But this combination of factors seems to be a common experience even in those communities that have a stable population. Though the situation seems less grave in Xcalakdzonot—today it is a reasonably prosperous community of more than a thousand people—similar problems have faced the kaj where Felipe Alcocer Castillo and several villagers were "martyred" in the struggle against the dissident faction of San Nicolás (see Chapter 4). As with Nicté Há, the incorporation of Xcalakdzonot into the newly created municipality of Chan Kom in 1935 initiated a complex and often tense relationship with the authorities in the municipal seat. On at least one occasion, this aggression was targeted directly against the elements of a local historical memory that celebrates the village's claims to Revolutionary culture and heroism. The monument to the "Martyrs of Xcalakdzonot" was destroyed several years ago to make room for a bus stop commissioned by the municipal government of Chan Kom. There are no signs that the construction of a new monument is forthcoming, and the willful eradication of a cherished piece of local memory is consistent with a broader "abandonment" that the residents of many agrarian kajo'ob experienced over the second half of the twentieth century.

Popolá, Nicté Há, and Xcalakdzonot are just three examples of the tribulations faced by the ejidos that were created in the early 1920s. Given the range of ecological, demographic, and political factors, many such communities were mired in seemingly hopeless economic stagnation well before the neoliberal policies of the 1980s and 1990s undermined the agrarian reform on the national level (see Warman 1985). In this sense, it is surprising that the 1992 amendment of the agrarian reform, which permitted peasant communities to parcel off and sell their ejidos, did not lead to the quick demise of many communities. X-Tojil and several other villages ceased to exist altogether when the few remaining residents sold off their landholdings and moved in with relatives in larger towns (Mis Cobá 2006). However, the majority of the communities in Oriente cling tenaciously to collective land tenure. In agrarian kajo'ob—Nicté Há, Popolá, Xcalakdzonot, and so on—the ejido committee is still a powerful political institution and the basic body politic of local decision-making. Ongoing participation in the oral performance of written texts and other political rituals that characterize agrarian committee meetings has tended to help local people to frame contemporary projects in older institutional molds.

The legacy of twentieth-century agrarian politics, political conflict, and the new potentials of the tourist industry contribute to the ambivalence that contemporary forms of state-sanctioned multiculturalism have in these smaller agrarian communities. In the agrarian kajo'ob that I know best, Popolá and Xcalakdzonot, the political culture and collective memory of the agrarian reform continue to be the lens through which most people seem to make sense of their collective engagement with the Mexican state. The optimism that infused stories of ejido foundation—and much of Robert Redfield's ethnography—is difficult to reconcile with the memory of the later twentieth century. But these narratives still serve local people as they try to situate their own collective or factional agendas in relation to official institutions and urban politicians.

Popolá is an especially good example of this redressing of projects from the neoliberal era in older populist clothes. People there refer to the period of the 1980s and 1990s as "that time of change" (Ma. *u tiempoe' k'extalo'*), alluding to a series of infrastructural improvements that coincided with early migrations to Cancún and the beginnings of household production of handicrafts. During the first summers that I taught English and conducted research there (2000 to 2003), transportation to and from the Chichén Itzá corridor was complicated by the poor condition of the eighteen-kilometer dirt road, which was not paved until 2005. But even so, the weekly delivery of wood handicrafts to merchants in Pisté had been providing a source of cash for local families for a number of years. In the minds of many people in the village, this newfound economic prosperity coincided with a series of state-sponsored construction projects that, ironically enough, began amid the neoliberal reforms of Carlos Salinas de Gortari's presidency (1988–94). These projects are also strongly associated with the PRI governor Víctor Cervera y Pacheco (1984–88 and 1995–2001), a populist figure referred to by contemporaneous commentators as the classic PRI "dinosaur." Projects associated with this period included the construction of a new water tower, a new basketball court, and a government fund that provided free cement floors for pole-walled homes. Today, the floors of many houses in Popolá still bear the stamp that identifies them as the products of a project initiated by Cervera in 1996. They are a monument to the role of the popular governor in "the time of change."

The fact that people in Popolá characterize this time of change through a conflation of government-run development projects and the income from the sale of handicrafts also reflects their engagement with the Casa de las Artesanías de Yucatán. This is a state-level institution that promotes the development of sustainable handicrafts production in Mayan communities and sells the products of the communities that it sponsors in stores in Mérida and the archaeological zone of Uxmal. In the late 1990s, this organization facilitated the creation of an artisanry cooperative and sent recent university graduates to design new products that could be produced in Popolá and sold in the Casa's stores. Carefully managing their commitments to the Casa de Artesanías and middlemen in Pisté, residents of Popolá managed to secure funds for tools, training, and other resources that turned local handicrafts into a reliably profitable venture.

A time of change implies a newfound prosperity, but does not necessarily mark a perceived rupture with older models of citizenship and modernization. The vernacular narrative of Popolá's transformation still hinges on a concatenation of state-sponsored institutions, the organization of local families through the ejido committee or collective bodies such as the artisanry cooperative, and resources that are brought to the community through urban engineers and cultural promoters. At several points from 2001 to 2003, I was asked to take dictation and type up letters that a local cooperative was sending to different funding sources in Mérida. The members of the cooperative asked to be identified as "Mayan artisans," whereas Tranquilino Díaz and the other founders of the kaj had solicited an ejido as self-identified "peasants." However, there are important parallels in their adoption of the kind of collective voice that figures in both the written correspondence and oral commemoration of the agrarian reform. This is a political strategy that constitutes their rights as citizens in corporate terms, and shows a fundamental similarity between how the politics of peasant and Maya identity are experienced in these communities. As I will show below, the contours of modernity and class identity in larger communities have created a very different set of possibilities for a "postpeasant" iteration of Mayan identity politics.

"Postpeasant" Mayas

Economic prosperity and the politics of Maya identity look very different in the kajo'ob that are more strategically situated on the main tourist circuit, where a significant portion of the population is *not* dedicated to maize agriculture. Communities such as Pisté still have a viable ejido, and it is currently unlikely that the community would reach consensus on liquidating its collective landholdings (see Chapter 1). The local agrarian committee must still be consulted or appeased in issues dealing with the community's collective landholdings. However, this institution does not represent the kind of generalized male body politic that it does in the smaller agrarian kajo'ob. The ejidatarios of Pisté tend to figure in local politics as one more constituency that is not of more importance than the artisanry vendors or merchants who own stores downtown. Many people in Pisté seem to see the ejido committee as a conservative element of local politics, a group of older men who play a vital role in mitigating corrupt practices that might lead to the illegal sale of collective landholdings, but who are slow to realize the potential of new political and economic realities.

The sidelining of the ejido committee as a political authority is just one dimension of the broader social and cultural transformations that have been brought about by tourist wealth. Whereas Nicté Há is a depopulated shadow of its former self and Popolá experienced generations of decline before its tourism-fueled revival, Pisté sits at the opposite end of the spectrum of late twentieth-century prosperity. A village whose population had dwindled to sixty individuals during the violent summer of 1921, it is today a prosperous town of more than 5,000 souls with stores that cater as much to the local population as they do to the thousands of tourists who stream through every year. Though other towns on the main road linking Chichén Itzá to Cancún—including Xcalakoop, Kaua, Cuncunul, and Ebtún—have not prospered as dramatically, they have also benefited from their advantageous position on the main tourist circuit.

If people in Popolá speak of participation in the cash economy and government projects in the early 1990s as prompting a "time of change," residents of Pisté can cite even more dramatic commercial and infrastructural developments going back to the 1960s and 1970s. Doña Petrona Chan de Mukul, a seventy-year-old woman whose family was among the people who left Chan Kom and Nicté Ha to settle in Pisté in the 1950s, narrated a fairly typical description of these changes:

> Long ago here, when we were children, when I was seven years old, we arrived here [from Chan Kom]. This was different from today. Back then, I think . . . Around the Church, there were cows, there were horses, there were pigs that walked around. Everything [like that]. There was no, there was no order. Today, however, there is more [order]. You might see some here [or there], but fewer pigs, fewer chickens. Not like before.
>
> This road here, it wasn't here back then. They were still working on it when I was a child here. Back then, my father was the only one who owned a store, . . . he had a motor to give it electricity. There was no electricity here. Well, back then, people were poorer. There was no easy way for the people to earn a few cents. There were those who died [of hunger]![11]

The owner of the first electric mill in Pisté, Doña Petrona's father represented one of the better-off settler families who left agriculture to explore new commercial possibilities as full-time merchants and capitalists. When the tourist boom expanded in the 1970s and 1980s, these families were well established as a commercial elite. Doña Petrona's memories also reflect one of the most consistent elements of emerging middle-class identities in Oriente: a focus on escape from the life of need experienced by rural agriculturalists.

For many visitors from more rural villages, the lifestyle on display in Pisté's storefronts represents both the promises and the excesses of the prosperity that tourism offers to well-educated merchants and wage laborers. Whereas smaller agrarian kajo'ob tend to have one or two stores selling soft drinks, snacks, and other manufactured foods, the main street of Pisté boasts several large supermarkets that are patronized as much by locals as by tourists, with smaller stores in most neighborhoods. Since the later 1990s, these have been complemented by an electronics store and a cellular phone kiosk, both selling items that one "once had to go all the way to Valladolid to buy." A dozen or so family businesses sell fashionable clothes driven in from Mérida, enough locals own cars to create a growing parking problem, and weddings or *quinceañeras* have become lavish and competitive feasts (see Figure 6.3). Given that the grandparents of today's privileged *pisteil* lived with far more limited economic possibilities, the rapid urbanization of this kaj is often referred to with a degree of ambivalence. One of the stereotypes of people in Pisté is that their consumerist lifestyle is supported by "pure debt" (Sp. *pura deuda*; Ma. *Chen puro p'ax*), whereas their more responsible peasant grandparents earned money through thrift and the honest work of agriculture.

On the surface, this nouveau riche of Pisté seems to parallel the character of the "new *ts'ul*" that is parodied in much traditional theater and humor in Yucatán (see Armstrong-Fumero 2009a; Burns 1983; Gabbert 2004; Hervik 1999). This term refers to rural people who, after the acquisition of wealth, adopt Western clothes, urban habits, and the exclusive use of the Spanish language associated with a *ts'ul* identity. However, many elements of assuming this traditional ts'ul identity are now less common in Pisté than they were a generation ago. For example, even a few decades ago, it was common for a new ts'ul to Hispanicize his or her surname. Thus, a person with the surname Ek might assume the synonymous Spanish term Estrella. A person of the surname Pat might adopt the vaguely homophonous Padilla. This practice seems to be far less common now than it once was. Though I know several families who Hispanicized their surnames in the 1950s or 1960s, none of the families I know who have become wealthy through the tourist industry seem to have felt the need for this kind of ethnic rebranding.

The retention of Maya surnames may be more than just a sign of a greater appreciation for indigenous ethnic heritage; it also reflects the reality that middle-class identities in Oriente no longer depend on the emulation of the urban Hispanophone culture of Mérida and other major cities. The reorientation of the regional economy has also diminished the degree to which traditional urban centers are seen as an exclusive or privileged source of modern lifestyles. Note, for example, how Doña Petrona's daughter Antonia Mukul de Dzul responded to my question about how she compared ways of life in Pisté and Mérida:

> How would I compare them? There are dollars here! Whenever people come from Mérida to here, I think that they think that this is a town with no culture. I don't know—they call us Yucas [a pejorative term for Yucatecans], Nacos [a pejorative term for urban "Indians"]. That's how they see us. But they don't know that people here have more contact with tourists than they do, and are prospering more every day. (interview August 15, 2004)[12]

Her brother Mario was even clearer on this point. He observed:

> The difference is that here in Pisté, the people we live alongside are more liberal than others. All of the ideas that the [Anglo] Americans, the tourists bring, have been taken up by the town. There is modernism in Mérida, but it is not as liberal as here.
>
> The ideas that the Spanish, Italians, and other tourists bring are copied very much here. Even their food. You've seen that the food that they serve at parties here is the food of Americans, Spaniards, or French people. If you go to a normal party in Mérida, the food that they give . . . is only what is typical of there. There is nothing modern. (interview September 8, 2004)[13]

FIGURE 6.3. Main street (*top*) and municipal hall (*bottom*) of Pisté, 2011. Photos by author.

Notwithstanding stereotypes of pretentious and debt-riddled pisteil, the difference between the lifestyle of kajo'ob on the tourist circuit and their more isolated agrarian neighbors is more than just a question of conspicuous consumption. The diversification of the local economy provided unprecedented opportunities for people to make use of specialized training and advanced math or reading and writing skills. Many postings for service jobs in the tourist sector—which often involve some proficiency in English and other foreign languages as well as Spanish speech and literacy—state that applicants should show at least a secondary school diploma certificate (grades 6 through 9). The best-paying jobs, such as licensed tour guide, require that a person finish three additional years of preparatory school (grades 10 through 12) and additional vocational training. Whereas students in Popolá, Nicté Há, and Xcalakdzonot must commute to other communities if they want education beyond primary school (grades 1 through 6), Pisté, Xcalakoop, and other large communities have grown enough in population to successfully apply for the construction and staffing of secondary and even preparatory schools.[14] School choice is also an increasingly prominent element of cultural capital. As students from smaller communities commute to finish secondary and preparatory education in public institutions, wealthier families send their children to private schools in Valladolid or Mérida.

Even if secondary and preparatory education is more accessible to rural people in Oriente than ever before, the way in which it is experienced by people from different communities highlights hierarchies based on cultural capital. Recall that differences in Spanish fluency and literacy were already evident in the 1930s, when the Chan Kom elites moved to Nicté Há. These differences were even further entrenched when the wealthier "people from Nicté Há" (Ma. *nictehail*) sought new lives as merchants in larger towns, where their children and grandchildren would experience a range of different educational opportunities. Don Adalberto's observations about the distinguished careers of the children of some of his former neighbors are consistent with what seems to be a more general phenomenon. Even under the best circumstances, children from the smaller agrarian kajo'ob begin the quest for cultural capital with a number of clear disadvantages.

Language continues to be one of the densest points for reflection on class identity in rural Oriente. Fluency in Spanish is a prerequisite for entry into the more lucrative trades in the tourist industry, and is one of the most commonly cited differences between people in Pisté and their neighbors in more isolated communities.[15] This tendency seems to be exacerbated by the steady language shift to Spanish in Pisté and many larger communities. In the years since I have been conducting research, only children from the poorest families in Pisté or who have recently moved from more rural communities speak Maya upon entering school. This is in sharp contrast to education in Popolá, Xcalakdzonot, Nicté Há, or similar communities where many or most children are still essentially monolingual in Maya when they enter primary school.

In the next chapter, I will look more closely at how different conceptions and experiences of the Maya language figure in a range of different narratives about ethnic identity. But one final contrast underscores how public education tends to reproduce some of the hierarchies established by the geography of tourism. Primary schools in more isolated agrarian kajo'ob tend to use the Maya language, either by being mandated to employ official "bilingual and bicultural" curricula or through more pragmatic techniques by teachers (see Chapter 5). In contrast, children in Pisté, Xcalakoop, and other large communities encounter Maya only in the classroom as a "foreign language" that is taught to fulfill federal educational requirements for the inclusion of indigenous language. As I will show in the next chapter, the difference between rural Maya speakers for whom Yucatec continues to be the primary means of communication and their wealthier neighbors who encounter the language in more specialized contexts has contributed to two very different experiences of bilingualism.

Conclusions

Wealth, cosmopolitanism, and education form the basis for the "postpeasant" class identities that distinguish people in Pisté and other communities on the main lines of the tourist circuit from their neighbors in smaller agrarian kajo'ob. Still, this hierarchy has developed along lines that defy the expectations of classic studies of ethnicity in Mesoamerica. Robert Redfield saw modernization as the gradual incorporation of "Indians" into a Hispanic national society, whereas early ethnographers working among highland Maya groups focused on "ladinoization," the process through which social advancement compels people who once identified as "Indian" to assimilate into the ethnically unmarked Hispanic population (Tax 1942). The attitudes of many people in towns such as Pisté tell a somewhat more complicated story. A tourist industry in which "Maya culture" has become important economic capital, like new possibilities offered by the rise of multicultural institutions, has mitigated some of the stigma that was historically attached to speaking Maya or to other stereotypically "Indian" customs. So instead of a distinction between people who are identified as "Indian" and as "non-Indian," local assessments of the difference between people in more urbanized towns and the residents of agrarian villages often involve a more nuanced comparison of habits and character.

If certain factors have created the potential for an ethnic identity that crosscuts class boundaries, the realities of the tourist economy have contributed to the retrenchment of class hierarchies within the Maya-speaking communities. Education, which has a traditional association with rural schools and a pact between peasants and the state, includes a spectrum of new gradations that range from commuting to secondary and preparatory schools and access to prestigious private institutions. Combined with a division of labor that segregates manual artisans and unskilled servicepersons from capitalists and professionals, the hierarchy of cultural capital draws lines for a number of factional interests within the broader realm of Maya identity politics.

The combination of social hierarchy with a new value ascribed to Mayanness contributes to often unexpected vernacular iterations of the politics of "culture." The everyday narratives with which people make sense of identity politics are marked by tensions between nostalgia for the past and desire for more civilized lifestyles, or by a basic continuity with notions of citizenship that emerged in the very different realities of the early twentieth century. The realpolitik of contemporary multiculturalism develops at the intersection of these vernacular discourses and state-sanctioned definitions of indigeneity. Perhaps ironically, these state-sanctioned definitions are also marked by a great deal of ambiguity about who exactly "counts" as a member of the Maya ethnic group. These intersections between official multiculturalism and local understandings of identity will be the focus of the next chapter.

Notes

1. A striking example of the conflation of temporal and geographic distance that Johannes Fabian (1983) critiques in classic ethnographic writing, Redfield's folk-urban continuum is an attempt to neatly graph time (cultural "types" that reflect different stages of progress toward modernity) onto space (the conduits through which cultural traits were transmitted from more urban to more rural settings). Though this resembles an evolutionary hierarchy in many senses, Redfield refers to diffusion, not evolution, as the driving force in creating this geography of modernization.

2. One of the earliest works by Oscar Lewis was a restudy of Tepoztlán village in Central Mexico where Redfield first delved into the topic of folk culture. Lewis questioned the image of an egalitarian and strongly integrated village community that Villa Rojas and his coauthor would bring to Yucatán studies (Lewis 1960). A decade later, the Marxist Arnold Strickon would argue that Redfield's error was in assuming that his four sample communities could be so easily assimilated into a single process of "progress." He observed that the colonial city of Mérida, the emergent transit junction of Dzitas, the recently founded subsistence village of Chan Kom, and the economically diverse settlements of Quintana Roo all developed in such different ecological and social contexts that it was impossible to reduce them to a single evolutionary trajectory (Strickon 1965). More recently, Quetzil Castañeda composed an analysis of Redfield's text that focused on how these a priori assumptions of unilineal progress were coded

into Redfield's ethnography at different levels, overwriting much of the heterogeneity within and between Maya-speaking communities (Castañeda 1996).

3. Tourism also produced a rapid development of the once autonomous zones of Quintana Roo. After the Caste War of 1847, Valladolid had been seen as a provincial outpost of an urban culture that was concentrated far to the west in Mérida. Cancún emerged as a new urban core far to the east, in lands traditionally associated with the rebellious *cruzo'ob* (People of the Cross, descendants of Caste War rebels), such as the inhabitants of Tuzik. New possibilities for wage labor contributed to the integration of these semiautonomous communities into state-sanctioned development schemes, essentially succeeding where generations of urban military men and schoolteachers had had limited success (Redclift 2004).

4. Though my presence in these places certainly aroused more attention than it did in cosmopolitan Pisté, I found people to be gracious from the beginning of our interactions. The closest that a rural store owner came to refusing my business was in declining to spend all of her change breaking a two-hundred-peso bill. More than characterizing any generalized tendency in peasant communities, these statements about shy, stingy people reflect the same stereotypes of rural character that informed early schoolteachers' statements about "bashful Indians" (see this chapter). But where this "racial" association may have seemed like common sense to teachers who identified as Hispanic *ts'ulo'ob* in the 1930s, it is far less tenable for rural bourgeois in a kaj such as Pisté.

5. Original Spanish: *Cultura? Como el tipo de cultura de los mayas? Ya no hay, ya no hay tanta cultura antigua como antes. Antes oías cada tiempo, vamos a hacer Ch'a chaak, vamos a hacer que llueva. Otra cosa que hacían antiguamente era . . . ¿qué será otra cosa que hacían muy Antigua, de los mayas? Por ejemplo, tienes que buscar a alguien, que decían que hablan bonito, que hablan dulce. Y es un trabajo también porque le vas a cobrar. Y él llega [a la casa de novia], y tiene palabras agradables y dulces para el suegro o la suegra antes que te regañen a ti. Ya si vas a pedir tu novia, era que vas a pedirlo tres veces, cuatro veces, no una vez. Llegan con pan, refresco, chebas, chocolate. Así era antiguamente. Ahora no, ahora, nomas el novio y la novia le avisan, me voy a casar mañana.*

6. Original Spanish: *Y aquí entre los mayas usamos la palabra "tío" aun que no sea tu tío, se usa de respeto. Buenas noches tíos, o en Maya Noches tío. Los abuelitos, es el tipo de respeto. Ahora, pasas uno, te va a empujar, te va a atropellar. [No como antes] Te saluda, había más respeto. Ahora creo que tenemos más nosotros, hay más facilidad de estudiar, hay colegios más modernos, pero el respeto se perdió. Antes no había colegios o universidad, pero había más respeto.*

7. Original Spanish: *Bueno, la forma moderna de comerlo es con tostadas. Antiguamente se comía con pimes.*

8. Topógrafo Ramón López to Adán Cárdenas, Secretary of the Comisión Agraria Mixta, May 2, 1942, RAN, Popolá, exp. 654.

9. From descriptions and the ecological context of the cattle, this was likely the tick- and mosquito-borne illness anaplasmosis.

10. "Censo General," AHSEP, Dirección de Enseñanza Primaria en los Estados y Territorios, Referencia IV/161(IV/14)23158.

11. Original Maya: *Uuchi wayé. Ka'ach paalo'on, ka'ach taalen te waya' way mas siete años. Pues behlae mas diferencia yan, mas habitado waye. Min uuchile' mas . . . Te baanda le iiglesiao', yan waakaxo'ob, yan tsiimno'obi, k'ee'een ku maan. Tu laakal. Mina'an, mina'an oorden. En cambio behlae, mas pakchen. Chen u kawiilik wayé, pero menos k'eek'een, menos kaax. Ka'achi, ma. Le beh he'ela, mina'an le behe uuchi. Todabia ku meyajtaj ka'ach paalen wayé. Mina'an tienda. Uuchile, pues in papa, chen, leti u tial u meya; . . . yan u mootoro ku ts'a cooriente t[i l]e tienda. Mina'an kooriente uchi waye. Tu laakle . . . Pues uuchile, mas, mas, mas otsilchaj le geente. Mina'an u manera paasil u yaantaj jump'iit seentavo tio'ob. Yaan maak ku kiimil . . .*

12. Original Spanish: *¿Como compararía? Acá hay dólares. Pues la gente que viene de Mérida, siempre que vienen acá, creo que piensan que Pisté es un pueblo que no tiene cultura. No sé, cuando viene nos dicen Yucas, nos dicen nacos, así nos ven. Es que ellos no saben que la gente de acá tiene más contacto con el turismo, cada día va prosperando más.*

13. Original Spanish: *La diferencia es que acá en Pisté, el tipo de gente con que convivimos son más liberales que otros. Todas las ideas que traen los Americanos, que traen los turistas, el pueblo lo ha tomado para usar. En cambio en Mérida vas, hay modernismo, pero no tan liberal como acá.*

Las ideas que traen los turistas, Españoles, Italianos, todo. Lo copian mucho. Es más, hasta las comidas, como has notado acá, las comidas que hacemos en una fiesta, así pues, es comida de americanos, comida de españoles, comida de franceses. Si vas a Mérida, pues una fiesta normal, que de darán . . . Lo típico de allá. No hay nada moderno.

14. The population of Nicté Há, Popolá, and similar communities never expanded beyond the point at which federal education authorities would found anything other than primary schools or even more basic educational institutions. But in Pisté, the primary school founded in 1933–34 has since been joined by a secondary school, a kindergarten, and a preparatory school. Since at least the 1980s, children from Popolá, Xcalakoop, and other communities that have only primary schools have commuted or temporarily moved to Pisté to attain higher degrees. The expansion of higher education has also contributed to the use of school choice as a source of prestige. As people from rural communities make efforts to attain higher degrees in Pisté, well-to-do families in Pisté and other communities that have had a longer experience in the tourist trade send their children to private preparatory and even secondary school in the city of Valladolid.

15. In communities where the majority of students are fluent in Spanish, which rarely have bilingual schools, lack of fluency in Spanish also tends to exclude children in local families from even primary education. Most people in their twenties and thirties whom I've interviewed in Pisté remember attending classes in which a small minority of students rarely participated and often dropped out after a few years of school because they "didn't speak Spanish well" (Sp. *no hablaban bien el español*).

7

"What Does 'Culture' Mean?"

PROGRESSIVISM, PATRIMONIALISM, AND CORPORATISM
IN VERNACULAR DISCOURSE ON MAYA CULTURE

What makes the politics of "Mayan" identity distinct from older notions of citizenship and political organization? Some anthropologists have seen the appropriation of the term "Maya" by speakers of aboriginal languages as a redefinition of what it means to be indigenous in Mesoamerica. In particular, movements such as Guatemalan Pan-Mayanism have been interpreted as the rise of a collective identity that has the potential to transcend more localized, community-based ethnonyms (Fischer and Brown 1997; Montejo 2005; Warren 1998). On the surface, it seems that something similar might be happening in Oriente, as people from a range of different social classes and communities are increasingly likely to pledge their allegiance to "the Maya culture." But as I have argued throughout this book, the incorporation of this relatively new label into everyday speech does not necessarily involve more general changes

DOI: 10.5876/9781607322399:c07

in notions of citizenship and collective rights. Nor does it always signal the emergence of solidarities that crosscut social class and factional divides. Like the agrarian identities of the 1920s, the new currency of Maya identity discourse is often instantiated in rural communities through narratives and performances that redraw such divisions.

This chapter provides an ethnographic sketch of the conceptual toolkit used by people in the communities I study to make sense of their place amid the structural possibilities offered by state-sponsored multicultural institutions. I focus on some of the same tensions between the heritage of older peasant identities and "postpeasant" notions of indigeneity that I discussed in the previous chapter. As scholars working in other parts of Mexico have shown, it is difficult to disentangle the heritage of peasant identities from contemporary engagements with indigenous politics (Mattiace 2003; Stephen 2002). That said, my experience suggests that the structural realities of participating in contemporary multicultural institutions have provided some new tools with which certain individuals and factions can articulate politically potent identities consistent with emergent hierarchies that are based on education and occupation.

One major difference between agrarian and multicultural institutions stems from the fact that the latter have no single procedure that is equivalent to the donation of *ejidos*, a ritual that was repeated again and again in *kajo'ob* across the region. Even amid conflicts such as those that took place in Xcalakdzonot and Nicté Há, the general procedures of the agrarian reform became a broadly intelligible language of collective rights and political participation as "peasants." The structural possibilities for participating in politics as self-identified Maya are somewhat different. Though requests for funds and assistance from contemporary multicultural institutions also entail a series of bureaucratic procedures, these can involve a range of different institutions at the state and federal levels with broadly defined and overlapping mandates. This situation creates an array of possibilities that play out differently among communities. After a brief description of the formal institutional framework of contemporary multiculturalism, I will focus on three discursive or rhetorical strategies (which I will refer to under the heuristics of "progressivist," "patrimonialist," and "corporatist") that rural people in Oriente use to discuss this conceptual terrain in quotidian contexts. The often fluid relationship among these three iterations of culture in everyday speech is consistent with a broader series of ambiguities in the divergent interests that seem to mark the politics of culture in contemporary Yucatán.

Who Are the Maya People?

Given that agencies at the federal and state levels that work in Yucatán have invested significant political capital in promoting the welfare of "Maya people," official definitions of who exactly belongs in this group are remarkably vague. As I noted in Chapter 1, the development of state-sanctioned multiculturalism in Mexico is often associated with the processes that contributed to the decline of PRI authoritarianism. This included adherence to international discourses on human rights that helped to legitimate Mexico's evolving democracy on the global stage. Given the relative lack of grassroots activism in Yucatán (Armstrong-Fumero 2009a; Castillo Cocom 2005; Mattiace 2009), the expansion of discourse on the rights of the ethnic Maya community has leaned heavily toward the translation of international standards of cultural democracy to local realities.[1] In many cases, the ideas of "sustainable development" and "respect for cultural values" invoked by these institutions owe more to international charters—the Indigenous and Tribal People's Convention of 1989 (International Labor Organization Convention 169), for example—than they do to a bottom-up definition of local political identity.

In the communities where I have conducted fieldwork, four agencies have been most instrumental in constituting the institutional spaces through which most rural Maya speakers encounter the formal statutes of state-sponsored multiculturalism. First are the public schools still operated by the SEP, which have been charged with implementing new standards for inclusive education in their functional curricula. The first rural schools used bilingual classrooms to wean students gradually off of their native tongue, while contemporary schools in kajo'ob where most children speak Maya are employing a more self-consciously "pluricultural" pedagogy (Pfeiler and Zámišová 2006). Schools in Pisté and other large towns, where the majority of schoolchildren are more comfortable in Spanish than in Maya, have incorporated units on the Maya language into their Spanish-medium curriculum. In this sense, rural Yucatecans who have entered into the public school system since the 1980s are likely to have encountered official attitudes toward the Maya language and culture that are quite different from those experienced by their parents and grandparents.

Second and third federal institutions that are active in Yucatán focus explicitly on economic development in indigenous communities. These are descendants of the now-defunct National Indigenist Institute (Instituto Nacional Indigenista, INI), founded in 1948 to direct the assimilation of indigenous groups into a Hispanic national society. The dissolution of the INI in 2003 reflects the degree to which the heritage of this assimilationist project and of massive centralized federal institutions became politically untenable at the turn of the millennium. However, the idea of targeted economic development policies in areas with a high population of indigenous people continues to be an important political currency. The most direct institutional descendant of the INI is the National Commission for the Development of Indigenous Peoples (La Comisión Nacional para el Desarrollo de los Pueblos Indígenas, CDI), which describes its mission as to

> orient, coordinate, promote, support, foment, give continuity and evaluate programs, projects, strategies and public actions to reach the holistic and sustainable development and the exercise of rights of indigenous people and communities in accordance to the second article of the Mexican Constitution.[2]

Today the most visible projects associated with the CDI in Oriente include extensive works for improving rural infrastructure, such as the maintenance of roads and running water. Major CDI initiatives have appeared in many of the communities where I have worked in the last six or seven years, and are prominently advertised on billboards placed on the main street or in the municipal hall of a beneficiary *kaj*.

A related and somewhat older institution is the General Direction of Popular Cultures (Dirección General de Culturas Populares or simply Culturas Populares, DGCP). The DGCP was consolidated in the 1980s and focuses more specifically on the preservation of different elements of aesthetic and intangible heritage, such as traditional handicrafts, ethnic dance, and indigenous-language literature. It has a fairly prominent presence in rural communities through a grant known as the Program of Aid for Municipal and Community Cultures (Programa de Apoyo a las Cultural Municipales y Comunitarias, PACMYC), which funds a range of opportunities for developing the arts and local entrepreneurship. This particular grant will be discussed several times in this chapter.

These federal institutions are joined by a fourth state-level organization called the Institute for the Development of the Maya Culture of the State of Yucatán (El Instituto para el Desarrollo de la Cultura Maya del Estado de Yucatán, INDEMAYA).[3] Developing programs with its own limited funding, the INDEMAYA also facilitates the implementation of CDI and DGCP initiatives in local communities. Its own mission mirrors that of the federal institutions, though it includes a stronger provision for work with the Yucatec Maya language. In 2011, the website listed the goals of the INDEMAYA:

> Aid in the generation of development policies founded in clear respect of the cultural values of the Maya people, that through an *adequate institutional coordination* seeks to guarantee that the *human, material and financial resources* that are destined for the development of the ethnic group are adequately used, and to *promote greater access* to all public services and *diffuse and consolidate the Maya language.*[4]

Although the mandate of the INDEMAYA, the CDI, and other institutions seems quite clear, the exact definition of the population they serve in Yucatán is surprisingly vague. As I have stressed throughout this book, communities in rural Yucatán lack the tightly structured civic and ritual hierarchies or the clear-cut distinction between Indians and *ladinos* that are more common in the highlands of Chiapas and Guatemala. Determining who exactly counts as a Maya person in Yucatán has led official institutions to adopt broad and often vague definitions of ethnicity. Two general tendencies in contemporary institutional language are simply to assume that all or the majority of the rural population of Yucatán counts as "indigenous," or to consider members of the ethnic group to be individuals who speak the Maya language. Thus, for example, most federal census estimates of the ethnic Maya population are based on the number of indigenous-language speakers (*hablantes de lengua indígena*, HLI) over five years of age. Whether this criterion captures all of the individuals who would self-identify as Maya, or if most HLI persons self-identify as indigenous in Yucatán, is debatable (Ruz 2002a, 18–24). The linguistic definition of indigeneity is especially difficult to apply given the social heterogeneity of the rural population and the degree to which Yucatec Maya was historically a lingua franca for people who identified themselves as European descendants (see Armstrong-Fumero 2009b).

More recent legal frameworks have stressed self-ascription, the conscious assertion of a Mayan identity, as a chief criterion for membership in the ethnic group. Thus a 2007 reform to state-level laws for economic development states that "Consciousness of identity as a Maya of Yucatán is the fundamental criterion for determining if the dispositions regarding the Yucatec Maya people and their communities are applicable to an individual" (Gobierno del Estado de Yucatán 2007, 24). In theory, this legal definition of Mayanness as a self-conscious identity would enable people in agrarian kajo'ob and those who express more distinctly postpeasant Mayan identities to participate in the work of multicultural institutions. But, as will become evident, a number of informal policies and judgment calls by the directors of state and federal agencies place much narrower de facto limits on who can participate in state-sponsored cultural promotion.

This confusion about who "counts" as a Maya person is particularly evident in the Maya-language propaganda that is one of the most visible manifestations of contemporary multicultural politics. In texts produced by state agencies such as the INDEMAYA, one of the most common translations of the Spanish *el pueblo maya* (the Maya people) is *Maya winiko'ob*. This compounds *Maya*, a term that most native speakers associate with the language, with the plural form of *winik*, a term for "person," is formed from the same root that is used to refer to the physical body (*winkilil*). Many native speakers who are less familiar with academic and institutional notions of ethnicity tend to interpret this as a reference to the Maya speech community. On the surface, *Maya winik* seems analogous to the vernacular term *mayero*, which is used to refer to persons of any social class who speak the Yucatec language.

Other translations, however, seem to imply that the constituency of multicultural development and rights is not bounded by the community of *mayeros*. That is, they imply that this community is composed of a more narrowly defined body of economically disadvantaged people. For example, translations of the federal law pertinent to the protection of indigenous languages refer to the "Maya language" (*maya t'aan*) as one of many "indigenous languages." The latter term is translated as *máasewal t'aano'ob* (Briceño Chel 2004). A term borrowed into Maya from the Nahuatl language, *máasewal* has traditionally been translated into English as meaning "Indian." The equivalent Spanish term, *indio*, is universally pejorative in rural Yucatán, where it is used as a reference to poverty and ignorance, and can be used as the equivalent of calling someone "stupid." I have spoken to some native speakers who translate *máasewal* into more polite Spanish as "humble people" (*gente humilde*). Still, the conflation of *maya t'aan* with other *máasewal t'aano'ob* in the text of the federal language law interjects an assumption of class that would not necessarily be self-evident from the term *Maya* alone. That is, it implies that the Yucatec language is protected by the law as the language of poor or "humble" people, not just for its own sake as a language spoken by members of a socioeconomically diverse rural population.

This confusion of tongues is further compounded by the tendency of many institutions to use neologisms or to revive obsolete terms that are obscure to many native speakers in rural communities. During the governorship of Patricio Patrón Laviada (2001–7), the INDEMAYA used the term *ch'iibal* as a translation for the Spanish term for "ethnic group" (Sp. *etnia*).[5] *Ch'iibal* is a term for patrilineage, recorded in the sixteenth century, which became obsolete sometime in the seventeenth or eighteenth century and is currently obscure to the vast majority of Maya speakers.[6] This word was used in official texts in contexts where authors sought to contrast the heritage of Maya people with that of ethnically unmarked Yucatecans, as, for example, in this slogan that was used extensively in INDEMAYA propaganda as recently as 2006: "Yucatan, je'elasil u *ch'iibalo'ob*, jump'el u beh" (Yucatán, various *peoples*, and a single path). How this word was understood by rural Maya speakers is a more complicated matter. Few rural people I mentioned the term *ch'iibal* to seemed to be at all familiar with it. On the few occasions that someone recognized the word, that person translated it to the Spanish as "people" (Sp. *pueblo*), "ethnic group" (Sp. *etnia*) or even as "race" (Sp. *raza*). Whereas the first two terms reflect a contextual understanding of the rhetoric of multicultural institutions, the last translation shows the degree to which the vestiges of nineteenth-century "race" narratives are still commonplace in vernacular speech and figure in interpretations of the rhetoric of ethnicity.

The three examples above reflect the ambiguity of terms used as ethnonyms if they are taken outside of their broader narrative context. I should note that there are books, television broadcasts, and other indigenous-language media that do offer members of the Maya-speaking public the tools necessary to develop a consistent understanding of what official institutions consider to be the "stuff" of Mayanness.[7] But in spite of these more sensitive treatments, the use of *ch'iibal*, *etnia*, and other unfamiliar Spanish or Maya terms, as well as the lack of a single canonical definition of who counts as a member of the Maya people, makes the process of defining a constituency for rural politics difficult. Nowhere is this ambiguity more evident than in the semantic flexibility that terms such as "culture" and "Maya" have in the vernacular speech of rural communities.

In the next two sections, I will draw ethnographic vignettes of narratives that I characterize as progressivist, patrimonialist, and corporatist. I use these three categories as loose heuristics to distinguish among broad tendencies that I have observed in how rural people in Oriente situate institutional discourses on the Maya culture in their own lives. For most of my friends and informants in Yucatán, these diverse themes and tropes are fairly compatible devices that can be interwoven in attempts to make sense of the potentials of cultural politics. But as I will argue, they also reflect distinct historical and ideological legacies and an often contradictory series of ways in which members of this diverse society can inhabit the politically sanctioned status of "Maya person."

Progressivism, Patrimonialism, and Corporatism

In previous chapters, I discussed how everyday references to "culture" by people in rural Yucatán often equate this term with "civilization." This conflation has its origins in the assimilationist project of early twentieth-century schools and constitutes a vernacular iteration of culture that I refer to as "progressivist." The fact that it is still so common in the everyday speech of these communities reflects the degree to which official efforts to reframe Mexican nationality as being "pluricultural" have not radically transformed the ways in which many people think of "culture." Note, for example, the immediate response that Doña Petrona Chan gave when I asked her, "How do you see the culture of this town?" (Ma. *Bi'ix ka wilik u kúultura le kaja'*): "Its education? There is more education now [than before]" (Ma. *U éedukasion? Beyora mas yan éedukasión*). Asked a similar question, forty-year-old Rubén Dzul responded: "Now, the culture is improved, there are more schools" (Ma. *Beyora ku méejorar* [sic] *u kúultura, yan mas escuelas*).

This progressivist definition of culture is not necessarily limited to people who entered the public school system before the implementation of pluricultural curricula.

I have often heard rural Yucatecans as young as their twenties criticize bad behavior with the sentence "Show your culture!" (Sp. *Muestra tu cultura*). This popular sentence was used in a sign that stood for several years on the main street of Pisté, where it was placed by the municipal authorities. It read: "Show Your Culture, Do Not Throw garbage" (Sp. *Muestra tu Cultura, No Tires Basura*).

As I hinted in Chapter 1, this progressivist iteration of culture tends to be used to underscore divisions and hierarchies within the community of rural Maya speakers. In 2001, I had a memorable conversation about this kind of culture with Bartolomé Xiu, a wealthy merchant of artisanry who lived in Pisté. Xiu had finished several years of university education before seeking greener economic pastures in the tourist industry. A native speaker of Yucatec born in a town in the western part of the state, he self-identifies strongly as a Maya person. He also expresses the common attitude that the communities of his adopted home in Oriente have less "culture" than those of his native microregion:

> Here, [in Oriente] the cultural level of the people is very low. Those of us who have a
> level of culture that is a little bit higher try to take our children away from here. That's
> why my grandchildren go to school in Valladolid. The people who live here do not
> improve. I feel that this is because of culture. They find themselves stuck, dragged along
> by the lack of cultural promotion that the authorities do in the community. And they
> become addicted to alcohol. (interview July 14, 2001)[8]

Xiu's statement about different levels of culture in town, like Doña Petrona's and Rubén Dzul's observations that the community had acquired "more" culture, shows the degree to which progressivist ideas popularized through early schools are still alive and well in the age of multiculturalism. In this statement, "cultural promotion" by the authorities would be aimed to produce a quantitative *increase* in local people's level of culture.

That said, this kind of discursive continuity does not imply that the redefinition of national culture promoted by the CDI, the INDEMAYA, or like institutions has made no inroads into vernacular speech. Given the dynamics of everyday conversations, progressivist statements about culture such as these can segue quite seamlessly into what I refer to as "patrimonialism," a vernacular interpretation of culture that is more compatible with the definition promoted by multicultural institutions. This is exactly what Bartolomé Xiu did later in our 2001 interview, when he shifted from his critique of local vices to a discussion of heritage and archaeological tourism that echoed the rhetoric of UNESCO:

> This region is a cultural patrimony of humanity. We are all owners. The American tour-
> ists, that is, from the United States and from the South or Central American countries,

visit the archaeological zones to fill one more point in their package tour. But they are not tourists that truly interest themselves in our culture. Yucatán has distinguished itself for the many vestiges left to us by the Colonial Period, left to us by the Maya culture, which is of interest to that tourist who is interested in Maya culture. There is much to learn, much to see, much to live among the Mayas.[9]

In these passages, there is a notable shift in what Don Bartolomé refers to as "our culture" and "Maya culture." At this point in our conversation, culture became something that had deep local roots in Oriente and that preceded the foundation of rural schools and other institutions that would "increase" the level of culture. Patrimonialist statements like this tend to situate "the Maya culture" in objects and behaviors that are tangible within the quotidian world of rural Yucatán and that foreigners must travel to see. What's more, common sentences such as "We are all owners" posit a kind of culture that *can* be shared across boundaries of class and faction.

This patrimonialist iteration of culture is also clearly influenced by the tourist market, which developed several decades before the creation of formal multicultural institutions. Many of the objects and practices that take on a "cultural" charge in everyday speech are the ones that are most visible in the tourist circuit. The nature of some of the most popular metonyms of culture became especially evident to me in an offhand remark that a taxi driver made about the new park built in Pisté in 2004. The park was somewhat ambiguously named "The Park of Culture" (Sp. *El Parque de la Cultura*), and the taxi driver noted: "They say that it is the Park of Culture but it doesn't have anything of culture. I don't see a pyramid!" (Sp. *¡Dicen que es el parque de la cultura pero no tiene nada de cultura. No veo la pirámide!*).

Just as archaeological ruins have been enshrined as a privileged token of "culture," touristic marketing and a history of encounters with anthropologists have also imbued far more quotidian experiences with a distinctly "cultural" aura. During the course of my fieldwork, I met many people who had a limited formal education but had derived a working knowledge of the "stuff" of ethnography from their own experience of tourist and anthropological gazes (see also Breglia 2006; Castañeda 1996). A few examples from my fieldwork give a good sense of the kinds of practices and experiences that vernacular patrimonialism imbues with a cultural aura. While I was conducting research in Xcalakoop, a friend in his twenties found the easiest way to introduce me to some of the elders with whom I conducted oral history interviews: "He comes to see how people live here, so he can write his book" (Ma. *Leti ku tal u yilik bi'ix u kuxtal maak waye', tial u ts'iibt[ik] t[i] u liibro*). Don Daniel Mo, a fifty-year-old baker in Xcalakoop, drew an even more explicit connection between the observation of "how people live" and "culture" when he explained to his children what I did for a living: "An anthropologist studies the culture of people . . . how they live" (Sp. *Un antropólogo estudia la cultura de la gente . . . cómo viven*).

This equation of culture with how people live is consistent with a series of commonsense assumptions about the relationship between individual and social habits found in the speech of Yucatán. Central to this relationship are the notions of "custom" (Sp. *costumbre*) and "tradition" (Sp. *tradición*), which have a long history in regional writing about folklore. In rural Yucatán, many common uses of the Spanish word *costumbre* seem to be influenced by the Maya word *suk*. As a set, these two terms refer to an individual emotional state: the fact of being habituated, resigned, or content with a particular lifestyle. *Costumbre* and *suk* can also be applied in more general terms to refer to the "customs" of a kaj, which are understood as the sum of the habits that individuals in that community are *accustomed* to follow. In many cases, this commonsense language of "custom" becomes quite compatible with patrimonialist iterations of culture.

The fluid connection that many rural Yucatecans see between individual habits and social practices became evident when I discussed the revival of *jarana* dancing at Pisté's December fiesta with Carlos Cahum, a forty-year-old artisan (interview December 7, 2003). This dance had been in decline until several semiprofessional groups emerged to perform it for tourists, contributing to a minor revival of jarana as a recreational activity for young people. At the lively dance that took place in the *k'iwik*, the announcer made repeated references to the celebration of "folkloric dance" (Sp. *baile folclórico*), to this "traditional dance of the Mayas" (Sp. *baile tradicional de los mayas*) in this "picturesque community" (Sp. *pintoresca comunidad*). Carlos Cahum commented:

> **CP:** This *custom* was being lost, the young people dance disco now. But as you see, the tourists want to see *jarana*, so now they [the young people] want to learn. Now this *tradition*, this *custom*, will not be lost. Now the young people become *accustomed* to dance [the *jarana*] again.[10]
>
> **FA:** And you never go on out to dance?
>
> **CP:** I never go to dances. It is not my *custom*. I am not *accustomed* to go out.

Cahum makes a smooth transition between referring to the "tradition" of jarana dancing as a general "custom" of local society and referring to it as something that a given individual is "accustomed" to doing. Even if the highly formalized jarana that is performed in tourist venues and public celebrations bears little resemblance to older village dances (Pinkus Rendón 2005), the vernacular semantics of "custom" means that rural people can make a fairly fluid connection between the individual habit of dancing and collectively owned cultural patrimony like a "dance tradition."

This same commonsense understanding of the relationship between individual and collective customs figures in the way many of the people I have interviewed apply patrimonialist notions of culture to assessments of their own interaction with different state-sponsored programs. In 2003, I interviewed Román Puc, a thirty-five-year-old artisan from Pisté who had received a PACMYC grant for setting up a workshop in which to make archaeologically themed wood carvings and furniture. When I asked him what the goals of the grant were, he replied:

> I saw that the PACMYC was for preserving culture, fomenting culture. For preserving traditions. If you know a given kind of work, sadly there are others who do not but would like to learn it . . . I can teach it, and automatically you preserved your culture, because you deposited it in the hands of others.[11]

By the time I conducted this interview I had known Román for a number of years and decided to push him a bit on his definition of culture. Though he had limited formal schooling, he is an avid reader of books on archaeology from which he gleaned designs, and has a far better knowledge of anthropology than most of my beginning undergraduate students in the United States. In another conversation, Román had referred to the carving of wooden reproductions of pre-Hispanic sculptures as "culture" and to popular dances or foods as "folklore." I asked him if there was a distinction. He replied:

> **RP:** Because our culture and the folkloric began to blend together [Sp. *amestizarse*] with the arrival of the Spanish. The jarana dance is a mixture of Maya and Spanish dances. So it becomes folkloric; it is here where it becomes traditional. Also because they do it in a traditional way, not constantly [i.e., only on special occasions]. Jarana dancers do a performance here once a year. On the other hand, what we are making [archaeological reproductions] is constant, every day. It is our way of life. Today you wake up, you will design a new work, and make something new. That is culture, because it is bound to your life. It is your way of doing everything.
>
> **FA:** But there are those who speak of culture as if it were the same as education.
>
> **RP:** No. Culture has nothing to do with education. Yesterday, I was explaining to my son about the way of life that these boys here today have that dress like *cholos*. I tell him . . . that those clothes are from the poor barrios of Bronx in New York, where the blacks live. The blacks use clothes like that, with wide sleeves, and wide pants. They have it as a cultural form, but if we dress that way, we only look ridiculous. We also listen to their music, which is really good music, but [because it is in English] we don't understand a word.

This is a form of culture, then. It has nothing to do with education. Culture is your roots, where you come from. Those who come from Mexico say they have Aztec blood. We have Maya blood, we are Maya. What you understand that you are is your culture. What you represent is your culture. Not education. There are people with much education, but no culture. And there are people of much culture with no education.[12]

Román is not just repeating the multicultural rhetoric that he had encountered in his meetings with the INDEMAYA promoters and DGCP auditors who administered his PACMYC grant. He made the language of "preserving cultures" his own by reconciling it with two old Yucatecan standbys: commonsense notions about custom and romantic narratives about race. For him, the "cultural" value of wood carving comes from two sources. It is more "cultural" than "folkloric" traditions such as jarana dancing because it is an everyday practice, and because its subject matter comes from art that was made before the *mestizaje* promoted by the conquest. Unlike the progressivist statements that I quoted earlier, Román's idea of culture does not hinge on attaining a Western type of education, but on the "blood" and quotidian habits of people like Mayans and African Americans. For Maya people like himself, this culture is embodied in the artistic skills and images inherited from a time before the Spanish conquest. Though his emphasis on "blood" might seem out of place in the language of contemporary multiculturalism, this is nevertheless a patrimonialist definition of culture that is quite compatible with the idea of an intangible heritage employed by the INDEMAYA and similar institutions.

Román's use of this kind of patrimonialist discourse to make a claim on Mayan ethnicity reflects the strategies common among people who no longer practice agriculture or other traditionally "indigenous" economic pursuits. It is telling that the success of his PACMYC application hinged on his ability to transfer a "cultural" skill that he possessed as an individual onto others. Like Carlos Cahum's comments on the personal and collective "custom" of jarana dancing, this is a vision of culture as something that can be cultivated in individuals and will contribute to more collective solidarities.

But this dynamic between personal cultivation and collective identities is not the only means that rural Yucatecans have for conceptualizing their relationship to multicultural institutions. In smaller communities, amid the very different realities of a lifestyle in which maize agriculture and older agrarian institutions play a major role, I have encountered a more strongly "corporatist" iteration of the culture concept. Whereas someone like Román might attempt to highlight the authentic Mayanness of his own specialized niche in the local tourist market, agriculturalists in less economically diverse communities are more likely to assert their rights to certain resources and protections in the corporatist terms inherited from the agrarian reform.

This corporatist iteration of culture is, in some respects, more consistent with the expectations of a global imaginary that conflates indigeneity with communalism and subsistence agriculture. Whether in small agrarian kajo'ob or in urban newspapers, much of the public discourse on the rights and needs of the Maya ethnic group still tends to cite the preservation of pre-neoliberal agrarian institutions as necessary for the long-term survival of "traditional" culture. Though such demands for communitarian rights are often addressed to the same institutions that offer grants, such as the PACMYC, they often imply distinct vernacular ideas of political subjecthood. In particular, the claims made in rural communities often sideline the emphasis on the personal cultivation of intangible goods to focus on more traditional demands for resources and territorial rights.

One of the most interesting intersections I have observed between the contemporary politics of Maya culture and the heritage of agrarian corporatism involves a scandal that was reported in regional newspapers. It involved dishonest attempts to purchase ejido lands by developers who were reported to be associated with members of the family of the sitting governor, Patricio Patrón Laviada. By 2005, the residents of X-Tojil in the municipality of Chan Kom had sold their ejido and abandoned the kaj altogether, and it seemed as if Nicté Há and several other villages might soon follow. This episode happened to coincide with an unfolding struggle between federal heritage organizations and artisanry vendors from Pisté and other communities, who had set up illegal stalls in the archaeological zone of Chichén Itzá (Mis Cobá 2005). As I will discuss further in the next chapter, this was a conflict in which narratives of Maya identity came to play an important role.

In this atmosphere of antagonism among members of rural communities, governmental heritage institutions, and nonlocal businessmen, some disgruntled residents of villages whose ejidos were in the process of being sold consulted a lawyer. As it happens, this lawyer had been involved extensively with the artisanry vendors at Chichén, and was practiced in deploying the language of ethnic rights. I will quote at length from an interview that he gave to *Por Esto*, a Left-leaning regional newspaper:

> I consider the loss of lands by the peasants to be a very grave problem, since this is their only patrimony and without it, they will not have anywhere to cultivate their *milpas*, cut firewood, produce charcoal, obtain medicinal plants and other elements that nature supplies them with. The children of the peasants and their other descendants will immigrate toward urban centers and lose their customs, their language, and all of their identity . . .
>
> Cultural patrimony is intangible, and its loss represents something very grave for indigenous peoples. Unfortunately, this is happening in Yucatán with the accumulation of land in very few hands. (Mis Cobá 2006)

Having known a number of people from the communities in question, I doubt that the potential loss of language and customs was foremost among their concerns when they were faced with the breakdown of their ejido. But in framing the plight of rural Yucatán in these terms, the lawyer successfully translated a political agenda based on corporate agrarian territoriality into terms that have greater cachet in an age of multiculturalism. For communities where the old ejido framework continues to be the primary means through which people imagine and engage the state, this kind of marriage of the language of ethnicity to the practice of peasant corporatism becomes an important tool for facing changing political and economic realities.

To summarize, progressivism, patrimonialism, and corporatism are three tropes that rural Maya speakers use to advance a number of distinct political and ethical arguments in the name of "culture." Where progressivism tends to rank people and communities based on a degree of intellectual or moral attainment, patrimonialism posits a kind of primordial heritage that is potentially shared by all people with historical or "racial" roots in Yucatán, even if its preservation requires self-conscious effort. While I have observed these two discursive strategies employed on many occasions by individuals making claims on personal authority or authenticity, entire communities often mobilize around a corporatist iteration of culture that tends to conflate this kind of intangible heritage with the older forms of collective rights that were encoded in the agrarian reform.

Everyday narratives with which people make sense of multicultural politics often involve a fluid interplay between progressivism and patrimonialism, and have an ambiguous relationship to the corporatist traditions inherited from the twentieth century. These everyday iterations of Maya culture also tend to be rife with tensions between a series of communitarian and factional legacies. In the next chapter I look more closely at how these ambiguities have figured in the successes and failures of several individuals and communities that have sought to derive tangible benefits from multicultural institutions. But first I close this chapter by describing how the logics of progressivism, patrimonialism, and corporatism come into play in vernacular discourse on indigenous language, a field with particular importance for understanding who "counts" as a Maya person.

Progressivism, Patrimonialism, and the Maya Language

Language-based reforms have been some of the most visible results of post-1980s multiculturalism in Yucatán. Today there is an unprecedented range of radio and television programming in Maya. There has also been an expansion of officially sanctioned spaces for Maya-language writing, which is now included in state-funded lit-

FIGURE 7.1. The OXXO chain convenience store in Pisté (2011). Note the Maya-language sign on the poster on the door that translates roughly as "México, I believe in You." In urban OXXO locations, this same promotional campaign is rendered in Spanish. Photo by author.

erature contests and increasingly available in printed form (see Andrade and Máas Collí 1999; Berkeley 1998; Dzul Poot 1985; Mattiace 2009). This new openness to creating an official role for the Maya language is consistent with the Mexican state's avowed commitment to international standards of human rights that stress the need for ethnic minorities to preserve their maternal languages and use them to interact with governmental institutions (see Figure 7.1). In theory, the way in which such policies are experienced in rural communities forms the final link in a transnational chain that binds global juridical currencies to the quotidian life-worlds of indigenous language speakers.[13]

In practice, however, the ideological content of these policies is less clear when state-sponsored narratives about the promotion of indigenous languages come into contact with vernacular ideas about patrimonialism, progressivism, and corporatism. In spite of the growth of Maya-language media, it would be an exaggeration to say that there is a large Maya-reading public that holds some consensus regarding the value of official language promotion. Given budget shortfalls, schoolbooks and other publications sponsored by the state tend to have a small circulation (Hoil Gutiérrez, May, and Martínez Huchim 2008). For example, in spite of the widely celebrated development of new "bilingual and bicultural" pedagogies, only about a third of

Maya-speaking primary school students have access to comprehensive bilingual curricular material (Pfeiler and Zámišová 2006). The limited demographic reach of official Maya-language media means that these texts have exercised a fairly sporadic influence on vernacular discourse on language. What's more, my own experience suggests that there is a significant disconnect between the register of Maya that is used in official communications and the spoken vernacular used by most rural Yucatecans.[14] As I will show below, this disjuncture has tended to blur many rural Yucatecans' perception of differences between patrimonialist and progressivist narratives about the Maya language.

These ambiguities reflect both technical issues in the translation of speech to writing and more general questions about the role of "promoting" the use of indigenous languages. One technical issue that creates tension between official Maya-language literature and the quotidian experience of rural Yucatecans involves orthography that is used to render the sounds of spoken Maya. By the 1990s, all official documents translated into Maya were written in an "official" orthography based on a phonetic standard developed by Guatemalan Maya linguists in 1985. Although this orthography has definite advantages in representing tone and vowel length, most rural native speakers have a tacit knowledge of the older colonial-era orthography in which toponyms and surnames are still written. In my own experience, literate Maya speakers who are accustomed to writing their names and local toponyms using the traditional orthography often find learning the "official" orthography confusing.

A more general tension regarding the purpose of contemporary language policies emerges from the tendency of Maya-language writing to purge Spanish borrowings that are common in everyday speech.[15] For example, a translation of the federal law of linguistic rights (Briceño Chel 2004) renders the phrase "Federal Government of México" in Maya as *u jala'achil noj lu'umil meejikóo* (literally, "the rulership of the great land of México"). This phrase would be utterly unfamiliar even to monolingual Maya speakers, most or all of whom have grown up using the Spanish borrowing *féederasion* or *péederasion*. In this sense, the Maya language that is being promoted as the cultural right of an ethnic group will have many elements that seem foreign to native speakers. This results in confusion regarding the role of state-sanctioned Maya-language policy: Is the state's "promotion" of Maya a patrimonialist project that validates the quotidian speech of rural people, or is it a progressivist effort to "improve" the ways in which they use their native language?

I have seen this kind of confusion firsthand on a number of occasions. I remember watching a Maya-language news program on Mérida's Channel 13, in which a report of daily events was read by a middle-aged woman dressed in traditional *mestiza* costume. I was watching the broadcast with my landlady in Pisté, who is herself far more comfortable speaking Maya than speaking Spanish. Mouthing unfamiliar words read by the announcer, she turned to me and said, "That's *real* Maya, isn't it? I don't understand it" (Ma. *Letí jach maaya, mas[im]a? M[a] in naatiki'*).

Her statement reflects how this disjuncture between spoken and written Maya has contributed to a vernacular discourse about "good" Maya that denigrates vernacular standards in favor of what many native speakers refer to as *jach maaya* ("real Maya"). Neologisms that are common in Maya-language writing and obscure to people such as my landlady are often interpreted as elements of jach maaya that "changed" or "were lost" by recent generations (Armstrong-Fumero 2009b; Berkeley 1998). For example, many people cite Spanish borrowings such as *pero* (but) or *entonces* (and then) in spoken Maya as recent corruptions. Written texts often correct these terms by using older-sounding constructions such as *chen baale'* (roughly, "the thing is"). Interestingly, studies of colonial-era texts strongly suggest that many of these borrowings have been in place since the eighteenth century (see Lockhart 1999). But for speakers who understand jach maaya within the broader context of culture loss, commonly used Spanish words are signs that the language is gradually going the way of the *cha chaak* ceremony and traditional marriage customs.[16]

These differences between the language that is used in official media and the oral vernacular of rural Yucatán contribute to a more general ambiguity regarding where language promotion fits in amid the patrimonialist, progressivist, and corporatist understandings of cultural politics. Perhaps ironically, members of agrarian communities such as Xcalakdzonot, Popolá, and Nicté Há—where Maya is the primary means of communication—base their political identity more on the corporate territory of the ejido than on things like language use. However, people in larger towns who are not engaged in agriculture and cannot claim many of the more common markers of an "indigenous" lifestyle often treat language as a privileged site through which to express ethnic identity. But given the socioeconomic diversity of these larger communities, local interpretations of language promotion can be used to articulate some very different collective or factional identities.

A good example is Pisté, an economically diverse community where there is still a vigorous use of Maya among adults but a growing language shift to Spanish among school-age children. In most of the spontaneous references that I have heard about the need to "preserve" Maya, patrimonialism emerges as part of the more generalized nostalgia for the gradual "loss" of older lifestyles associated with the semi-mythic solidarity of the agrarian past. This was touchingly expressed by Santiago Ek, a fifty-five-year-old artisan and maize agriculturalist (interview March 9, 2004) when he talked about his difficulty in communicating jokes and parables to his younger children. He noted that "the fact that Maya is being lost is very sad. [The children] must learn

Spanish to defend themselves, but Maya is also beautiful" (Ma. *Jach tríiste le ku saʼatal le maayajoʼ. Kʼabeet u kaankoʼob eespanyol tial u defendert[i]kubaoʼob, pero jatsuts le maaya xan*).

If Santiago Ek expresses nostalgia for the wit and wisdom that still have broad currency in Pisté, other laments for the "loss" of the language hint at a less egalitarian past. I have often noticed that many middle-class women in Pisté who speak only Spanish in public make a point of speaking Maya to the women, often bilingual themselves, who wash their clothes or clean their homes. While this gesture can mark solidarity with women who represent a collective rural heritage, it also serves to reinstate the class boundaries between members of extended bilingual households. The class-marking potentials of code switching were obvious when the matriarch of a wealthy Pisté family frowned at her daughter's alleged monolingualism in Spanish and said, "It's nice to speak Maya, because you can converse with anyone" (Sp. *Es bonito hablar Maya porque puedes conversar con cualquier persona*). Her own language choice on a number of occasions made it clear that the "anyone" that she speaks Maya to tends to be an outsider to her well-off, Spanish-speaking in-group.

Whether Maya serves to preserve old stories or to present a useful way of talking down to the help, reflections on the "loss" of the language play a role in how many people in Pisté situate official efforts to promote the use of Maya within their everyday lives. Like the pyramids of Chichén Itzá or the "custom" of jarana dancing, language is a tangible metonym for a patrimonial iteration of culture. The parallel between archaeological zones and living languages was made quite explicit by Don Hernán Tuyub, a Pisté man in his fifties:

> We cannot forget Maya, because it is the most precious heritage that our ancestors left us. It is the language that our grandparents spoke, and to respect them we cannot forget it. But how can we forget it, if the ruins of Chichén Itzá are right there?[17]

A similar observation by Rubén Dzul, a forty-year-old butcher from the same town, underscored the degree to which the value of the language is certified by the work of people who are experts on questions of culture:

> And thanks to what the anthropologists say, we know that Maya is important. Now we know that it is important and that it has grammar. Not like before, when it was said that it was a dialect. We know now that it is important to preserve, because Maya is being lost. The way we speak it has become very mixed.[18]

Both of these statements seem consistent with the centrality of language preservation in the patrimonialist discourse of the INDEMAYA and similar institutions. But the language ideology that is shared by many people in rural Oriente often veers into a more distinctly progressivist narrative about the need to cultivate "good" Maya. When he observed that people used to refer to Maya as a mere "dialect," Dzul was referring to an old racist stereotype that indigenous speech forms lack the subtlety and internal consistency of "languages" such as Spanish and English. But it is just as telling that he notes that the language that is *actually* spoken in the community is a degraded version of the original. In his comments, unenlightened speakers of Yucatec Maya are as much of a threat to the integrity of the language as prejudiced school-teachers, and the "promotion" of correct forms of Maya has many parallels in other projects that "increase" the culture of local people.

Many rural Yucatecans with whom I've spoken don't seem to think that the language that deserves preservation and that is a heritage of Maya culture is the one being used by people in the streets and swidden fields. Hernán Tuyub was even more explicit about this hierarchy among different kinds of Maya. Later in the above conversation, he segued from his characterization of Maya as a "heritage of the grandparents" to a discussion of a project of his church to translate didactic materials into Maya for use in rural communities: "It should be in the legitimate Maya language. It cannot be in the Maya of Pisté or in the Maya of [the village of] San Francisco, because these are dialects."[19]

This statement about the value of Maya reproduces a logic that was very similar to the assimilationist language policies of early rural schools denigrating local speech forms as mere "dialects." In effect, Hernán Tuyub situates "legitimate" Maya within a progressivist model of culture in which local people need to cultivate a proper use of the language that they do not necessarily possess.

The actual practice of cultivating the use of "good" Maya seems to flow along class-marked lines. In over a decade of fieldwork, I have observed that well-off and better-educated people in Pisté use the idea of jach maaya for the same kind of "linguistic terrorism" that Jane Hill (1985) documented in urbanized, upwardly mobile Nahuatl speakers. For example, these people are more likely to make a point by excising Spanish borrowings from common Maya phrases. One of the most frequent of such performances concerns the Maya equivalent of "thank you." For a monolingual peasant, this term is uttered as *Dios bo'otik* (God will pay you). Many bilingual, well-educated Maya speakers have corrected my use of this phrase to *Yum bo'otik* (The Lord/Owner will pay you), a term that is rarely if ever used in speech between native speakers. On a similar note, I was often warned by middle-class friends in Pisté to take any Maya that I learned from members of the local community of wood carvers and ambulant handicrafts vendors with a large grain of salt. Many characterize this group, an underclass to whom the tourist economy offers little more than an alternative to peasant agriculture, as the epitome of the community's ills (see Castañeda 1996;

Armstrong-Fumero 2000). In many cases, it has been described to me as a dangerous lumpen proletariat whose "lack of culture" is evident from their constant vulgar joking and from the fact that they can speak neither Spanish nor Maya well.

To summarize, the authors of state-sponsored indigenous-language media have not always been explicit in stating that Yucatec Maya is an important heritage because it is actually spoken by self-identified Maya people. Thus, the register of the language that is used in these media, which is different from the everyday speech of most rural Yucatecans, is often perceived as a more "correct" form of the language that must be cultivated through specialized study. This vernacular progressivist interpretation of multicultural policy enables certain kinds of elitist narratives that contradict the democratizing goals of contemporary Mexican language policy. And rather than promote solidarity among a community of people united by a shared language, it tends to legitimate the habits cultivated by some elite segments who denigrate the speech of their poorer neighbors.

This sketch of the everyday politics of speaking Yucatec Maya is a good example of the conceptual spaces in which rural people in Oriente make sense of their own relationship to contemporary multicultural politics. It is not simply a case of there being multiple ways of claiming Maya identity. The emphasis on linguistic and cultural criteria in official definitions of the Mayan ethnic group, like the continuity of corporate agrarian institutions in most communities, has created two fairly distinct and potentially opposed modes of claiming Mayanness. Some individuals, factions, and communities seek to reconcile the political potential of ethnic identity with the older heritage of agrarian corporatism. Others can opt for an often ambiguous play between patrimonialist and progressivist claims of language and culture. The irony in the latter case is that the contemporary politics of language tends simultaneously to provide tools for constituting both solidarity and factional divisions. As a vernacular medium for communication, the Yucatec language is a form of patrimony shared by people occupying a range of different classes and communities. But many popular interpretations of the jach maaya used in written media turn these into tools asserting elitist and essentially progressivist claims of "Maya culture."

In theory, both conceptions of Mayan politics can be incorporated within the broadly defined institutional framework of official multicultural politics. This is particularly the case given the degree to which self-ascription has gained acceptance as a means of defining the Maya ethnic group. But in practice, these two vernacular iterations of Mayan culture can be difficult to reconcile with the structural realities of contemporary indigenist institutions and urban public opinion. The inevitable tensions will be the focus of the next chapter.

Notes

1. For a discussion of how similar phenomena have played out in both grassroots and state-sponsored indigenous politics, see Ramos 2002.

2. Http://www.cdi.gob.mx/index.php?option=com_content&task=view&id=2&Item id=4.

3. Http://www.indemaya.gob.mx/noticias/index.php, accessed June 2011.

4. Emphasis in original. http://www.indemaya.gob.mx/info.php, accessed June 2011.

5. I have looked carefully at INDEMAYA's current websites and texts and have not found this term. Many jobs at INDEMAYA are patronage positions. Thus, much of the institute's staff—including several Maya-language authors who wrote much of its propaganda—was replaced at the end of Patrón's tenure as governor. The change in official terminology probably reflects the preferences of current staff writers.

6. The URL for INDEMAYA's website is http://www.indemaya.gob.mx/. The slogan has since been changed, but references to *ch'ibalo'ob* were used as late as 2008.

7. A good and fairly early example is *La Milpa en Muxupip* by Salvador Aké (1979), a bilingual edition of an original Spanish-language ethnographic study by a native-speaker anthropologist. Aké uses the term "Maya" extensively, and tends to refer to the "Maya culture" throughout the Spanish text. In the Maya-language version, he translates most of the references to "culture" in the Spanish text with the Maya phrase "how people live" (Ma. *bey u kuxtal maak*) (Aké 1979). This is consistent with commonsense understandings of the work of ethnography among the people of many of the communities where I have conducted fieldwork (see below).

8. Original Spanish: *Aquí, [en el Oriente] el nivel cultural de la gente es muy bajo. Nosotros, que tenemos un nivel de cultura un poquito más elevado de los demás tratamos de sacar a nuestros niños de aquí. Por eso mis nietos estudian en Valladolid. Estas personas que viven aquí no mejoran. Siento que es por parte de cultura. Se ven estancados, arrastrados por la falta de promoción cultural de las autoridades hacia la población. Y se envician en el alcohol.*

9. Original Spanish: *Esta región es un patrimonio cultural de la humanidad. Todos somos dueños. El turista Americano, ya sea de los estados de Norteamérica o de los países Sudamericanos o Centroamericanos, pues ellos visitan a las zonas arqueológicas para llenar un punto más en el paquete. Pero no son turistas que realmente se interesen en nuestra cultura. Yucatán se ha distinguido por sus muchas vestigios que nos dejo la colonia, que nos dejo la cultura maya, que le interesa a aquel turista que se interesa en la cultura maya. Hay mucho que aprender, hay mucho que ver, hay mucho que convivir con los Mayas.*

10. Original Spanish:

> **CP:** *Esta* costumbre *se estaba perdiendo, ya los jóvenes bailan disco. Pero ya que ven que el turismo quiere ver jarana, lo quieren aprender. Ya no se va a perder esta* tradición*, esta* costumbre*. Ya los jóvenes se* acostumbran *a bailar otra vez.*
>
> **FA:** *Y tú nunca te animas a salir a bailar?*
>
> **CP:** *No voy nunca a los bailes. No es mi* costumbre*. No estoy* acostumbrado *a salir.*

11. Original Spanish: *Vi que el pacmyc sirve para preservar la cultura, fomentar la cultura. Si tú sabes que es el trabajo, lamentablemente hay otros que no saben el trabajo y quisieran aprenderlos . . . Yo lo puedo enseñar, automáticamente ya preservaste tu cultura, porque ya se la depositaste en manos de otras personas.*

12. Original Spanish:

RP: *Porque nuestra cultura y lo folklórico se fue amestizando con la llegada de los españoles. Que la jarana es amestizada. Con danzas Mayas o danzas españolas. Entonces se vuelve folklórico. Es allí donde se vuelve tradicional. Ya lo hacen de una manera tradicional, que no es constante. Que cada año hay vaquerías, que presentan un grupo de jaraneros. En cambio, lo que nosotros estamos haciendo es constante, es día por día. Es nuestra forma de vida. Hoy amaneces, vas a diseñar un nuevo trabajo, vas a labrar algo nuevo. Eso ya es la cultura, porque es parte de la vida va ligada a tu vida. Es tu modo de todo.*

FA: *Hay quienes que cuando hablan de cultura, lo usan como si fuera lo mismo que la educación.*

RP: *No. La cultura no tiene nada que ver con la educación. Al menos yo, hasta anoche le estaba explicando a mi hijo las formas de vida que llevan los muchachos de ahora, que se visten de cholos, y le digo . . . Esas, son las vestiduras de los barrios bajos, de Bronx en Nueva York, donde habitan los negros. Los negros son los que usan ropa así, mangas gordas, pantalones anchos. Pero ellos lo tienen como una forma de cultura. Porque si nosotros nos vestimos como se visten los negros, lo único que hacemos es vernos ridículos. Escuchamos a su música, que es a todo dar esa música, pero no le entiendes nada.*

Entonces, eso es una forma de cultura. No tiene nada que ver con educación. Cultura es tus raíces, es donde provienes. Los que provienen de México dicen que tengan sangre Azteca. Nosotros tenemos sangre Maya, somos Maya. Lo que tú entiendes que eres, ésta es tu cultura. Lo que tú representes es tu cultura. No educación. Hay gente que tiene mucha educación, pero no tiene cultura. Y hay gente que no tiene nada de educación, pero tiene cultura.

13. For a similar discussion of this relationship between transnational institutions and local experience of language policies in Bolivia, see Gustafson 2009.

14. Here, it is important to recall that Maya-language writing is not, in and of itself, a novel development of post–Cold War Yucatán. Yucatec has been written since the sixteenth century by a small minority of the regional population, composed of authors who self-identified as "Indians" and "white" (see Armstrong-Fumero 2009b; Berkeley 1998). As I noted in Chapter 2, Maya was a common language for public administration and record keeping in rural communities until at least the nineteenth century. Though this notarial tradition has been replaced by Spanish-language record keeping, the colonial orthography survives in the spelling of Maya-language toponyms and surnames. This means that rural Yucatecans who can read and write in Spanish generally have an intuitive knowledge of how to read in Maya.

15. This is a phenomenon common in other revitalization and standardization projects (see Bratt Paulston 1997; Urla 1988).

16. In reality, there is a less direct relationship between processes that have accelerated the pace of language shift in the twentieth century and those that prompted selective lexical borrowing over the centuries since colonization. In Pisté and other towns near tourist sides sites on the main road between Cancún and Mérida, the fact that two or more generations of residents have participated in wage labor in sectors that entail some knowledge of Spanish, the fact that nonagriculturalist parents are less likely to take their children out of school to help in fieldwork, and the opening of new educational opportunities through tourism income have all contributed to the expansion of Spanish. Since I began fieldwork in Pisté and Xcalakoop, another large community that is intensely invested in the tourist sector, I've observed that only the children of families who practice agriculture or were recent transplants from agrarian villages make extensive use of Maya by the time they enter primary school. In contrast, in Xcalakdzonot, Nicté Há, Popolá, and other small agrarian villages, the majority of schoolchildren are more fluent in Maya than in Spanish when they enter school, and some form of bilingual education is a necessity. But as I will show below, the relationship between these sociolinguistic processes and the narratives that people tell about language loss often says more about vernacular models of modernization than about the realities of language shift.

17. Original Spanish: *No nos podemos olvidar del Maya, porque es la herencia más preciosa que nos dejaron los antepasados. Es la lengua que hablaban los abuelos, y para respetarles no lo podemos olvidar. ¿Pero como vamos a olvidarlo, si allí tenemos las ruinas de Chichén Itzá?*

18. Original Spanish: *Y gracias a lo que dicen los antropólogos, sabemos que es importante que es el Maya. Ya sabemos que es un idioma y que tiene gramática. De antes no, se decía que era un dialecto. Sabemos ahora que es importante que se preserve, porque ya se está perdiendo el Maya, ya está muy revuelto como lo hablamos.*

19. Original Spanish: *Debe ser en la lengua maya legítima. No puede ser en el maya de Pisté, o en el maya de en San Francisco, porque estos son dialectos.*

8

The Realpolitik of Yucatecan Multiculturalism

Historically, tension between unity and discord has characterized each regime of state-sanctioned identity politics
experienced by the rural people of Oriente. In the 1920s,
the leftist discourse associated with the Socialist Party
forged a fragile paramilitary coalition between diverse
kajoʼob, but also provided an ideological gloss for factional
struggles that fractured this fleeting alliance. In that same
decade, the agrarian reform offered an incentive for communities to come together and solicit title to their lands,
even as it enabled some dissident factions to stake com-
peting claims that fragmented the population and land
base of many older kajoʼob. In the 1930s, schools became
monuments of a community's investment in modernity,
even as their foundation often figured in struggles between
intra-*kaj* factions. The schools also instituted a series of
"cultural" standards that enabled manifestations of intra-

161

DOI: 10.5876/9781607322399:c08

community class distinctions at the same time that they promoted the emergence of a unifying nationalist identity. A similar tension between factionalism and solidarity seems to be emerging in the vernacular discourses on Mayan identity that have developed along with the tourist industry and the emergence of Mexico's official multiculturalism. In other words, despite what have been significant reformulations of Mexico's state-sanctioned cultural projects, the everyday politics of Mayan culture in rural Oriente seems to be reproducing the ambivalence of earlier collective labels.

This ambivalence, along with the ambiguity about who counts as a Maya person, is contributing to a series of tensions between the expectations of rural Maya speakers and the material benefits that can be derived from ethnic identity politics. As I discussed in the previous chapter, there is not a single and consistently applicable official definition of a "Maya person." Thus, determining if an individual or group of individuals forms part of the constituency for multicultural politics is more complicated than it was to determine the usufruct rights of peasants to land for participants in the agrarian reform. In this sense, people in rural Oriente who hope to derive tangible benefits from the politics of Mayan identity must tangle with both factional tensions within their communities and the ambiguity of a new set of discourses that is being imposed from the top down.

One important aspect of this ambiguity concerns the scope of political concessions that people can expect from the politics of ethnicity. Many rural Maya speakers tend to frame contemporary political events and processes through concepts that they inherited from older regimes of agrarian politics, or by drawing parallels to events that are familiar from the collective memory of the twentieth century. Some invoke a corporatist model of Mayan identity that draws important parallels between older agrarian institutions and the discourse of indigenous rights. Even in "postpeasant" communities such as Pisté, people often articulate progressivist or patrimonialist ideas of culture to stake territorial claims to major tourist sites, claims that echo the radical redistribution of resources during the agrarian reform.[1] But is engaging the state as "Mayas" today necessarily yielding the same kind of concessions that engaging the state as "peasants" and "workers" did in the 1920s and 1930s?

This question is a familiar one to students of post–Cold War multiculturalism. In her classic analysis of late twentieth-century political movements, Nancy Frazer (1996) situates multiculturalism within a broad transition away from a "politics of redistribution" to a "politics of recognition." She argues that the twentieth-century politics of redistribution had been characterized by class-identified subaltern groups clamoring for a radical systemic transformation that would lead to a more equitable distribution of capital and resources. In contrast, recognition-based politics gained prominence after the 1960s, when groups that were identified with different ethnic, sexual, or ideological minorities asserted their own right to be different within an existing system. Frazer's discussion of the difficulties of reconciling the politics of difference with the desire for a more humane distribution of economic resources is mirrored in discussions of Latin American multiculturalism. Since the late 1990s, authors working in the region have documented a range of cases in which the mobilization of indigenous identity has been appropriated and "domesticated" by neoliberal politicians (Bartra 2002b; Hale 2005). In many cases, indigenous identity politics seems to offer rural communities a means of seeking limited concessions amid the decline of traditional welfare institutions (Hale 1999; Warren and Jackson 2002; Yashar 2005).

Frazer's dichotomy between recognition and redistribution hints at one of the chief elements of ambiguity that is built into state-sanctioned multiculturalism and affects the strategic value of Mayan identity politics for local communities. The evolution of multicultural policy in Mexico has engendered a series of tensions between the state's constitution of indigenous rights in terms of antidiscrimination policies and grassroots organizing that demands a more radical redistribution of resources. Collective entitlement to resources and real estate within traditional ethnic territories has been a theme in literature on indigenous rights since the late 1960s (Díaz-Polanco 1991). Such claims became a prominent part of the manifestos published by the EZLN of Chiapas in the years that followed the group's highly publicized rebellion. However, these strictly territorial demands proved a sticking point in negotiations between the Zapatistas and the Mexican state, and were ultimately excluded from the concessions that were formally incorporated in the Mexican Constitution at the turn of the millennium (Collier and Quaratiello 2005). Developments like these have important implications for the experience of multicultural policies in communities in Oriente. Although rural Maya speakers are now more likely to encounter official spaces in which their language and customs are celebrated as a valuable heritage, the more tangible benefits of recognition can be elusive.

The ambiguous relationship between recognition and redistribution is further complicated by the fact that policies for the promotion of Maya culture or the rights of Maya people are experienced very differently in different communities. There are important contrasts between the contours of vernacular identity politics in smaller agrarian villages and in postpeasant kajo'ob that are deeply invested in the heritage industry. Whereas a number of factors make the smaller communities more attractive to official institutions, residents of the larger ones tend to be more invested in deploying a strictly cultural idiom of identity and rights. Nevertheless, both types of communities are often united by a similar investment in a regional tourist economy that has become one of the primary spaces for performing a politicized ethnic identity, but that is difficult to reconcile with the logic of indigeneity in state-sanctioned multiculturalism. An event that took place at the archaeological site of Chichén Itzá seems to exemplify the ambivalence of contemporary multiculturalism as a "politics of recognition." Tensions that bubbled beneath the surface of this celebration of Mayan heritage expressed the disjuncture between the multicultural celebration of linguistic and cultural diversity and local desires for the distribution of more tangible resources. It also set the stage for a series of events that would have major impacts on the politics of Mayan culture in turn-of-the-millennium Oriente.

"Because They Don't Know Him"

The event in question was called the Second Linguistic and Cultural Encounter of the Mayan People of Belize, Guatemala, and Mexico (Sp. *Segundo Encuentro Lingüístico y Cultural del Pueblo Maya de Belice, Guatemala y México*), held at Chichén Itzá in the summer of 2002. As with many events geared explicitly toward the celebration of language and culture, the relationship between the goals and political agendas developing among the local communities of Maya speakers was somewhat vague. The stated goal of the encounter was to reach a series of conclusions for the promotion and preservation of the Mayan languages. However, some of the murmurs of dissent at this event hinted at desires for an identity politics that would yield a more tangible outcome, desires that would have a more militant expression just two years later.

I was invited to attend by Julio Hoil Gutiérrez, a close friend and colleague. Julio is a Maya-language author of short stories who trained as an archaeologist and is currently a doctoral student in history. He was born and raised in Xcalakoop and is a member of several activist institutions. His insights on local cultural institutions and activists have informed my work for years. Yet even he seemed to be at a loss to explain the full range of ironies that we would observe on that day.

The sponsors of the event were a typical alphabet soup of state, federal, and municipal agencies. These included the National Institute of Anthropology and History (Instituto Nacional de Antropología e Historia, INAH), the INI (still extant as such in 2002), the INDEMAYA, the state government of Yucatán, and the municipal government of Tinúm. Mayaon, a Valladolid-based NGO that has been less active in recent years, played a major role in organizing the event.[2] Local civil society was represented by businesses—mostly owned by entrepreneurs who lived in Mérida or Cancún—that contributed different kinds of logistical and financial support.

Among the most prominent financial sponsors of the event were the Barbachano family. A tight-knit clan with deep roots in the Mérida aristocracy, they had purchased the hacienda at Chichén Itzá in the 1930s (see Breglia 2006). This purchase included most of the land on which the current archaeological zone is situated.

Having conceded control of the archaeological remains on their land to the INAH, the Barbachanos operate a chain of luxury hotels (Hotel Mayaland) and other businesses that employ a large number of people from surrounding communities. Though the lands on which the archaeological zone is located were purchased by the state government in Yucatán in 2010, in 2002 they were the legal property of the Barbachanos.

This connection between the event and wealthy private interests hints at the somewhat ambivalent place of civil society in Yucatecan multiculturalism, at least in major tourist zones such as the periphery of Chichén Itzá. The Barbachanos' sponsorship of the event was prompted by the patriarch of the family, who was making plans for creating a new NGO that would promote education and Maya culture in surrounding communities. At that particular moment in history this philanthropic gesture seemed somewhat ironic. Recently, the Barbachanos had fired a significant portion of their kitchen and waiting staff—the vast majority of whom were Maya-speaking natives of Pisté and Xcalakoop—over conflicts regarding unionization. They also had an ambivalent relationship with the INAH, which had legal custody of archaeological remains that were officially on Barbachano-owned land. But in the years since the *encuentro*, the Barbachano clan has found that philanthropic support of the Mayan cultural heritage serves as powerful moral capital. They have even reinvented one of their luxury hotels as an "ecoresort" that sponsors several NGOs.[3]

Setting aside the motives behind Barbachano sponsorship, something else that seemed fairly unclear at this event was precisely who was the intended audience for the Second Linguistic and Cultural Encounter of the Mayan People of Belize, Guatemala, and Mexico. The inaugural event was open to the public, and on the afternoon that I spent there I ran into a number of INAH custodians. Though some people from Pisté, Xcalakoop, and other neighboring communities were in attendance, the majority of the people at the conference seemed to be representatives of the INAH and the INDEMAYA, of Mayaon, and of a number of smaller community-based organizations from different parts of the state. In keeping with the title of the event, there were also several invited delegations that represented Maya-speaking ethnic groups from other countries. But the most notable attendee—at least from the perspective of the journalists who were present—was Patricio Patrón Laviada, the governor of the state of Yucatán.

As we milled around the different events at the archaeological zone, Julio introduced me to a number of language activists from other parts of the state whom he had met before at conferences in Mérida and at the university. At the very least, this event seemed to be a useful place for networking for these different activists, and there was much catching up, talk about current projects, and exchanging of business cards and e-mails. This also seemed to be a space where young professionals whose education and lifestyle had distanced them from the life of rural communities had an opportunity to express Mayan identities through the wearing of traditional dress. I remember thinking that I had never seen so many people in their twenties and thirties dressed in traditional clothes: men in all-white cotton outfits and straw hats, women in brightly embroidered *huipiles* (dresses). Men from a community-based music group from the neighboring state of Quintana Roo called New Song (Ma. Tumben K'ay) were wearing outfits with bright embroidery on the cuffs and hems, a style of ceremonial men's clothing that had not been used for decades.

Though the community activists seemed to be making the most of the event, they were also fairly candid about the fact that this was a convenient photo opportunity for the governor, his political cronies, and local businessmen. Many of those in attendance expressed disappointment that more emphasis seemed to be on the governor's visit than on the various working-group roundtables that were to take place in the following days. This skepticism was even more evident in the snarky comments made by some of the attendees regarding a *saká* ceremony, for the blessing of corn gruel, that was held on the road to the sacred cenote. Initially, participants in the encuentro were told that women would not be allowed to attend the ritual. This is a common element of ceremonies that involve the use of "virgin water" (Ma. *sujuy ja'*) taken from caves or wells hidden deep in the forest. But the other men in attendance and I soon noticed that the saká was being made with purified water, gallon jugs of which could be seen behind the altar of the ritual practitioner (Ma. *jmeen*). A tour guide said, to a chorus of chuckles, "That's fine. Did you think that you can just give Patricio [Patrón] well water to drink?" This joke had a double irony: just as well water might expose the governor to parasitic infection, drinking the water of a community's well is a gesture of solidarity often associated with establishing a personal commitment to the place (see Chapter 2).

The jmeen who conducted the ceremony raised some eyebrows himself. He *was* praying in Maya, but he did so facing the audience and in a loud and declamatory voice, an act that seemed more consistent with the New Age mystics who brought foreign tourists to the ruins during the equinox than with the "unintelligible speech" (Ma. *xwalat'an*) in which *jmeeno'ob* normally muttered their prayers while facing their altar, their mouths half covered by a hand.

The gender segregation of the ritual didn't last long either. A group of four European tourist women in shorts and bikini tops elbowed their way through the crowd to snap a flurry of photos by the jmeen's altar. A group of young Maya women in huipiles, visibly annoyed at having been pushed to the margins of the ritual in the first place, seemed to take this as their cue and pushed their way into the audience alongside the men.

The tourists' interest in the saká ritual was prophetic in another sense: the particular piece of political theater seemed more credible to nonlocal audiences than to people who were familiar with all of the players. During the inaugural event, many people from Pisté drifted in to catch a glimpse of the governor. The conversation in the stands consisted mostly of thinly veiled heckling at the speeches given by various visiting dignitaries. Particular derision was aimed at the speech made by Efrén Nahuat Dzib, the municipal president of Tinúm and executive representative of the municipality that includes Chichén Itzá and Pisté. Adopting the language of ethnic awakening and democratic transitions, Nahuat stated that the indigenous people of Mexico would no longer "tolerate dark paternalism, much less being used by politicians to scale political positions." He stressed the right of Mayan communities to "enjoy all of the forms of help provided by the government, including running water, electricity, paved roads and productive projects." Nahuat proposed the creation of "a legal framework that is equitable for Indian peoples and respects their ideals and particularities, as this is a live, driven culture that is not afraid to work."[4]

This speech was striking in that it made such explicit references to infrastructure and access to tangible goods, when the stated themes of the event all focused on the promotion of language and other forms of intangible heritage. But be this as it may, the municipal president's call for a better distribution of resources elicited a chorus of angry groans and whistles from the Pisté people in the audience. In 2002, Nahuat Dzib was not a well-liked figure there. All federal and state funds for infrastructural improvement in the municipality must first pass through Tinúm. In spite of the fact that Pisté was a larger, wealthier, and more vibrant town, in 2002 it probably had fewer paved roads than the sleepy municipal seat. One of the INAH custodians shouted, loudly enough for everyone seated around him to hear, "He's lying! When has he ever paved a road in Pisté?"

After this opening event, the substance of the encuentro consisted of a series of roundtable discussions regarding language policy. Julio decided not to attend, and I did not feel comfortable inviting myself. However, the conclusions of these work sessions were published in regional newspapers. Major points raised in the conference included the creation of policies for the preservation of indigenous language and culture analogous to frameworks that had been adopted in Guatemala. Other points in the declaration called for the promotion of local forms of autonomy for indigenous communities and regions, and the development of a collective Mayan identity that would unite communities across the borders of four nation-states.

In the years since this event, I have spoken candidly to many of the people who attended. Some of the Maya-speaking scholars and activists have expressed skepticism at what exactly was accomplished at the 2002 roundtables. The abstract conclusions of the working group covered familiar ground. Calls for adherence to international codes of language and ethnic rights had been common in Mexico since the 1990s, and were well on their way to being written into the national constitution by 2002. Arguments for a Pan-Maya identity that would bridge social and political gaps among different language groups *were* something of a novelty. But while this political agenda had gained considerable currency in Guatemala (Montejo 2005; Warren 1998), it would be relatively difficult to communicate to rural Yucatecans, for whom ideas of indigeneity tend to be much more ambiguously defined. The most significant criticism of the event was the degree to which the discussion was limited to a small and fairly exclusive group of Maya-language authors. One reporter who wrote about the event observed that there was a notable absence of rural schoolteachers, whose efforts in bilingual education often represented the "front lines" in linguistic and cultural revitalization (*Por Esto* 2002).

If Maya-identified scholars and activists expressed some ambivalence about this event, laypersons in Pisté and other communities that neighbored Chichén seemed even more skeptical. Language policy might be one of the cornerstones of official discourse on multiculturalism, but its benefits are often less immediately tangible to members of local communities. Critics of official takes on multiculturalism have noted that the willingness of states to incorporate questions of language rights into political reforms reflects the assumption that the work of cultural revitalization is largely "apolitical" (Warren 1998) and that the emphasis on "traditional" heritage over contemporary social issues contributes to the "domestication" of grassroots agendas (Hale 2005). This kind of critique is just common sense to people in Pisté. Although the call for Maya-language revitalization clearly resonates with vernacular ideas of patrimonialism and nostalgia, the reaction to the municipal president's speech regarding a more tangible redistribution of resources of Maya-speaking communities reflects the skepticism that many residents have regarding the end products of contemporary policy toward indigenous peoples.

In the end, however, this event was a success for the Barbachano family. They have since spent considerable resources to promote events that highlight their philanthropic activities in Maya-speaking communities. But if anything, these activities are viewed with even greater skepticism by the rural Yucatecans who form most of the hotels' workforce, or who offer competition through their own independent tourism ventures. For example, the Hotel Mayaland stages yearly meetings for practitioners of traditional medicine. One man from Pisté—himself a practitioner of bone setting and massage (Ma. *yot', kax bak*)—described the event in this way:

> Barbachano brings these people in from far away, Xocen or Chichimilá or by Yaxcabá,
> [places far from Chichén] where they don't know him. He gives them a big meal,

takes them for a tour of the Mayaland, and tells them about all that he is doing for the Mayas. Then, they're saying "Wow!" because they don't know how he is. Then he takes their picture for the newspaper, and they go back home. (interview August 6, 2006)

The politics of recognition in contemporary Yucatán has created a series of spaces in which businesspeople like the Barbachano clan can pander to the regional newspapers, contributing to the ambivalence of cultural recognition for many rural Maya speakers. Still, these kinds of events are a learning experience; they demonstrate how the combination of a famous site such as Chichén Itzá and references to Mayan identity can be the basis for high-profile public performances. These lessons would be put to work by a local movement in Chichén Itzá just three years after the 2002 encounter. However, the mixed results of this group also reflect the limits that public opinion and urban people's assumptions about indigeneity have placed on emergent forms of grassroots organizing.

Illegitimate Artisans and the Impossibility of Middle-Class Maya

Three years after the language conference at Chichén Itzá, a feud between the owners of Mayaland, the local community of artisanry vendors, and INAH employees created the conditions for a new collective claim based on ethnic identity. In 2004 and 2005, the Barbachano family sought to create a new entrance to the archaeological zone from the Hotel Mayaland. Though the land on which the new entrance was to be built was on their property, strict INAH regulations limited the degree to which private constructions could affect access to the zone. Wrangling over the rights to the new entrance coincided with a conflict between the Barbachanos and a group of INAH employees who had been born and raised in Pisté and who operated two concession stands in the archaeological zone (see Breglia 2006). Although the Barbachanos were thwarted in their initial attempts to create a new entrance, they were more successful in employing a range of maneuvers to take control of the two cooperative businesses.[5]

By 2005, several hundred ambulant artisanry vendors had set up illegal posts inside of the archaeological zone. Many people have suggested to me that the vendors had the tacit approval of INAH custodians who were seeking some form of revenge against the Barbachanos. The occupation of the archaeological zone also reflected some of the local resentment that was bubbling beneath the surface of the 2002 encuentro. Sales of souvenirs or refreshments in the archaeological zone are tightly regulated by the INAH, and the exclusion or removal of ambulant artisanry vendors from surrounding communities has been an ongoing struggle since the late 1980s (Armstrong-Fumero 2000; Castañeda 1996; Peraza López and Rejón Patrón 1989).

The new entrance proposed by the Barbachanos would have made more tourists pass through handicrafts stores attached to the hotel, creating competition for the state-sponsored artisanry market that had been made at the main entrance of the ruins as a concession to local vendors, who began selling in the zone in the 1980s and 1990s. Frustrated with the lack of access to a place that many considered to be part of their traditional lands, people in the surrounding communities took action.

This latest occupation of the archaeological zone by vendors has had more success than similar movements in the 1980s and 1990s (see Castañeda 1996), and participants have made more extensive use of an explicit rhetoric of ethnic resurgence.[6] Nevertheless, those who are still selling their wares in the archaeological zone have had to contend with a negative press campaign that has accompanied attempts to dislodge them. Several articles and public declarations have characterized the vendors as nonlocal people who rallied opportunistically under the banner of indigenous rights, or as profiteering vandals who harassed tourists and defaced the ruins. The handicrafts that were being sold—most of which are produced locally—were dismissed as factory-made knickknacks imported from China. Rumors represented the committee that was formed among the artisans as a cynical protection racket, whose leaders pocketed the 100-peso fee collected from each merchant to hire the group's lawyer. The fact that this lawyer—the same whose statements against the sale of *ejido* lands in Nicté Há I quoted in Chapter 7—had previously been on the INAH payroll was also cited to discredit this group.

In the public statements of the artisans and artisanry vendors, appeals to a territorial right based on an ancestral connection to the ruins were used in response to these accusations. Silvia Cimé Mex, the leader of the artisans' association, was quoted in the Left-leaning *Por Esto* newspaper as saying:

> The INAH has always used defamation and calumny to discredit us through all the media. They make sweeping statements that we rob tourists and produce garbage, but we will now show to the world that we are not the kind of people that they say we are. Because of this, we ask the communities that surround Chichén Itzá to make solidarity with our just cause, where the government and a few rich people try to trample upon once again, in the very place where our ancient grandparents were born and died amidst struggle. (Mis Cobá 2005, 10)

In the summer of 2005, I heard rumors in Pisté, often spoken in a half-joking and incredulous tone, that the leaders of the artisans' committee had "gone to Chiapas to talk to [Subcomandante] Marcos," the charismatic spokesman of the EZLN movement. This was during a period when, having walked away from negotiations with the Mexican government and lost much of their initial momentum as a national political phenomenon, the Zapatistas were seeking to cultivate a broader oppositional con-stituency. Months later I learned that a delegation from the Artisans of Chichén Itzá had, in fact, conferred with Subcomandante Marcos. An independent online media source circulated a "Declaration from Chichén Itzá at 158 Years from the Caste War," a brief document that frames the demands of the vendors selling within the archaeo-logical zone in the rhetoric of the EZLN and its "Other Campaign." Dated July 30, 2005, the declaration states:

> Today, we the Mayan artisans and small sellers from the towns that surround Chichén Itzá are the legitimate heirs to this ceremonial center, built with the blood of our ances-tors. Nevertheless, we live under threats from neoliberal governments who discriminate against us and use their authoritarianism to abuse laws and presume to drive us from our own house.[7]

This document states the adherence of the Artisans of Chichén Itzá to the sixth declaration from the Selva Lacandona, a text released earlier in the summer of 2005 in which the EZLN announces changes to its organizational structure that were meant to develop broader forms of solidarity across leftist groups. This collabora-tion between the Artisans of Chichén Itzá and the EZLN culminated in late January 2006, when Subcomandante Marcos himself made a visit to the ruins of Chichén Itzá (Giordano 2006).

Though the exchange of visits between Subcomandante Marcos and the leaders of the artisans' organization is common knowledge in Pisté, I have not gotten a sense that the written text of the "Declaration from Chichén Itzá" was widely circulated within the kaj. Still, something that seems remarkable about this document is the blend of specific references to contemporary types of indigenous identity politics and narratives that resonate with the heritage of Revolutionary-era nationalism. The parallel between a contemporary struggle and the Caste War of 1847 is perfectly consistent with the "flattened" notion of national history that emerged in the public ritual and pedagogy of the 1930s and 1940s (see Chapter 5). As Lynn Stephen (2002, 310–16) has noted, this is precisely one of the strengths of neo-Zapatista rhetoric: the ability to reformulate familiar Revolutionary-era narratives to address contemporary oppositional struggles.

Still, the odds are stacked against Chichén Itzá becoming another regional pocket of EZLN activity. The sellers have succeeded in remaining in the archaeological zone despite persistent threats from state and federal authorities. However, contacts with the EZLN seem to have fizzled, and the movement of local people to sell their wares amid the ruins built by their ancestors has failed to attract the same kind of national and international enthusiasm as did the charismatic agrarian rebels from the jungles of Chiapas.

The legitimacy crisis of the vendors at Chichén Itzá is twofold. First, there is the simple fact that local traditions of tourist art have tended to be characterized as "inauthentic" by many connoisseurs (Castañeda 2004) of "folk" arts. But just as important is the complex web of production, resale, and processing that is involved in the artisanry trade. This is a microregional economy that involves a range of economic positions difficult to reconcile with official assumptions about "native" craftspersons. Somewhat ironically, this same diverse economy plays an important role in many contemporary engagements between rural people in Oriente and official institutions for the promotion of Maya culture.

Viewed within the broader context of multicultural realpolitik in Yucatán, the lack of public sympathy garnered by the Artisans of Chichén Itzá is consistent with a series of de facto policies that have effectively excluded certain kinds of work from the realm of acceptable "indigenous" activity. This informal exclusion takes place even as official statutes posit a fairly broad definition of membership in the Mayan ethnic group (see Chapter 7). Prejudice against "nontraditional" occupations is one of the reasons why Román Puc, whose interview I referred to in Chapter 7, has been the only recipient of a PACMYC grant out of the hundreds of people who have been involved in handicrafts artisanry in Pisté since the 1970s. Representatives of different state institutions sometimes express this prejudice quite openly, referring to the handicrafts market at Chichén Itzá as a quintessentially inauthentic cultural phenomenon.

In 2001, I interviewed the assistant director of a state-level organization, the Casa de las Artesanías, which promotes the development of ethnic crafts by providing small capital loans to rural cooperatives (interview July 24, 2001). When I arrived in the assistant director's office, I noticed that the molded cement figurine that he was using as a paperweight came from the workshop of Guillermo Macal, an artisan and merchant I knew from Pisté. When I mentioned it, the assistant director picked up the piece and said, "Ah, yes, the eternal pal from Pisté," before launching into a discussion of why he did not consider the output of Macal's workshop to be worth pursuing. Shaped in a silicon mold with commercial cement, hand-painted with commercial pigments, and sprayed with shellac, these pieces fell well outside of the range of artisanry that the Casa de las Artesanías considered worthwhile. Repeating an assessment that I had heard many times before, the assistant director suggested that the community of artisans and artisanry vendors in Pisté was too large, fractious, and competitive to create successful cooperative organizations.

This attitude seemed ironic at a time when cultural institutions were envisioning an identity politics that avoided the pitfalls of earlier corporatist institutions—what the municipal president of Tinúm referred to as the "dark paternalism" of earlier decades. Guillermo Macal fit the criteria that laws written at the state and federal levels use to designate members of "the Maya people." He was a native of a rural Yucatecan community, a native speaker of Maya with a Mayan surname. His store provided a viable retail venue for more than a dozen artisans who were themselves native speakers of Maya with Maya surnames and who lived in rural communities. What's more, Macal is part of a class of local capitalists whose growing influence in the artisanry trade emerged from their rejection of state-sponsored sales outlets. Facing fierce competition from other vendors, a number of the more successful merchants built shops in the neighboring communities of Kaua, Ebtún, and Cuncunul on the main road from Cancún (Armstrong-Fumero 2000). By paying generous commissions to tour guides, the owners of these stores have secured a captive market even before tourists reach Chichén Itzá.

But however much it was the product of native entrepreneurship, this enterprise reflected a reality of the contemporary artisanry market that was difficult to reconcile with stereotypes that are deeply rooted in institutions for the development of "indigenous" societies in Mexico. The owners and operators of these stores have rarely been hailed as successful indigenous capitalists. More often than not, they have been accused of a range of wrongdoings, from illegally purchasing the land where their stores are built, to contributing to the downfall of vendors in the state-sponsored market, to profiting from exorbitant markups at the expense of local producers.

It is clear from my experience that a fair bit of exploitation does occur in the locally controlled artisanry market and that wealthier vendors have done all that they can to press their advantage over less fortunate local competitors. However, the fact that local entrepreneurs are dismissed as potential partners in promoting indigenous crafts, whereas the Barbachanos and other larger moneyed interests are granted a great deal of legitimacy as philanthropists, suggests that other prejudices might be at work. I have heard many capitalists such as Guillermo Macal referred to as *caciques*, the term used for local "Big Men" such as Lorenzo Barrera and Santiago Beana in the 1920s. This is a loaded term in Mexico, alluding as much to political power brokering and corruption as to the "traditional" source of a rural leader's power (Lomnitz 1992). As a label, it alludes to the double bind of Macal and merchants like him who do not embody the markers of "authentic" indigeneity, even as they lack the legitimacy that is given to Hispanic business moguls such as the Barbachanos.

These same prejudices are applied even to penny capitalists who are far less privileged than Macal, that is, the vast majority of the people who are currently selling handicrafts inside the archaeological zone of Chichén Itzá. The idea of the "indigenous artisan" that permeates institutional discourse revolves around craftspersons who sell objects that they themselves fabricate directly to tourists. This form of production and sale had been common in the early years of the local handicrafts trade in the 1970s and 1980s, and is still practiced by technically talented artisans who create high-end pieces and wish to cut the middle agent out of their profits. But what about the artisanry vendors who, despite being local people and meeting the official criteria for membership in the "Maya ethnic group," choose to invest their limited capital in marketable products that they have not produced themselves? The lack of public sympathy they garner, like the adversarial tone that continues to mark their interactions with the INAH and state-level heritage institutions, suggests that assumptions about the precapitalist nature of authentic indigenous behavior place de facto limits on the kinds of commercial activities that can become the basis for credible claims on "traditional" or "ethnic" rights.

Seen against the vernacular narratives of culture that I discussed in the previous chapter, this exclusion of artisanry vendors from the realm of "legitimate" identity politics is particularly ironic. Younger people and those involved in the tourist circuit are far more likely to adopt patrimonialist narratives of culture that mirror those employed by the INDEMAYA, the CDI, and related institutions. But the experiences of many of those who have deployed these narratives to assert their right to points of sale in the archaeological zone are ambivalent at best. While discourse on ethnic rights has made the latest wave of artisanry vendors more successful than previous ones, they have not necessarily secured the kind of permanent and legally sanctioned territorial concession that their grandparents and great-grandparents attained as self-identified "peasants."

Not only has the use of ethnic identity discourse with the vendors met equivocal success in terms of formally sanctioned territorial concessions; it has not necessarily generated consensus on political identity in their home communities. Juan Canul (interview August 15, 2004), a native speaker of Yucatec and a self-identified Maya, is a licensed tour guide in the archaeological zone and someone who has experienced enough of local politics to have fairly negative opinions about both the Barbachano clan and the INAH. However, he is also ambivalent about the artisans. Though the people selling in the zone are neighbors he has known for years or fairly recent transplants from neighboring communities, he said there is a need for institutions to distinguish "legitimate artisans" from the well-off capitalists who sell pieces that they have bought from others.

The fact that this statement was made by someone who is himself a native of the community and a self-identified Maya demonstrates the degree to which ideas about authenticity are not simply a product of the relationship between "external constructions" of Mayanness (Hervik 1999, 59) and the lived realities of rural Yucatecans. In effect, the artisanry vendors do not have a monopoly on Mayan identity, and their invocation of discourse on ethnicity does not speak for the entirety of the kajo'ob that they call home. As I noted in the previous chapter, artisans and artisanry vendors are one interest group in large communities such as Pisté, just as are subsistence agriculturalists, tour guides, service workers, and other skilled and unskilled laborers. Each of these groups includes its own internal factions and agendas that don't always overlap with those of the artisanry vendors. For example, guides such as Canul have a vested interest in traffic flows within the archaeological zone, and have a complicated relationship with the vendors who compete for the attention of "their" tour groups (Castañeda 1996).

Just as the artisanry vendors do not speak for the community at large, they do not have a monopoly on the use of Mayan identity. In the previous chapter, I discussed how the ambiguity of "culture" in the vernacular speech of Oriente creates a range of possibilities for the use of patrimonialist, progressivist, and corporatist articulations of Mayanness. Juan Canul's comment is typical of many people in his own community who, like those who warned me away from learning vulgar Maya from "the artisans," cast doubt on the handicrafts vendors' cultural credentials.

This apparent lack of kaj-level consensus on what constitutes the substance of politicized Mayan identity has been a recurring problem for artisans from Pisté in their attempt to solicit aid from state and federal multicultural institutions. Just as the factional divisions and socioeconomic complexity of the local community of artisans have made Pisté less attractive to institutions like the Casa de las Artesanías or administrators of grants like the PACMYC, it has made grassroots movements that invoke indigenous identities somewhat of a tough sell. These tensions are a good reflection of how, notwithstanding the expansive membership that contemporary institutions posit for "the Maya people," the tangible benefits of ethnic politics have been elusive for many self-identified Maya.

Corporate Ejidos and Individual Artisans

If people such as the "illegitimate artisans" of Chichén Itzá must seek ways to reconcile their own expectations with institutional stereotypes of "indigeneity," people in smaller agricultural communities face a different set of tensions between traditional corporatist institutions and new uses of Mayan identity. As I discussed in Chapters 6 and 7, the explicit invocation of Mayan identity that is common in larger communities is often less intelligible in agrarian kajo'ob, where notions of citizenship and territorial patrimony tend to be expressed in terms of the ejido. But, perhaps ironically, it is these same small communities that are more attractive to the CDI, the INDEMAYA, and other institutions that see them as better representatives of "indigenous" lifestyles.

Another reason these institutions seem to prefer communities such as Popolá, Xcalakdzonot, and Nicté Há is a matter of the scale and the potential reach of projects. That is, government institutions seem to have an easier time engaging these communities as organic corporate entities in which land and other resources are managed collectively, and in which a shared identity is derived from the "traditional" relationships among land, labor, and society. The ejido committee creates a space in which, at least in principle, members of most or all local households have a right to vote and give input. By extension, programs organized with the ejido committee or parallel cooperative structures have the potential to impact the community as a whole, not just particular groups or factions. In some communities, particularly in Popolá, local people have organized fairly successful cooperative ventures built on a simple model of shared decision-making, in which women have played an especially prominent role.

That said, engaging the contemporary heritage industry as an ejido committee or community-level cooperative entails some of the same frictions that people in Pisté encounter when they try to reconcile the image of the agrarian indigene with the postpeasant economy of tourism. In spite of the superficial appearance of corporatism and "tradition," agrarian kajo'ob are products of the same processes that shaped the social and political organization of Pisté and other similar communities. Given soil depletion, population growth, and related factors, the vast majority of families in smaller agrarian kajo'ob have engaged in some form or other of outside work for decades, whether this is geared toward the production and sale of handicrafts or wage labor (Castellanos 2010b; Warman 1985). This diverse economy has played an important role in how people envision labor, by drawing a sharp distinction between work that takes place "at home" in lands held collectively by community and more individualistic forms of participating in the cash economy.[8] Recently, Bianet Castellanos has written a sensitive study of the experience of women from rural communities in the east of Yucatán who migrate to work in the service industry in Cancún. As she notes, tourist zones such as Cancún are understood as more than merely a source of income; they embody a series of assumptions about personal discipline and "civilization" whose roots in the vernacular consciousness span to the educational project of the early twentieth century (Castellanos 2010b).

The expansion of the local tourist hub at Chichén Itzá has meant that many people in agrarian kajo'ob can experience this dual nature of labor in their own backyards. Although official criteria such as language use would constitute Pisté and Popolá as members of the same Maya ethnic group, the eighteen-kilometer trip from their home village to larger tourist areas can represent significant cultural and social distance. This was a persistent theme in my research in Popolá, which I began after three years of work in Pisté. Knowing that I had many friends in Pisté, Popolá residents were in general fairly circumspect when characterizing these differences, often commenting that people there "had a different way of living" (Ma. *díiperente u porma u kuxtal*). One artisan, however, was fairly blunt in saying that "Pisté is screwed up" (Sp. *Pisté está cabrón*). He noted that there was only one car in Popolá, but that his visits to Pisté were marred by the constant worry of being run down. This sense of danger was compounded by other disconcerting experiences, including the time he was nearly robbed while drinking in a local cantina, or when he learned that the sexually aggressive waitress was actually one of about a dozen locally born people who were openly gay or transgender.

These encounters with the "otherness" of Pisté punctuate a contrast between the activities that take place in the spaces that are controlled by the ejido committee of Popolá and those in which individual *popolail* must seek out business deals with the residents of larger and more cosmopolitan kajo'ob. Artisans are granted access to wood by the ejido committee of Popolá, where local men and women can rely on the influence of uncles and cousins who have an officially sanctioned voice in the management of collectively held lands. But from the 1980s to around 2005, the process of selling these crafts to second parties from Pisté involved far less advantageous conditions. With access to motor vehicles and lucrative sites of sale, and having a better command of Spanish and foreign languages, these intermediaries were historically able to buy at prices that permitted them to sell to tourists at a 250 percent markup (Armstrong-Fumero 2000). Careless drivers and thieves were not the only hazards faced by *popolailo'ob* on the unfamiliar ground of Pisté. It is common knowledge that wholesalers of handicrafts that travel to Pisté from smaller kajo'ob have to sell their wares before returning home, or face the loss of all of the time and money invested in the trip down the unpaved road. Along with the fact that many *pisteil* view people from neighboring communities as naive country bumpkins, this need for a quick sell has made artisans from Popolá vulnerable to a range of exploitative business practices. Thus there is a sharp difference between the relative security that carvers experience during the production of handicrafts and the dangers involved in selling to middlemen. One friend from Pisté summed up these facts of the handicrafts market when he drove me to Popolá. When we passed a group of wood carvers who had taken a break from their work to hang out under the shade of a tree, he smiled and said: "Look at those guys! Mayan Princes. In Pisté or Mérida, people discriminate against them. But here, they give the orders."[9]

In the late 1990s, the Casa de las Artesanías, the same parastatal agency whose representatives had declined to develop a project with Guillermo Macal of Pisté, began a project in Popolá. One of their stated goals was to provide a sales outlet for local artisans that would give them an alternative to the market at Pisté. Through this project, people of Popolá received a collectively controlled credit for the purchase of tools. They also collaborated with design students brought from Mexico City to develop and produce crafts that conformed to the institution's criteria of "authentic" folk art. Thus, where more than a decade of participation in the Chichén Itzá tourist sphere had taught them to produce archaeologically themed carvings based on ruins from the ancient site, the Casa de las Artesanías taught them to make crosses and chests decorated with colonial designs. The products of the cooperative were collected on a regular basis and sold in the institution's stores at a fixed price.[10]

The history of this project from the late 1990s to early 2000s illustrates some of the tensions that can emerge when the logic of contemporary multicultural institutions meets the realities of the Maya culture industry. The adoption of a cooperative structure for the artisanry project was familiar to community members who were raised in a tradition of ejido politics, particularly given the fact that the local agrarian committee played a significant role in directing harvesting procurement of carving material from collectively controlled lands. But this cooperative structure was a more awkward fit for the processes that take place at the site of sale. Though people whom I spoke with in Popolá were generally pleased with the credit offered by the Casa de las Artesanías, it was soon evident that the prices that the institution was able to offer for the wholesale of their pieces were not significantly higher than what they could expect from the middlemen in Pisté. Ironically, the fact that the Casa offered fixed prices that were negotiated with the collective body of the community was counterintuitive to many local carvers. Despite the odds being tilted in favor of middlemen in Pisté, some carvers from Popolá have been able to exploit the heightened demand for handicrafts at certain high-traffic times of the year to haggle with middlemen and get more value for their work. This was impossible in the relationship that they established with the Casa de las Artesanías.

This arrangement seemed even less attractive after the occupation of the archaeological zone by vendors in 2005, an event that was quickly followed by the paving of the hilly eighteen-kilometer dirt road that connected Popolá to Pisté. Though a number of local families still produce artisanry for wholesale, many explored a range of new roles in the tourist industry. At first, this consisted of work as teamsters and porters, carrying merchandise for vendors who operated stands within the archaeological zone. Now there are a number of sellers from Popolá who operate their own stalls, or who sell merchandise directly to tourists in stalls maintained by merchants from Pisté.

I don't intend my critical observations about the Casa de las Artesanías intervention in Popolá to be interpreted as saying that cooperative projects in small agrarian kajo'ob are generally a failure. In my time in the field, I have seen a number of very successful state-funded projects of apiculture, cattle, and pig raising in Popolá, Xcalakdzonot, and other communities. What seems evident in the current state of the handicrafts market is that models that work well for projects that focus on agriculture are difficult to apply to handicrafts production in Oriente.

The frictions I've described are important for two primary reasons. First, as part of the most vibrant dimension of the regional economy, Popolá's niche in the tourist industry holds far greater promise for economic prosperity amid the diminishing returns of agriculture. Second and more important is the central role of Chichén Itzá in the emergence of an explicitly ethnic politics. The demands of artisans from Pisté, Popolá, and other kajo'ob are historically important insofar as they are not justified by the kind of usufruct claims that defined generations of agrarian politics. Instead, they are claims based on an ethnic connection to the original builders of Chichén, claims that would have been difficult to imagine a generation earlier. The outcome of struggles over access to the archaeological zone is a significant test of how Mexican multiculturalism can encompass the experience of individuals who do not conform to traditional stereotypes of indigeneity. Similarly, how local residents and government officials navigate the tensions between corporate land management and individual haggling that mark Popolá's engagement with the tourist market has important implications for the realpolitik of multiculturalism in smaller agrarian communities. These outcomes can determine whether actual policy decisions can live up to official definitions of minority ethnic rights that are not necessarily grounded on traditional models of "Indian" lifestyles.

Conclusions

In a study called *The Trouble with Unity*, the political theorist Cristina Beltrán (2010) has argued that the idea of a coherent political agenda and ideology that unites self-identified U.S. Latinos is difficult to reconcile with the democratic representation of different groups within this broadly defined "community." A similar argument could be made for Maya identity politics in Yucatán. The idea that a single ethnic and linguistic identity can override the differences between communities such as Popolá and Pisté, or the class and factional divides that exist within different kajo'ob, tends to overlook some of the most significant challenges facing rural people in Oriente. What's more, the "stuff" of this imagined cultural unity—like speaking the Maya language—provides a comfortable space for a politics of recognition that is difficult to reconcile with grassroots demands for tangible resources.

The two experiences of cultural politics and the handicrafts market that I discussed above embody a sort of double bind faced by both rural Maya speakers and representatives of official multicultural institutions. At least on paper, the rights of Maya people that are currently protected by state and federal governments are not limited to agrarian communities that are organized through corporate institutions such as the ejido or that lead traditional rural lifestyles. That is, the ability to claim certain rights as a descendant of the ancient Maya should be independent of occupation. By extension, and even if certain forms of exploitation take place in the artisanry markets of Pisté and Chichén Itzá, the categorical dismissal of the vendors' right to profit from sites that were constructed by their ancestors seems contrary to the stated purposes of the law. A similar disconnect between institutional models and the economic realities of the Maya culture industry is evident in the difficulties that the people of Popolá have faced in reconciling, on the one hand, the cooperative structure of their engagement with the Casa de las Artesanías with, on the other hand, the potentials of the handicrafts market. Again, the recognition of people's right to produce artisanry in an authentically "Mayan" way is circumscribed too strictly by institutional assumptions about the corporate nature of indigenous production.

As I hinted above, the importance of both of these cases is that they represent the current challenges faced by the theory and practice of a politics based on ethnic, rather than peasant, identity. They test the ability of official multicultural institutions and local communities to successfully act within a regional culture industry that has become one of the principal spaces for the performance of politicized indigeneity in Oriente. These cases also test the degree to which the politics of indigeneity can move beyond the neoliberal politics of recognition to offer tangible results based on ethnicity.

As rural communities, activists, government officials, and scholars examine the new possibilities and limitations of identity politics, there are some useful lessons to be learned from history. Throughout this book, I have stressed the ambivalence and ambiguity of identity politics, the fact that rural people in Oriente have tended to engage semantically flexible concepts such as peasant and Maya to explore a range of possibilities for factionalism and solidarity. Here, the parallels between the contemporary politics of ethnicity and the agrarian politics or educational projects of the early twentieth century become particularly important. The ambivalence of local uses of national institutions has not limited the degree to which these institutions are successfully and meaningfully integrated into people's lives. The range of factional struggles that marked the agrarian reform of the 1920s defies the ideas of organic and corporate unity that politicians and scholars ascribed to the "peasant village," but it did set up a series of precedents for a political culture that is still empowering many rural people. Public schools instituted the idea that rural citizens can demand a range of cultural goods from the state, even as their foundation and operation often reinstituted factional and class divides within different kajo'ob. In this sense, the complexities and contradictions of contemporary Mayan identity politics are hardly new. Generations of rural people in Oriente gained a number of key concessions and asserted their rights as Mexican citizens even though their understanding of the key terms "peasant," "community," "culture," and so on was not necessarily what urban politicians had had in mind.

The challenge faced by the multiple actors who are engaged in the contemporary field of multicultural politics is not simply one of testing the boundaries between the neoliberal politics of recognition and more radical forms of resource distribution. Nor is it simply a question of recognizing the heterogeneity that exists within the community of people who might self-identify as Mayan. It is also a question of making sense of these demands for material resources and the heterogeneity of rural Yucatecans in a way that can accommodate mobilizations articulated at different scales, and without forcing an imagined unity on the politics of ethnicity. Only coming years will tell if a radically new rethinking of cultural and social democracy will emerge amid the new possibilities of multiculturalism and rural Oriente's heritage of factionalism and solidarity.

Notes

1. As Lisa Breglia has noted, rural Yucatecans in several parts of the state have mobilized these forms of territoriality to stake a claim on archaeological zones that federal agencies have legally expropriated from their collective landholdings (see also Breglia 2006). One of the most successful cases of such claims has been the Yucatec Maya–speaking kaj of Cobá in the neighboring state of Quintana Roo, which has maintained significant control over management and the tourist industry in the ruins of the same name located within their original *ejido*. Still, this is a relatively rare success story. For example, the ejidatarios of Xcalakoop have relatively little direct involvement in tourism at the caves of Balankanche, which are managed by the National Institute of Anthropology and History (Instituto Nacional de Antropología e Historia, INAH) within the kaj's ejido.

2. For discussions of Mayan activities in the late 1990s and early 2000s, see Berkeley 1998 and Mattiace 2009.

3. See the Hotel Hacienda website: http://www.haciendachichen.com/special-services .htm, accessed August 13, 2011.

4. These quotations are translated from excerpts from the regional newspaper *Por Esto*, which chronicles the *encuentro*, cited in the bibliography under *Por Esto* 2002. The quotations that I copy here come from newspaper reports of the event, which correspond to the few notes that I'd jotted down.

5. More than one person has told me that a representative of the Barbachanos got the operators of the concession stand drunk and tricked them into signing papers that terminated their lease.

6. For an account of previous occupations of the archaeological zone and local movements that did not rely on the discourse of indigeneity, see Castañeda 1996, 2003.

7. The full text of the declaration was posted at the following URL until some point in 2007: http://arn.espora.org/article.pl?sid=05/08/01/1033206.

8. For a comparative analysis of rural people's consciousness of mixed economies, see García Canclini 1989; Gordillo 2004; Nash 1993.

9. Original Spanish: *¡Mira a esos chavos! Príncipes Mayas. En Pisté o en Mérida, les discriminan. Pero acá, ellos mandan.*

10. In 1998 and 1999, the Casa de Artesanía's orders consisted of small boxes decorated with colonial-style flower motifs, which had no market at Chichén Itzá but were sold in the institution's stores in the state capital, Mérida. They later relaxed their standards somewhat and purchased a few archaeologically themed carvings.

Aguilar Camín, Héctor, and Lorenzo Meyer. 1993. *In the Shadow of the Mexican Revolution: Contemporary Mexican History 1910–1989*.

Ai Camp, Roderick. 2002. *Mexico's Mandarins: Crafting a Power Elite for the Twenty-First Century*. Berkeley: University of California Press.

Aké, Salvador. 1979. *La milpa en Muxupip*. Mérida: Universidad de Yucatán.

Albó, Xavier. 2002. *Los pueblos indios en la política*. La Paz: Editores Plural.

Alexander, Rani. 2005. *Yaxcaba and the Caste War of Yucatan: An Archaeological Perspective*. Albuquerque: University of New Mexico Press. http://dx.doi.org/10.1525/jlat.2005.10.2.478.

Alexander, Rani. 2006. "Maya Settlement Shifts and Agrarian Ecology in Yucatán, 1800–2000." *Journal of Anthropological Research* 62: 449–70.

Alexander, Rani. 2010. Personal communication in Mérida, Yucatán, June 13, 2010.

Alvarado, Salvador. 1994. *Salvador Alvarado: Estadista y pensador, compilación*. Ed. José Paoli Bolio. Mexico City: Fondo de Cultura Económica.

Alvarez, Sonia, Evelina Dagnino, and Arturo Escobar. 1998. "Introduction: The Cultural and Political in Latin American Social Movements." In *Cultures of Politics/Politics of Cultures: Re-visioning Latin American Social Movements*, ed. S. Alvarez, E. Dagnino, and A. Escobar, 1–30.

Alvarez Barret, Luis. 1972. *Origen y evolución de las escuelas rurales en Yucatán*. Mérida: Luis Alvarez Barret.

Amaro Gamboa, Jesús. 1999. *Vocabulario del uayeísmo en la cultura de Yucatán*. Mérida: Universidad Autónoma de Yucatán.

Anderson, Benedict. 1983. *Imagined Communities: Reflections on the Origin and Spread of Nationalism*. London: Verso.

Andrade, Manuel J., and Hilaria Máas Collí, eds. 1999. *U tsikbalilo'ob mayab (uuchben tsikbalo'ob)*. Mérida: Universidad Autónoma de Yucatán.

Armstrong-Fumero, Fernando. 2000. "Making Maya Art in Pisté: Art and Experimental Ethnography in a Yucatec Maya Community." MA thesis, University of Pennsylvania.

Armstrong-Fumero, Fernando. 2009a. "A Heritage of Ambiguity: The Historical Substrate of Vernacular Multiculturalism in Yucatan, Mexico." *American Ethnologist* 36 (2): 300–16. http://dx.doi.org/10.1111/j.1548-1425.2009.01136.x.

Armstrong-Fumero, Fernando. 2009b. "Old Jokes and New Multiculturalisms: Continuity and Change in Vernacular Discourse on the Yucatec Maya Language." *American Anthropologist* 111 (3): 360–72. http://dx.doi.org/10.1111/j.1548-1433.2009.01138.x.

Baños Ramírez, Othon. 1978. *Yucatán: Ejidos sin campesinos*. Mérida: Universidad Autónoma de Yucatán.

Baños Ramírez, Othon, and Arcadio Sabido Méndez. 2008. *Democracia? Procesos electorales y participación ciudadana, Yucatán 2001–2007*. Mérida: Universidad Autónoma de Yucatán.

Bartra, Roger. 1987. *La jaula de la melancolía: Identidad y metamorfosis del mexicano*. Mexico City: Grijalbo.

Bartra, Roger. 1999. *La sangre y la tinta: Ensayos sobre la condición postmexicana*. Mexico City: Océano.

Bartra, Roger. 2002a. *Anatomía del mexicano*. Mexico City: Plaza Janez.

Bartra, Roger. 2002b. *Blood, Ink, and Culture: Miseries and Splendors of the Post-Mexican Condition*. Durham, NC: Duke University Press.

Basso, Keith. 1996. *Wisdom Sits in Places: Landscape and Language among the Western Apache*. Albuquerque: University of New Mexico Press.

Bauman, Richard, and Charles Briggs. 2003. *Voices of Modernity: Language Ideologies and the Politics of Inequality*. Cambridge: Cambridge University Press. http://dx.doi.org/10.1017/CBO9780511486647.

Beer, Caroline C. 2002. "Institutional Change in Mexico: Politics after One-Party Rule." *Latin American Research Review* 37 (3): 149–61.

Beltrán, Christina. 2010. *The Trouble with Unity: Latino Politics and the Creation of Identity.* New York: Oxford University Press.

Benítez, Fernando. 1956. *Ki: El drama de un pueblo y de una planta.* Mexico City: Fondo de Cultura Económica.

Benjamin, Thomas. 2002. *La Revolución: Mexico's Great Revolution as Memory, Myth, & History.* Austin: University of Texas Press.

Benjamin, Thomas, and Marcial Ocasio-Meléndez. 1984. "Organizing the Memory of Modern Mexico: Porfirian Historiography in Perspective, 1880s–1980s." *Hispanic American Historical Review* 64 (2): 323–64.

Berkeley, Anthony. 1998. "Revitalization and Remembrance: The Archive of Pure Maya." PhD dissertation, Department of Anthropology, University of Chicago.

Betancourt Pérez, Antonio. 1951. *Cuatro corrientes filosóficas en las escuelas de Yucatán.* Mérida: Gobierno del Estado.

Betancourt Pérez, Antonio. 1965. "La escuela de la Revolución Mexicana." Conferencia sustentada por su autor, la noche del 18 de diciembre de 1965, ante la Academia Mexicana de la Educación, Ciudad de Mexico. Mérida: Ediciones de Gobierno de Yucatán.

Betancourt Pérez, Antonio. 1969. *La pedagogía del anarquismo en México: La escuela racionalista.* Mérida: Universidad de Yucatán.

Betancourt Pérez, Antonio. 1983. *Memorias de un luchador social.* Mérida: Instituto de Cultura de Yucatán.

Beuchot, Mauricio. 1998. *The History of Philosophy in Colonial Mexico.* Washington, DC: Catholic University of America Press.

Bonfil-Batalla, Guillermo. 1987. *México profundo: Una civilización negada.* Mexico City: Grijalbo.

Boyer, Christopher. 2003. *Becoming Campesinos: Politics, Identity and Agrarian Struggle in Postrevolutionary Michoacán, 1920–1935.* Stanford, CA: Stanford University Press.

Bracamonte y Sosa, Pedro. 2001. *La conquista inconclusa de Yucatán: Los Mayas de la montaña.* Mexico City: Centro de Investigaciones y Estudios Superiores en Antropologia Social.

Bracamonte y Sosa, Pedro, and Gabriela Solís Robleda. 1996. *Espacios mayas de autonomía: El pacto colonial en Yucatán.* Mérida: Universidad Autónoma de Yucatán.

Brading, David. 1973. *Los orígenes del nacionalismo mexicano.* Mexico City: Ediciones Era.

Bratt Paulston, Christina. 1997. "Language Policies and Language Rights." *Annual Review of Anthropology* 26 (1): 73–85. http://dx.doi.org/10.1146/annurev.anthro.26.1.73.

Bravo Lira, Bernardino. 1985. "Feijoo y la ilustración católica y nacional en el mundo de habla castellana y portuguesa." *Jahrbuch für Geschichte von Staat, Wirtschaft und Gesellschaft Lateinamerikas* 22: 100–22.

Breglia, Lisa. 2006. *Monumental Ambivalence: The Politics of Heritage.* Austin: University of Texas Press.

Briceño Chel, Fidencio. 2004. *Noj A'almaj T'aanil u Páajtalil u T'a'anal Máasewal T'aano'ob ich Maya yetel Káastlan T'an.* Mérida: Gobierno del Estado.

Briggs, Charles, and Richard Bauman. 1992. "Genre, Intertextuality and Social Power." *Journal of Linguistic Anthropology* 2 (2): 131–72. http://dx.doi.org/10.1525/jlin.1992.2 .2.131.

Brito Sansores, William. 1987. "¡Adiós Maestro Rural!" In *Los maestros y la cultura nacional*, 39–72. Mexico City: Secretaría de Educación Pública.

Britton, John A. 1976. *Educación y radicalismo en México, los años de Bassols*. Mexico City: Secretaría de Educación Pública.

Brunhouse, Robert L. 1973. *In Search of the Maya: The First Archaeologists*. Albuquerque: University of New Mexico Press.

Burns, Allan F. 1983. *An Epoch of Miracles: Oral Literature of the Yucatec Maya*. Austin: University of Texas Press.

Cámara Zavala, Gonzalo. 1953. *Reseña histórica de la industria henequenera*. Mérida: Liga de Acción Social.

Campos, García. 2003. *Sociabilidades políticas en Yucatán*. Mérida: Universidad Autónoma de Yucatán / Consejo Nacional de Ciencia y Tecnología.

Cancian, Frank. 1965. *Economics and Prestige in a Maya Community: The Religious Cargo System in Zinacantan*. Stanford, CA: Stanford University Press.

Castañeda, Jorge. 1994. *Utopia Unarmed: The Latin American Left after the Cold War*. New York: Vintage.

Castañeda, Quetzil E. 1996. *In the Museum of Maya Culture: Touring Chichén Itzá*. Minneapolis: University of Minnesota Press.

Castañeda, Quetzil E. 2003. "New and Old Social Movements: Measuring Pisté, from the 'Mouth of the Well' to the 107th Municipio of Yucatán." *Ethnohistory [Columbus, Ohio]* 50 (4): 611–42. http://dx.doi.org/10.1215/00141801-50-4-611.

Castañeda, Quetzil E. 2004. "'We Are Not Indigenous': Introduction to the Maya Identity of Yucatán." *Journal of Latin American Anthropology* 9 (1): 36–63.

Castellanos, Bianet. 2010a. "Don Teo's Expulsion: Property Regimes, Moral Economies, and Ejido Reform." *Journal of Latin American and Caribbean Anthropology* 15 (1).

Castellanos, Bianet. 2010b. *A Return to Servitude*. Minneapolis: University of Minnesota Press.

Castillo Cocom, Juan. 2005. "'It Was Simply Their Word': Yucatec Maya PRInces in YucaPAN and the Politics of Respect." *Critique of Anthropology* 25 (131): 132–55.

Chuchiak, John F. 1997. "Intelectuales, los indios y la prensa, el periodismo polémico de Justo Sierra O'Reilly." *Saastun* 1 (2): 3–49.

Clendinnen, Inga. 1987. *Ambivalent Conquests: Maya and Spaniard in Yucatan, 1517–1570*. New York: Cambridge University Press.

Cohen, Bernard. 1987. *An Anthropologist among the Historians and Other Essays*. London: Oxford University Press.

Cole, Jennifer. 2001. *Forget Colonialism?: Sacrifice and the Art of Memory in Madagascar*. Berkeley: University of California Press.

Collier, George. 1987. "Peasant Politics and the Mexican State: Indigenous Compliance in Highland Chiapas." *Mexican Studies / Estudios Mexicanos* 3 (1): 71–98. http://dx.doi.org/10.2307/4617032.

Collier, George, and Elizabeth Lowery Quaratiello. 2005. *Basta: Land and the Zapatista Rebellion in Chiapas*. Oakland: Food First Books.

Connaughton, Brian Francis. 2003. *Clerical Ideology in a Revolutionary Age: The Guadalajara Church and the Idea of the Mexican Nation, 1788–1853*. Calgary: University of Calgary Press.

Córdova, Arnaldo. 1973. *La ideología de la Revolución Mexicana: La formación del nuevo régimen*. Mexico City: Era.

Córdova, Arnaldo. 1986. *La política de masas y el futuro de la izquierda en México*. Mexico City: Era.

El Correo. 1921. "Indios asaltan al pueblo de Yaxcabá." June 23.

Darnton, Robert. 1984. *The Great Cat Massacre and Other Episodes in French Cultural History*. New York: Basic Books.

Dawson, Alexander E. 1998. "From Models for the Nation to Model Citizens: *Indigenismo* and the 'Revindification' of the Mexican Indian, 1920–1940." *Journal of Latin American Studies* 30 (2): 279–308. http://dx.doi.org/10.1017/S0022216X98005057.

Dawson, Alexander E. 2001. "'Wild Indians,' 'Mexican Gentlemen' and the Lessons Learned in the Casa del Estudiante Indígena." *Americas* 57 (3): 329–61. http://dx.doi.org/10.1353/tam.2001.0006.

De la Cadena, Marisol. 2000. *Indigenous Mestizos: The Politics of Race and Culture in Cuzco, Peru, 1919–1991*. Durham, NC: Duke University Press.

Díaz-Polanco, Héctor. 1991. *Autonomía regional: La autodeterminación de los Pueblos Indios*. Mexico City: Siglo Veintiuno Editores.

Domínguez, José. 1979. "Luchas campesinas de Yaxcabá." Licenciatura thesis, Facultad de Ciencias Antropológicas, Universidad Autónoma de Yucatán.

Donham, Donald. 1999. *Marxist Modern: An Ethnographic History of the Ethiopian Revolution*. Berkeley: University of California Press.

Dzul Poot, Domingo. 1985. *Cuentos mayos*. Mérida: Maldonado.

Echeverria, Ramón. 1996. *Historia de la educación en Yucatán*. Mérida: Universidad Autónoma de Yucatán.

Eiss, Paul. 2004. "Deconstructing Indians, Reconstructing *Patria*: Indigenous Education in Yucatan from *Porfiriato* to the Mexican Revolution." *Journal of Latin American Anthropology* 9 (1): 119–50. http://dx.doi.org/10.1525/jlca.2004.9.1.119.

Eiss, Paul. 2010. *In the Name of the Pueblo*. Durham, NC: Duke University Press.

Fabian, Johannes. 1983. *Time and the Other: How Anthropology Makes Its Object*. New York: Columbia University Press.

Falla, Ricardo. 2001. *Quiché Rebelde: Religious Conversion, Politics, and Ethnic Identity in Guatemala*. Trans. Phillip Berryman. Austin: University of Texas Press.

Fallaw, Ben. 2001. *Cárdenas Compromised: The Failure of Reform in Postrevolutionary Yucatán*. Durham, NC: Duke University Press.

Fallaw, Ben. 2004. "Repensando la resistencia maya: Cambios de las relaciones entre maestros federales y comunidades mayas en el Oriente, 1929–1935." In *Estrategias identitarias: Educación y la antropología histórica en Yucatán*, ed. J. Castillo Cocom and Q. Castañeda, 91–120. Mérida: Universidad Pedagógica Nacional / Open School of Ethnography / Secretaría de Educación Pública.

Farriss, Nancy. 1984. *Maya Society under Colonial Rule: The Collective Enterprise of Survival*. Princeton, NJ: Princeton University Press.

Fischer, Edward, and R. McKenna Brown, eds. 1997. *Maya Cultural Activism in Guatemala*. Austin: University of Texas Press.

Fischer, Ted. 1999. "Cultural Logic and Maya Identity: Rethinking Constructivism and Essentialism." *Current Anthropology* 40 (4): 473–500. http://dx.doi.org/10.1086/200046.

Foster, George. 1987. *Tzintzuntzan: Mexican Peasants in a Changing World*. New York: Waveland Press.

Fox, Jonathan. 2000. "State-Society Relations in Mexico: Historical Legacies and Contemporary Trends." Latin American Research Review 35 (2): 183–203.

Frazer, Nancy. 1996. *Justice Interruptus*. New York: Routledge.

Gabbert, Wolfgang. 2004. *Becoming Maya: Ethnicity and Social Inequality in Yucatán since 1500*. Tucson: University of Arizona Press.

Gallo Martínez, Víctor. 1966. *Política educativa en México*. Mexico City: Ediciones Oasis.

Gamio, Manuel. 1916. *Forjando patria (pro nacionalismo)*. Mexico City: Porrúa Hermanos.

García, Maria Elena. 2005. *Making Indigenous Citizens: Identities, Education, and Multicultural Development in Peru*. Stanford, CA: Stanford University Press.

García Canclini, Néstor. 1989. *Culturas híbridas: Estrategias para entrar y salir de la modernidad*. Mexico City: Grijalbo.

Gawronski, Vincent T. 2002. "The Revolution Is Dead. '¡Viva la Revolución!' The Place of the Mexican Revolution in the Era of Globalization." *Mexican Studies / Estudios Mexicanos* 18 (2): 363–97. http://dx.doi.org/10.1525/msem.2002.18.2.363.

Gilbert, Dennis. 2003. "Emiliano Zapata: Textbook Hero." *Mexican Studies / Estudios Mexicanos* 19 (1): 127–59. http://dx.doi.org/10.1525/msem.2003.19.1.127.

Gilly, Adolfo. 1979. "La guerra de clases en la Revolución Mexicana (revolución permanente y auto-organización de las masas." In *Interpretaciones de la Revolución Mexicana*, 21–54. Mexico City: Nueva Imagen.

Giordano, Al. 2006. "Marcos rompió el guión: 'Vamos a Chichén Itzá.'" Electronic document, http://www.narconews.com/Issue40/articulo1570.html, accessed May 20.

Gobierno del Estado de Yucatán. 2007. "DECRETO NUMERO 755." *Diario oficial del Estado de Yucatán* CX (30,902).

Goldkind, Victor. 1965. "Social Stratification in the Peasant Community: Redfield's Chan Kom Reinterpreted." *American Anthropologist* 67 (4): 863–84. http://dx.doi.org/10.1525/aa.1965.67.4.02a00010.

Goldkind, Victor. 1966. "Class Conflict and Cacique in Chan Kom." *Southwestern Journal of Anthropology* 22 (4): 325–45.

Gordillo, Gastón R. 2004. *Landscapes of Devils: Tensions of Place and Memory in the Argentinean Chaco*. Durham, NC: Duke University Press.

Gossen, Gary. 1998. *Telling Maya Tales: Tzotzil Identities in Modern Mexico*. New York: Routledge.

Greenblatt, Stephen. 1992. *Marvelous Possessions: Wonders of the New World*. Chicago: University of Chicago Press.

Guemez Piñeda, Arturo. 1994. *Liberalismo en tierras del Caminante: Yucatán 1812–1840*. Morelia: El Colegio de Michoacán.

Guemez Piñeda, Arturo. 2005. "Ciudadanía indígena y representación en Yucatán, 1825–1847." In *Encrucijadas de la ciudadana y la democracia: Yucatán 1812–2004*, 83–108. Mérida: Universidad Autónoma de Yucatán.

Gupta, Akhil. 1995. "Blurred Boundaries: The Discourse of Corruption, the Culture of Politics, and the Imagined State." *American Ethnologist* 22 (2): 375–402. http://dx.doi.org /10.1525/ae.1995.22.2.02a00090.

Gustafson, Brett. 2009. *New Languages of the State: Indigenous Resurgence and the Politics of Knowledge in Bolivia*. Durham, NC: Duke University Press.

Gutmann, Matthew. 2002. *The Romance of Democracy: Compliant Defiance in Contemporary Mexico*. Berkeley: University of California Press.

Hale, Charles. 1968. *Mexican Liberalism in the Age of Mora, 1821–1853*. New Haven, CT: Yale University Press.

Hale, Charles R. 1994. "Between Che Guevara and the Pachamama: Mestizos, Indians and Identity Politics in the Anti-Quincentenary Campaign." *Critique of Anthropology* 14 (1): 9–39. http://dx.doi.org/10.1177/0308275X9401400102.

Hale, Charles R. 1999. "Travel Warning: Elite Appropriations of Hybridity, Mestizaje, Antiracism, Equality and Other Progressive-Sounding Discourses in Highland Guatemala." *Journal of American Folklore* 112 (445): 297–315. http://dx.doi.org/10.2307 /541364.

Hale, Charles R. 2005. "Neoliberal Multiculturalism: The Remaking of Cultural Rights and Racial Dominance in Central America." *Political and Legal Anthropology Review* 28 (1): 10–28.

Hanks, William. 1990. *Referential Practice: Language and Lived Space among the Maya*. Chicago: University of Chicago Press.

Hawkins, John. 1983. "Robert Redfield's Culture Concept and Mesoamerican Anthropology." In *The Heritage of Conquest: Thirty Years Later*, ed. C. Kendall, J. Hawkins, and L. Bossen, 299–35. Albuquerque: University of New Mexico Press.

Hervik, Peter. 1999. *Mayan People within and beyond Boundaries: Social Categories and Lived Identity in Yucatán*. Amsterdam: Harwood Academic Publishers.

Hill, Jane. 1985. "The Grammar of Consciousness and the Consciousness of Grammar." *American Ethnologist* 12 (4): 725–37. http://dx.doi.org/10.1525/ae.1985.12.4.02a00080.

Hoil Gutiérrez, Julio. 2010. Personal communication, July 25, 2010.

Hoil Gutiérrez, Julio, Ismael May, and Patricia Martínez Huchim. 2008. "Translating, Preserving and Promoting Minority Languages: The Case of Yucatec Maya." Public presentation at the Louise W. and Edmund J. Kahn Liberal Arts Institute, Smith College, Northampton, November 14.

Jameson, Fredric. 1972. *The Prison House of Language: A Critical Account of Structuralism and Russian Formalism*. Princeton, NJ: Princeton University Press.

Jones, Grant D. 1989. *Maya Resistance to Spanish Rule: Time and History on a Colonial Frontier*. Albuquerque: University of New Mexico Press.

Jones, Grant D. 1998. *The Conquest of the Last Mayan Kingdom*. Stanford, CA: Stanford University Press.

Joseph, Gilbert. 1985. *Revolution from Without: Yucatán, Mexico and the United States, 1880–1924*. Durham, NC: Duke University Press.

Keen, Benjamín. 1971. *The Aztec Image in Western Thought*. New Brunswick, NJ: Rutgers University Press.

Knight, Alan. 1997. "The Ideology of the Mexican Revolution, 1910–40." *Estudios Interdisciplinarios de América Latina y el Caribe* 8 (1).

Kovic, Christine. 2005. *Mayan Voices for Human Rights: Displaced Catholics in Highland Chiapas*. Austin: University of Texas Press.

Kray, Christine. 1997. "Worship in Body and Spirit: Practice, Self, and Religious Sensibility in Yucatán." PhD Dissertation, Department of Anthropology, University of Pennsylvania.

LaCapra, Dominick. 1984. "Is Everyone a *Mentalité* Case? Transference and the 'Culture' Concept." *History and Theory* 23 (3): 296–311. http://dx.doi.org/10.2307/2505077.

LaCapra, Dominick. 1988. "Charier, Darnton and the Great Symbol Massacre." *Journal of Modern History* 60 (1): 95–112. http://dx.doi.org/10.1086/243336.

Lewis, Oscar. 1960. *Tepoztlán: Village in Mexico*. New York City: Harcourt College Publishers.

Lockhart, James. 1999. *Of Things of the Indies: Essays Old and New in Early Latin American History*. Stanford, CA: Stanford University Press.

Lomnitz, Claudio. 1992. *Exits from the Labyrinth*. Berkeley: University of California Press.

Lomnitz, Claudio. 2001. *Deep Mexico, Silent Mexico: An Anthropology of Nationalism*. Minneapolis: University of Minnesota Press.

López Bárcenas, Francisco. 2005. *Los movimientos indígenas en Mexico: Rostros y caminos*. Mexico City: MC Editores.

Loyo, Engracia. 2003. "La empresa redentora de la casa del estudiante indígena." *Historia mexicana* 46 (1): 99–131.

Manzanilla, Dorantes. 2004. "Identidad y resistencia: La educación para los Mayas de Yucatán." In *Estrategias identitarias: Educación y la antropología en Yucatán*, ed. J. Castillo Cocom and Q. Castañeda, 147–70. Mérida: Universidad Pedagógica Nacional / Open School of Ethnography / Secretaría de Educación Pública.

Mattiace, Shannan. 2003. *To See with Two Eyes*. Albuquerque: University of New Mexico Press.

Mattiace, Shannan. 2009. "Ethnic Mobilization among the Maya of Yucatán Today." *Latin American and Caribbean Ethnic Studies* 4 (2): 137–69.

McDonald, James H. 1997. "Fading Aztec Sun: The Mexican Opposition and the Politics of Everyday Fear in 1994." *Critique of Anthropology* 17 (3): 263–92. http://dx.doi.org/10.1177 /0308275X9701700304.

Mediz Bolio, Antonio. 1934. *La tierra del faisán y del venado.* Mexico City: Editorial México.

Mediz Bolio, Antonio. 1951. *Raíces y frutos de la Revolución en Yucatán.* Mérida: Yikal Maya Than.

Mena, José de la Luz. 1919. *De las tablillas de lodo a las fracciones de primer año.* Mérida: Departamento de Escuelas.

Mignolo, Walter. 2000. *Local Histories/Global Designs.* Princeton, NJ: Princeton University Press.

Miller, Marylin. 2004. *Rise and Fall of the Cosmic Race: The Cult of* Mestizaje *in Latin America.* Austin: University of Texas Press.

Mis Cobá, Rafael. 2005. "Chichén Itzá y los artesanos." *Por Esto*, August 1: 4–10.

Mis Cobá, Rafael. 2006. "Sin tierra y sin futuro." *Por Esto*, online edition, September 23. Electronic document, http://www.poresto.net/valladolid, accessed May 11, 2007.

Montejo, Victor. 2005. *Maya Intellectual Renaissance: Identity, Representation and Leadership.* Austin: University of Texas Press.

Montroy Huitron, Guadalupe. 1975. *Política educativa de la Revolución 1910–1940.* Mexico City: Cien de México.

Moreau, Joseph. 2004. *Schoolbook Nation: Conflicts over American History Textbooks from the Civil War to the Present.* Ann Arbor: University of Michigan Press.

Moreno, Roberto. 1975. "La ciencia de la ilustración mexicana." *Anuario de Estudios Americanos* XXXII: 25–41.

Morris, Stephen D. 2003. "Corruption and Mexican Political Culture." *Journal of the Southwest* 45 (4): 671–708.

Nash, June. 1993. "Introduction." In *Crafts in the World Market: The Impact of Global Exchange on Middle American Indians*, ed. June Nash, 1–23. Albany: State University of New York Press.

Nash, June. 2001. *Mayan Visions: The Quest for Autonomy in an Age of Globalization.* New York: Routledge.

Nelson, Diane. 1999. *A Finger in the Wound: Body Politics in Quincentennial Guatemala.* Berkeley: University of California Press.

Norá, Pierre. 1996. *Realms of Memory: Rethinking the French Past.* New York: Columbia University Press.

Paley, Julia. 2001. *Marketing Democracy.* Berkeley: University of California Press.

Paoli, Francisco José. 1984. *Yucatán y los orígenes del nuevo estado mexicano: Gobierno de Salvador Alvarado, 1915–1918.* Mexico City: Ediciones Era.

Patch, Robert. 2002. *Maya Revolt and Revolution in the Eighteenth Century.* Armonk, NY: M. E. Sharpe.

Peniche Vallado, Leopoldo. 1985. "Sobre Justo Sierra O'Reilly." In *Justo Sierra O'Reilly*, 15–20. Mérida: Consejo Editorial de Yucatán.

Peraza López, María Elena, and Lourdes Guadalupe Rejón Patrón. 1989. *El comercio de artesanías en Chichén Itzá y algunos efectos del turismo en la región*. Mérida: Centro Regional Yucatan del Instituto Nacional de Antropología e Historia, Sección de Antropología Social.

Pfeiler, Barbara, and Lenka Zámišová. 2006. "Bilingual Education: Strategy for Language Maintenance or Language Shift of Yucatec Maya?" In *Mexican Indigenous Languages at the Dawn of the Twenty-First Century*, ed. Margartia Hidalgo, 294–313. Berlin: Mouton de Gruyter. http://dx.doi.org/10.1515/9783110197679.3.294.

Pinkus Rendón, Manuel Jesús. 2005. *De la herencia a la enajenación: Danzas y bailes "tradicionales" en Yucatán*. Mexico City: Universidad Nacional Autónoma de México.

Por Esto. 2002. "Segundo encuentro lingüístico y cultural de los Pueblos Mayas de Belice, Guatemala y México." July 28 edition. Online, www.poresto.net, accessed September 28, 2004.

Postero, Nancy. 2006. *Now We Are Citizens: Indigenous Politics in Post-multicultural Bolivia*. Stanford, CA: Stanford University Press.

Povinelli, Elizabeth. 2002. *The Cunning of Recognition*. Durham, NC: Duke University Press.

Purnell, Jennie. 1999. *Popular Movements and State Formation in Revolutionary Mexico: The Agraristas and Cristeros of Michoacán*. Durham, NC: Duke University Press.

Quezada, Serio, and Inés Ortiz Yam. 2003. "Introducción: Por la senda del liberalismo." In *Yucatán en la ruta del liberalismo mexicano, siglo XIX*, 11–28. Mérida: Universidad Autónoma de Yucatán.

Quintal, Ella F., Juan Bastarrachea, Fidencio Briceño, Martha Medina, Beatriz Repetto, Lourdes Rejón, and Margarita Rosales. 2003. "U lu'umil Maaya Wíiniko'ob: A Tierra de los Mayas." In *Diálogos con el territorio: Simbolización sobre el espacio en las culturas indígenas de México*, ed. Alicia M. Barabás, 273–359. Mexico City: Instituto Nacional de Antropología e Historia.

Quintal Martín, Fidelio. 2002. *Autobiografía de un maestro rural*. Mérida: Delegación Yucatán.

Rabasa, José. 2004. "Of Zapatismo: Reflections on the Folkloric and Impossible in a Subaltern Insurrection." In *The Latin American Cultural Studies Reader*, ed. Ann Del Sarto, Alicia Ríos, and Abril Trigo, 561–82. Durham, NC: Duke University Press.

Rama, Angel. 1996. *The Lettered City*. Durham, NC: Duke University Press.

Ramírez Carrillo, Luis Alfonso. 2002. "Yucatán." In *Los Mayas peninsulares: Un perfil socioeconómico*, ed. Mateo Humberto Ruz, 47–78. Mexico City: Universidad Autónoma de México.

Ramos, Alcida Rita. 2002. "Cutting through State and Class: Sources and Strategies of Self-Representation in Latin America." In *Indigenous Movements, Self-Representation and the State in Latin America*, ed. K. Warren and J. Jackson, 251–78. Austin: University of Texas Press.

Rappaport, Joanne. 1993. *Cumbe Reborn: An Andean Ethnography of History*. Chicago: University of Chicago Press.

Re Cruz, Alicia. 1996. *The Two Milpas of Chan Kom*. Albany: State University of New York Press.

Redclift, Michael. 2004. *Chewing Gum: The Fortunes of Taste*. London: Oxford University Press. http://dx.doi.org/10.4324/9780203311202.

Redfield, Margaret Park. 1935. "The Folk Literature of a Yucatecan Town." *Carnegie Institute of Washington Publication* 456: 1–50.

Redfield, Robert. 1941. *The Folk Culture of the Yucatan*. Chicago: University of Chicago Press.

Redfield, Robert. 1950. *A Village That Chose Progress: Chan Kom Revisited*. Chicago: University of Chicago Press.

Redfield, Robert, and Alfonso Villa Rojas. 1934. *Chan Kom: A Maya Village*. Washington, DC: Carnegie Institute of Washington.

Reed, Nelson. 1962. *The Caste War of Yucatán*. Stanford, CA: Stanford University Press.

Restall, Mathew. 1997. *The Maya World: Yucatec Culture and Society, 1550–1850*. Stanford, CA: Stanford University Press.

Restall, Mathew. 2003. "A History of the New Philology and the New Philology in History." *Latin American Research Review* 38 (1): 113–34. http://dx.doi.org/10.1353/lar.2003.0012.

Ricoeur, Paul. 1990. *Time and Narrative*. Vol. 1. Chicago: University of Chicago Press.

Rockwell, Elsie. 1994. "Schools of the Revolution: Enacting and Contesting State Forms in Tlaxcala, 1910–1930." In *Everyday Forms of State Formation*, ed. G. Joseph and D. Nugent, 170–206. Durham, NC: Duke University Press.

Rodríguez, Victoria E. 1997. *Decentralization in Mexico: From Reforma Municipal to Solidaridad to Nuevo Federalismo*. New York: Westview.

Rodríguez Llosa, Salvador. 1991. *Geografía política de Yucatán, Tomo III: División territorial, categorías políticas y población 1900–1990*. Mérida: Ediciones Universidad Autónoma de Yucatán.

Rodríguez O, Jaime, ed. 2007. *The Divine Charter: Constitutionalism and Liberalism in Nineteenth-Century Mexico*. New York: Rowman and Littlefield.

Rosaldo, Renato. 1980. *Ilongot Headhunting, 1883–1974: A Study in Society and History*. Stanford, CA: Stanford University Press.

Roys, Ralph. 1983. *The Titles of Ebtun*. New York City: AMS Press.

Rugeley, Terry. 1996. *Yucatán's Maya Peasantry and the Origins of the Caste War*. Austin: University of Texas Press.

Rus, Jan, et al., eds. 2003. *Mayan Lives, Mayan Utopias: The Indigenous Peoples of Chiapas and the Zapatista Rebellion*. New York: Rowman and Littlefield.

Russel, Philip. 1994. *Mexico under Salinas*. Austin: Mexico Resource Center.

Ruz, Mario Humberto. 2002a. "Los Mayas peninsulares." In *Los Mayas peninsulares: Un perfil socioeconómico*, ed. Mario Ruz, 7–45. Mexico City: Universidad Nacional Autónoma de México.

Ruz, Mario Humberto, ed. 2002b. *Los Mayas peninsulares: Un perfil socioeconómico*, 7–45. Mexico City: Universidad Nacional Autónoma de México.

Sahlins, Marshall David. 1981. *Historical Metaphors and Mythical Realities: Structure in the Early History of the Sandwich Islands Kingdom*. Ann Arbor: University of Michigan Press.

Sawyer, Suzana. 2004. *Crude Chronicles: Indigenous Politics, Multinational Oil, and Neoliberalism in Ecuador*. Durham, NC: Duke University Press.

Sherzer, Joel. 1987. "Discourse-Centered Approach to Language and Culture." *American Ethnologist* 89 (2): 295–309.

Sierra O'Reilly, Justo. 2002 [1861]. "Diario de nuestro viaje a los estados unidos." In *La Guerra de Castas*. Mexico City: Consejo Nacional para la Cultura y las Artes.

Silverstein, Michael, and Greg Urban, eds. 1996. *Natural Histories of Discourse*. Chicago: University of Chicago Press.

Slyomovics, Susan. 1998. *The Object of Memory: Arab and Jew Narrate the Palestinian Village*. Philadelphia: University of Pennsylvania Press.

Spivak, Gayatri. 1987. *In Other Words: Essays in Cultural Politics*. New York: Methuen.

Steggerda, Morris. 1932. "Anthropometry of Adult Maya Indians." *Carnegie Institute of Washington Publications* 434.

Steggerda, Morris. 1941. "Maya Indians of Yucatán." *Carnegie Institute of Washington Publications* 531.

Stephen, Lynn. 2002. *Zapata Lives: Histories and Cultural Politics in Southern Mexico*. Berkeley: University of California Press. http://dx.doi.org/10.1525/california/9780520222373 .001.0001.

Stocking, George. 1968. *Race, Culture, and Evolution: Essays in the History of Anthropology*. Chicago: University of Chicago Press.

Strickon, Arnold. 1965. "Hacienda and Plantation in Yucatan." *América Indígena* 25 (1): 35–63.

Sullivan, Paul R. 1989. *Unfinished Conversations: Mayas and Foreigners between Two Wars*. New York: Knopf.

Tax, Sol. 1937. "The *Municipios* of the Midwestern Highlands of Guatemala." *American Anthropologist* 39 (3): 423–44. http://dx.doi.org/10.1525/aa.1937.39.3.02a00060.

Tax, Sol. 1942. "Ethnic Relations in Guatemala." *América indígena* 2: 43–47.

Taylor, Charles. 2007. *A Secular Age*. Cambridge: Belknap Press of Harvard University.

Tenorio-Trillo, Mauricio. 2009. *Historia y celebración: México y sus centenarios*. Mexico City: Tusquets.

Thompson, Richard. 1974. *The Winds of Tomorrow: Social Change in a Maya Town*. Chicago: University of Chicago Press.

Tonkin, Elizabeth. 1992. *Narrating Our Pasts: The Social Construction of Oral History*. Cambridge: Cambridge University Press. http://dx.doi.org/10.1017/CBO9780511621888.

Trejo Lizama, Ileana Inés. 1988. "La educación primaria y rural en el periodo de gobierno alvaradista: 1915–1918." Licenciatura thesis, Facultad de Ciencias Antropológicas, Universidad Autónoma de Yucatán.

Trouillot, Michel-Rolph. 1995. *Silencing the Past: Power and the Production of History.* Boston: Beacon Press.

Turner, Brian. 2002. "Liberating the 'Municipio Libre': The Normalization of Municipal Finance in Yucatan." *Mexican Studies / Estudios Mexicanos* 18 (1): 101–31. http://dx.doi.org /10.1525/msem.2002.18.1.101.

Uc Dzib, Andrés. 1987. "La escuela rural: Una nueva escuela de la época de oro de la educación en México." In *Los maestros y la cultura nacional,* 17–38. Mexico City: Secretaría de Educación Pública.

Urias Horcasitas, Beatriz. 2008. "El poder de los símbolos: los símbolos en el poder: Teosofía y 'Mayanismo' en Yucatán (1922–1923)." *Relaciones* XXIX (115): 179–212.

Urla, Jacqueline. 1988. "Ethnic Protest and Social Planning: A Look at Basque Language Revival." *Cultural Anthropology* 3 (4): 379–94. http://dx.doi.org/10.1525/can.1988.3.4 .02a00030.

Vansina, Jan. 1942. *The Historian in Tropical Africa.* London: Oxford University Press.

Vansina, Jan. 1985. *Oral Tradition as History.* Madison: University of Wisconsin Press.

Vasconcelos, José. 1926. *La raza cósmica.* Paris: Agencia Mundial de Librería.

Vaughan, Mary Kay. 1997. "Cambio ideológico en la política educativa de la SEP: Programas y libros de texto, 1921–1940." In *Escuela y sociedad en el periodo cardenista,* ed. M. Vaughan and S. Quintanilla, 47–110. Mexico City: Fondo de Cultura Económica.

Vaughan, Mary Kay, and Susana Quintanilla. 1997. "Presentación." In *Escuela y sociedad en el periodo cardenista,* ed. M. Vaughan and S. Quintanilla, 7–46. Mexico City: Fondo de Cultura Económica.

Vogt, Evon Z. 1974. *The Zinacantecos of Mexico: A Modern Maya Way of Life.* New York: Holt, Rinehart and Winston.

Voloshinov, V. N. 1973. *Marxism and the Philosophy of Language.* Translated by Ladislav Matejka and I. R. Titunik. New York: Seminar Press.

Voz de la Revolución. 1915. "Se celebra Primer Congreso Pedagógico en Mérida." *Voz de la Revolución* 1 (1): 115. July 16.

Warman, Arturo. 1985. *Estrategias de sobrevivencia de los campesinos mayas.* Mexico City: IIS–Universidad Autónoma de México.

Warren, Kay. 1998. *Indigenous Movements and Their Critics: Pan-Maya Activism in Guatemala.* Princeton, NJ: Princeton University Press.

Warren, Kay, and Jean Jackson. 2002. "Introduction: Studying Indigenous Activism in Latin America." In *Indigenous Movements, Self-Representation and the State in Latin America,* ed. K. Warren and J. Jackson, 1–45. Austin: University of Texas Press.

Wells, Allan. 1985. *Yucatán's Gilded Age: Haciendas, Henequen, and International Harvester, 1860–1915.* Albuquerque: University of New Mexico Press.

Wells, Allan, and Gilbert M. Joseph. 1996. "Summer of Discontent: Economic Rivalry among Elite Factions during the Late Porfiriato in Yucatán." *Journal of Latin American Studies* 18: 255–82.

White, Hayden V. 1975. *Metahistory: The Historical Imagination in Nineteenth-Century Europe*. Baltimore: Johns Hopkins University Press.

White, Hayden V. 1990. *The Content of the Form: Narrative Discourse and Historical Representation*. Baltimore: Johns Hopkins University Press.

Wiarda, Howard. 2003. *Civil Society: The American Model and Third World Development*. New York: Westview.

Williams, Raymond. 1977. *Marxism and Literature*. Oxford: Oxford University Press.

Wolf, Eric. 1959. *Sons of a Shaking Earth*. Chicago: University of Chicago Press.

Woolard, Kathryn A., and Bambi Schieffelin. 1994. "Language Ideology." *Annual Review of Anthropology* 23 (1): 55–82. http://dx.doi.org/10.1146/annurev.an.23.100194.000415.

Yashar, Deborah. 2005. *Contesting Citizenship in Latin America: The Rise of Indigenous Movements and the Past Liberal Challenge*. Cambridge: Cambridge University Press.

Index

Page numbers in italics indicate illustrations.

Activism, 165; religious, 12–13
Age of Politics, 45; violence dur-
    ing, 35–43, 62, 70
agrarian associations, 16
agrarian reform, 2, 10, 23–24, 78,
    126; in Chan Kom, 43–44;
    and collectivism, 25–26,
    127–28; land tenure and, 28,
    36, 38, 40; oral narratives of,
    51–52
agriculture, 21(n8), 46(n7),
    114, 119, 122; commercial, 11,
    21(n8), 28; and public educa-
    tion, 84–85; swidden, 32–33,
    84–85
Akula, 24
Alcocer Castillo, Felipe, 90,
    86–87, 125
Alvarado, Salvador, 66, 79, 81
ambiguity, 2, 5, 8, 19(n3), 162, 163
anthropology, 159(n18); commu-
    nity exposure to, 145–46
artisanry vendors, 13, 117; at
    Chichén Itzá, 169–75, 180
artisans, 182(n10); direct sales by,
    173–74; Popolá, 177–78
Artisans of Chichén Itzá, 171, 172
assimilation, 77, 78
autonomy, 27, 38

Aztecs, and national history,
    102–3
Barbachano family, 181(n5); and
    Chichén Itzá, 164–65, 169–75;
    on Maya-centered events,
    168–69
Barrera, Lorenzo (Lol), 59,
    74(nn23, 25), 84; Burning of
    Yaxcabá and, 61, 70; and Lauro
    Dzul, 62–63
Bassols, Narciso, 89
Beana, Santiago (San), 58–59, 61,
    63, 70, 72(n8), 80
bilingualism, 107–8, 133, 157(n7);
    promoting, 151–52
Bohom, 39
books, 80, 99
boundaries, 30
Bubul, 38
Buenfil, Martín, 107

Cahum, Carlos, 146
Cancún, 116, 126, 128, 135(n3),
    164, 176
Canul, Damasio, 40
capitalists: artisanry vendors,
    172–74
Cárdenas, Lázaro, 73(n20), 81

Carnegie Institute of Washington, 89

Carrillo Puerto, Felipe, 58, 61, 63, 67, 71–72(nn3, 4, 10), 81; as governor, 53–54; and Indians, 55, 56, 70–71

Casa de las Artesanías de Yucatán, 127, 172; and Popolá project, 177–78, 180, 182(n10)

Castellanos, Bianet, 44

Caste War, 19–20(n4), 28–29, 30, 65, 98, 102

Catholicism, 12–13, 119

cattle husbandry, 123

CDI. *See* National Commission for the Development of Indigenous Peoples

Cen, Martiniano, 40

Cen family, 34, 35, 40, 44

Cervera y Pacheco, Victor, 127

ch'a chaak rain ceremony, 119

Chamulas, 33

Chan, Carlin, 54

Chan, Juan, 67

Chan de Mukul, Petrona, 5, 6, 128–29

Chan Ichmul, 24

Chan Kom, 14, 15, 24, 34, 45(n1), 48(n30), 49(n36), 69, 73(n14), 78, 117, 120, 134–35(n2), 149; agrarian reform, 43–44; factionalism in, 40–43, 59; founding of, 30, 68; land claims, 37–38; modernization, 114–15; as municipal seat, 39, 122, 123; and Nicté Há, 49(nn36, 37), 132

Chan Kom: A Maya Village (Redfield and Villa Rojas), 114–15, 117

Chan Santa Cruz, 29

Chemax, 78

Chiapas, 11, 33, 163

Chichén Itzá, 3, 12, 19(n4), 102; artisanry vendors at, 169–75, 180; Barbachano family and, 164–65; communities near, 13, 14; cultural patrimony and, 149–50; infrastructure around, 126–27; tourism, 16, 89, 116, 128

Chichén Itzá hacienda, 57

Cimé, Anacleto, 43

Cimé, Eustaquio, 40, 41, 42, 43, 48(nn30, 31), 49(n36), 73(n20), 84; Burning of Yaxcabá and, 58, 59, 60, 61, 63

Cimé Mex, Silvia, 170

Cimé family, 40, 41, 42

class hierarchies, 28, 98, 162; culture, 144–45; language and, 132–33; tourism and, 13–14, 133–34

class struggle, collective memory of, 57–58

Cocom, Nachi, 53

Cocom Maya, 98

code switching, 96

collective identity, 8, 96, 127–28

collective memory, 10, 53; abandonment of, 125–26; of class struggle, 57–58; of conflict, 45, 52; and national history, 101–2, 103–4; toponyms, 30–31

collective rights, collectivism, 1–2, 4, 126–27

colonial period, 38; political geography, 26–28

Comisión Agraria Mixta, 37, 39

Comisión Nacional para el Desarrollo de los Pueblos Indígenas, La (CDI), 139–40

committees: parents', 85, 93(n15)

communities, 24, 25, 85, 162; Caste War, 28–29; collective voice, 16–17; factionalism, 36–43; founding narratives of, 33–34; governance structures, 10, 19(n3); identity politics in, 163–64; indigenous, 139–43, 175–76

construction projects, 12, 127

cooperatives: artisanry, 117, 177–78; success of, 178–79

corporatism, 143, 150; culture and, 148–49

Cruz, José, 82, 86, 90

Culturas Populares (DGCP). *See* Dirección General de Culturas Populares

culture, 6, 80, 96; corporatism, 148–49; education and, 78–79; hierarchies of, 110, 120, 155–56; and identity politics, 180–81; Maya, 8, 114, 135(n5); Mexican state and, 77–78; and modernization, 115–16; patrimony, 144–47, 149–50, 157(n9), 158(n11); progressivist definition, 143–44; and tradition, 118–19; uses of terms, 8–9, 157(n8); varying definitions of, 5–6, 147–48

Cuncunul, 24, 38, 46(n9), 47(n10), 60, 85, 128, 173; factionalism, 36, 37; founding of, 67, 68; municipal affiliations, 39, 40

customs, 5, 146, 148, 157(n9); traditional, 117–19

dance traditions, 146

debt peonage, 64–65

decentralization, 27

"Declaration from Chichén Itzá at 158 Years from the Caste War," 171

DGCP. *See* General Direction of Popular Cultures

Díaz, Tranquilino, 69, 70, 122, 127; debt peonage of, 64–65; as ejidatario, 66–67

Díaz family, 65, 66–67, 74(n23)
Dirección General de Culturas Populares
    (Culturas Populares; DGCP), 140
document reading, communal, 17
Dzitas, 73(n15), 79, 114, 117
Dzucmuc, 37
Dzul, Lauro, 62–63
Dzul, Rubén, 55, 57, 62, 154–55

Ebtún, 28, 36, 38, 47(n13), 73(n14), 128, 173; and
    Chan Kom, 37, 40; families in, 34, 46(n9),
    47(n10)
economic development: indigenous communi-
    ties, 139–43; narratives of, 33–34
economies, 9, 11–12; tourist, 13, 132
education, 5, 134, 152; examinations, 99–101,
    111(nn4, 5); public, 78–84; resistance to, 87,
    92(n12); rural, 6, 82, 84–85; Spanish-language,
    104–10, 136(n15); tourist industry and,
    92(n10), 132
Ejército Zapatista de Liberación Nacional
    (EZLN), 10, 11, 20–21(nn5, 7), 163, 170–71
ejidos, 12, 23, 24, 30, 46(n9), 114, 128, 176; con-
    flicts in, 36–43; foundation of, 52–53, 63–70,
    74(n32), 122; land tenure, 43–44, 73(n20);
    settlers of, 34–35; territoriality and, 33–34;
    Xcalakdzonot, 25, 86
Ek, Santiago, 153–54
elites, 28
employment, in tourist industry, 12, 13, 132
Escuela Felipe Alcocer Castillo, 85, 88
ethnicity, 7–9, 98, 114, 130, 174–75
ethnic labels, 6; in Yucatan, 7–9
ethnic movements, 2–3, 9
evangelicals, 42
examinations, national, 99–100, 101, 111(nn4, 5)
exiles, from Yaxcabá, 61–62
EZLN. See Zapatista Army of National
    Liberation

factionalism, 4, 6, 68, 122; Burning of Yaxcabá
    and, 58–60; Chan Kom, 40–43; com-
    munity, 25, 35; out-migration and, 36–37;
    Xcalakdzonot, 86–87, 90
fallow (in swidden agriculture), 32
families, 47(n10), 130; on ejidos, 34, 40, 46(n9)
feuds, San Nicolás–Xcalakdzonot, 86–88, 90
folk community, 4, 134–35(n2)

folk-urban continuum, 115, 134(n1)
fomenting, land use and, 33–34

General Direction of Popular Cultures (DGCP),
    140
geography, political, 26–30
Goldkind, Victor, 73(n20); and Chan Kom, 40,
    42, 48(n30)
governance, community, 10, 19(n3)
Guatemala, Pan-Mayanism, 168

haciendas, 29, 57
Haimil, 81, 85
handicraft cooperatives, 16
handicraft industry, 3, 116–17, 127, 177; cultural
    politics and, 179–80; culture and, 147, 148;
    tourism and, 169–75
Hau, Álvaro, 40
henequen industry, 29
henequen zone, 21(n8), 29
heroes, in national history, 99–101
Hidalgo y Costilla, Miguel, in national history,
    99, 100–101, 103, 111(n5)
Hidalgo y Costilla, Escuela Miguel, 85, 89
Hispanic(s), 28, 77; as racial identity, 8,
    19–20(n4)
history: collective memory and, 101–2, 103–4;
    national, 95, 96, 97–101; official Mexican,
    54–55; origin myths, 102–3; solidarity in,
    70–71. See also oral narratives
Hoil Gutiérrez, Julio, 164
honey-production cooperative, 17
Huitzilopochtli, 102

INAH. See National Institute of Anthropology
    and History
INDEMAYA. See Institute for the Development
    of the Maya Culture of the State of Yucatán
identity, 1, 3, 20(n5), 114, 120, 153, 168; of arti-
    sans, 174–75; collective, 8, 96; indigenous,
    10–11; language and, 7, 130, 132–33; Maya,
    156, 162, 166; national, 97–98, 111(n2); and
    national history, 99–101; state-sanctioned,
    4–5, 24
identity politics, 1, 2, 9, 26, 113–14, 127–28, 163;
    culture and, 180–81; Mayan, 18, 137–38,
    164–69; municipalities and, 120, 122
independence, 102

Indians (indios), 46(n8), 98; and Carrillo Puerto, 55, 56, 70–71; colonial period, 27–28; identity of, 8, 18–19(n1), 29, 115, 141; as term, 7, 142
Indian Republics, 27–28, 46(n8)
indigeneity, 9, 28–29
indigenous movements, 137; post-Cold War, 2–3
indigenous peoples: and economic development, 139–43; identity politics of, 10, 162–63, 167; promotion of language, 151–52; small communities, 175–76
INI. See National Indigenist Institute
Institutional Revolutionary Party (PRI), 9, 20(n5), 122
Institute for the Development of the Maya Culture of the State of Yucatán (El Instituto para el Desarrollo de la Cultural Maya del Estado de Yucatán; INDEMAYA), 140, 142, 148, 157(n5), 164, 165
Instituto Nacional de Antropología e Historia (INAH), 164, 165, 181(n1); artisanry vendors and, 169–75
Instituto Nacional Indigenista (INI), 139, 164
Iturralde Traconis, José María, 60, 61

jarana dancing, 146

k'aax, 32, 33, 39, 47(n13)
kaj, kajo'ob, 31–32, 33, 34, 38, 47(n13)
kajtal, kajtalo'ob, 31, 32, 33, 59; autonomy, 38, 47(n11); occupation of, 37–38
Kancabdzonot, 59, 117
Kaua, 15, 34, 36, 37, 38, 46(n9), 47(nn10, 17), 66, 67, 103, 128, 173; conflict with Ticimul, 68–69, 81
knowledge, landscape, 30
kool, 32
Kuyoc, José [Concepción?], 40

labor, 28, 57, 122; collective, 36, 47(n15); nonagricultural, 11–12; tourist industry, 116–17
land: access to, 11, 17, 28–29; agrarian reform and, 23–24, 36; claims to, 37–38; community management of, 29–30; swidden agriculture and, 32–33; use of, 33–34
land grants, 63–64, 73(n20). See also ejidos
landscape, 24, 25; remembered, 30–35
landscape knowledge, 30
landscape memory, 17

land tenure, 37, 120; collective, 12, 17; colonial protection of, 27–28; conflicts over, 38–39, 40–43; Mayan-language and Mexican state, 24–25; and territoriality, 9–10
land titles, 26, 28, 37; and agrarian reform, 43–44; ejidos, 38, 68
language(s), 17, 159(n16), 168; class identity and, 132–33; education and, 104–10; and identity, 130, 135(n6), 141; indigenous, 142, 151–56; and land tenure, 24–25
language ideology, 95, 96
languaging, 108–9
leadership, 10; colonial period, 27–28
letter reading, communal, 17, 21–22(n9)
library, public, 80
literacy, 82
literature contests, Maya language, 150–51
López, José Angel, 60

Macal, Guillermo, 172–73
maize (corn) agriculture, 32, 114
maize zone, 11, 21(n8), 29–30
Marcos, Subcomandante, 170, 171
Maya, 7, 98: cultural hierarchies, 155–56; culture, 5–6, 114, 119–20, 135(n5), 144, 159(n18); grassroots movements, 3–4; identity as, 1–2, 18–19(n1), 29, 127, 130, 137–38, 139–43, 162; identity politics, 9, 164–69, 180–81; postpeasant identity, 128–33
Mayaland, Hotel, 165, 168–69
Maya language, 5, 17, 135(n6), 158(n14), 159(n19); activists, 165–66; education and, 105, 106–7, 139; and identity, 7, 8, 96, 141–42; and land tenure, 24–25; multicultural reforms and, 150–56; and Spanish, 106–10, 112(nn13, 14); toponyms in, 31–32; use of, 133, 159(n17)
Mayanness, 134, 141
Mayaon, 164, 165
Mediz Bolio, Antonio, 98
Mérida, 27, 29, 43, 115, 127, 132, 135(n3), 136(n12), 164
mestiza/mestizo, use of term, 7–8, 29, 98
Mex, Adalberto, 41, 122–23, 125
Mex family, 42
Mexican Constitution, 12, 163
Mexican Revolution, 29, 40, 47(n11), 51, 66, 69; and education, 79, 80–81; national identity and, 97–98; violence during, 53–54

Mexico, 77–78, 82; origin myth, 102–3; state culture, 77–78
microregions, 14–16, 46(n7)
middle class, 13
migration, 30, 34–35, 36, 59, 73–74(n22)
Mis Dzib, Reynaldo, *3*
missionaries, Protestant, 12–13
Mixed Agrarian Commission, 37, 39
Mo, Daniel, 145–46
modernization, 116; Chan Kom and, 114–15; infrastructure, 126–27; Pisté, 128–30; and traditional culture, 118–20
Morely, Sylvanus, Pisté school, 89, 93(n23)
Muchukux, 64, 65, 66
Muchukux-caj, 67
Mukul, Mario, 5, 6, 118–19, 130
Mukul de Dzul, Antonia, 130
multiculturalism, 6, 8, 11, 114, 138, 142, 165, 168; language-based reform and, 150–56; politics of, 162–63
municipalities, 38–39, 46(n8), 120, 122. *See also by name*
myths, origin, 102–3

NAFTA. *See* North American Free Trade Agreement
Nah Santos, Pedro, 106
Nahuat, Rodrigo, origin myth and oral history, 102–3
Nahuat Dzib, Efrén, 167
name tagging, in national history, 100–101
National Action Party (PAN), 122
National Agrarian Registry (RAN), 34
National Commission for the Development of Indigenous Peoples (CDI), 139–40
National Indigenist Institute (INI), 139, 164
National Institute of Anthropology and History (INAH), 164, 165, 181(n1); artisanry vendors and, 169–75
nationalism, 89, 96, 111(n2); Revolutionary, 20(n6), 97–98, 111(n2)
neoliberalism, 6, 9, 114, 127
neoliberal reforms, 9, 10
Nicté Há, 15, 34, 44, 47–48(n18), 59, 64, 68, 74–75(n33), 116, *124*, 125, 126, 128, 132, 149, 153, 176; and Chan Kom, 49(n37), 122–23; ejido founding in, 66, 67; language use of, 133,

159(n16); schools in, 80, 136(n14); settlement of, 40–43
Noh Pereira, Álvaro, 105–6
North American Free Trade Agreement (NAFTA), 10, 20–21(n7)

oral narratives, 20(n6), 33, 71(n1), 74(n27); of agrarian reform, 51–52; of Burning of Yaxcabá, 60–62; of class struggle, 57–58; of community founding, 63–70, 74(n32); of landscape, 30–35; of national history, 98–99, 101–2; and official Mexican history, 54–55
Oriente, 1, 2, 46(n7); political geography of, 26–30
Osorio, Consuelo, 82
out-migration, factional violence and, 36–37

PACMYC. *See* Program of Aid for Municipal and Community Cultures
PAN. *See* National Action Party
Panbá, 39
Pan-Mayanism, 137, 168
paramilitary, 52, 161
parents' committees, 85, 93(n15)
Partido Acción Nacional (PAN), 122
Partido Liberal Yucateco (PLY), 58–59, 61, 72(n10)
Partido Socialista de Yucatán (PSY), 58–59, 60, 72(nn10, 12), 73(n15), 161
Partido Revolucionario Institucional (PRI), 9, 20(n5), 122
Pat, Andrea, 117
Pat, Petrona, 42–43
Pat, Primitivo, 42–43, 122, 125
Pat family, 42–43
patrimonialism, 143; culture and, 144–48, 149–50, 157(n9); language and, 153–55
Patrón Laviada, Patricio, 142, 149, 165
peasants, 1, 2, 4, 9, 12, 29, 69; identity as, 18–19(n1), 127
Pech, Mathilde, 118–19
Pisté, 3, 5, 12, 13, 14, 15, 30, 43, 46(n9), 47(n10), 57, 73(n15), 123, 125, *131*, 145, 136(n13), 167; artisanry vendors from, 172–73, 175; Burning of Yaxcabá and, 60, 61; cultural hierarchies in, 155–56; handicraft industry, 116–17, 127; Maya language use in, *151*, 153–54; modernization, 117–19,

128–30; school in, 85, 88–89, 90; Spanish language use in, 132–33; tourism and, 92(n10), 162, 177; Yaxcabá exiles in, 62, 73–74(n22)

Pixoy (Uayma), 34, 44, 65

place names, Mayan language, 30–32, 47(n14)

places, named, 24–25

PLY. *See* Yucatecan Liberal Party

political rituals, 17–18, 21–22(n9)

politics, 10, 19–20(n4), 111(n2); agrarian and ethnic, 2, 11, 114; and Burning of Yaxcabá, 58–59; cultural, 179–80; multiculturalism and, 162–63; municipal, 120, 122; national, 9, 20(n5); violence and, 35–43

Pom, 85

Popolá, 14, 15, 17, 35, 44, 117, 118, 119, 122, 128, 135(n4), 153; artisans in, 177–78, 180, 182(n10); founding of, 64–70; language use in, 133, 159(n16); modernization, *121*, 126–27; schools in, 80, 136(n14); tourist industry, 92(n10), 132, 176–77

Popolá, Rancho, 35

poverty, and identity, 7, 8

Presbyterians, 13, 49(n36), 62, 119, 122; and Nicté Há settlement, 41–42, 43

PRI. *See* Institutional Revolutionary Party

Program of Aid for Municipal and Community Cultures (Programa de Apoyo a las Cultural Muncipales y Comunitarias; PACMYC), 140; grants, 147–48, 172

progressivism, 150; on culture, 143–44

Protestantism, Protestants, 62, 119; Chan Kom families, 41–42, 49(n36); conversions to, 12–13

PSY. *See* Yucatecan Socialist Party

Puc, Román, 147–48, 172

Puc family, 34, 35, 44

Quintana Roo, 29, 60, 115; tourism, 116–17, 135(n3)

RAN. *See* National Agrarian Registry

reading, communal, 17, 21–22(n9)

rebellion, EZLN, 10–11

Redfield, Robert: autobiography of Eustaquio Cimé, 58, 63; and Chan Kom, 40, 134–35(n2); *Chan Kom: A Maya Village*, 30, 114–15, 117; on modernization, 115–16

reductions (reducciones), 27–28

Registro Agrario Nacional (RAN), 34

religion, 119; activism, 12–13; conflicts, 41–42

religious activism, 12–13

Repúblicas de Indios, 27–28, 46(n8)

resistance, 78; to schools, 86, 87, 88–89, 92(n12)

rituals, 17–18, 21–22(n9)

Rodríguez, Abelardo, 89

saká ritual, 166–67

Salamanca de Bacalar (Bacalar), 27

Salinas de Gortari, Carlo, 20(n5), 127

San Felipe, 116

San Francisco, 80

San Francisco de Campeche, 27

San Nicolás (X-Lab Kaj; X-Lab Cah), 24, 25, 39, 125; and Xcalakdzonot ejido, 86–88, 90

San Rigoberto, 85

Santa María, 37

schools, 92(n13), 93(n15), 132; cultural standards, 161–62; language use, 133, 136(n15); national and linguistic identity and, 95–96; Pisté, 88–89, 93(n23); public, 79, 139; rural, 78, 79–84, 85, 90, 91(nn1, 2), 99–100, 136(n14), 180; supplies for, 80–81; Xcalakdzonot, 86–87, 88

Second Linguistic and Cultural Encounter of the Mayan People of Belize, Guatemala, and Mexico, identity politics at, 164–69

Secretariat of Public Education (Secretaría de Educación Pública; SEP), 79–80, 86; rural schools and, 82, 85, 88–89, 90, 91(nn1, 2), 139

Selva Lacandona, 171

SEP. *See* Secretariat of Public Education

service industry, 176–77

settlers, on ejido, 34–35

Seventh-Day Adventists, 119

Siete Pilas, 24, 34

social hierarchy, 134

socialism, 57, 58

Socialist Party of Yucatán, 53, 58

social justice, 35

solidarity, 4, 6, 54, 70–71, 92(n11), 120

Spanish, colonial period, 26–28

Spanish language, 95, 96, 130, 159(n16); education in, 104–10, 112(nn7–11), 136(n15), 139

speech, and writing, 17

Tacchibichen, 62

teachers, rural, 81–84, 85, 86, 91–92(nn8, 10, 11), 105

Tec, Dagoberto, 83
Tec, Francisco: on ejido foundation, 64–70; on schools, 80, 81
Tekom, 47(n10), 60, 82
Temax, 80
territoriality, 9–10, 24, 25, 26, 33–34, 181(n1)
Thompson, Edward, 57, 58
Ticimul, 15, 34, 36, 37, 59, 64, 73(n14), 103, 116, 123; conflict with Kaua, 68–69; ejido formation in, 66, 67; school in, 80, 81
Tinúm, 14, 15, 38, 67, 72(n9), 164; Burning of Yaxcabá and, 60, 61; schools in, 79, 85
Tizimín, 43, 125
toponyms, 30–32, 47(n14)
tourism, 2, 11, 114, 135(n3); Chichén Itzá, 16, 89; and class hierarchies, 13–14, 133–34; cultural patrimony and, 144–45, 149–50; impacts of, 130, 132, 159(n16)
tourist industry, 9, 92(n10), 116–17, 120, 128, 162, 181(n1); artisanry vendors and, 169–75; Barbachano family, 165, 168–69; employment in, 13, 176–77; labor in, 11, 12
Traconis, Daniel, 64–65, 70
Traconis clan, 65
traditions, 5, 9, 118–19, 146
Tun, José, 40, 41
Tuyub, Hernán, 155
Tuzik, 115, 117
Tzeal, 37, 39, 44

Uayma (Pixoy), 34, 44, 65
Uc, Aurelio, 53, 58–59, 61
Uc, Doroteo Balam, 87–88
Uc, Miguel, 86, 87
Uc Couoh, José Santos, 87–88
United States, 19–20(n4), 29
Uxmal, 19(n4), 127

Valladolid, 27, 39, 79, 132, 135(n3)
Villa Rojas, Alfonso, 40, 58, 83–84; *Chan Kom: A Maya Village*, 30, 114–15
violence: Age of Politics, 35–43, 70, 73(n14), 74(n14); Burning of Yaxcabá, 58–60; collec-
tive memories of, 52–53; Mexican Revolution-era, 53–54; out-migration and, 36–37; in Xcalakdzonot, 86–88; Yaxcabá exiles, 62–63

word substitution, 106–7, 108–9, 112(n14)
writing, speech and, 17

Xalau, 81
X-Lab Kaj (X-Lab Cah). *See* San Nicolás
Xcalakoop, 13, 15, 35, 92(n10), 119; school in, 82, 136(n14); tourist industry, 116, 128, 132, 181(n1)
Xcalakdzonot, 15, 17, 34, 39, 44, 47(n13), 64, 85, 89, 117, 125–26, 132, 133, 153, 159(n16), 176; factionalism in, 86–88, 90; landscape of, 24–25
X-Katun, 64, 103
Xcocail, 37, 85
Xiu, Bartolomé, 144–45
Xkatun (X-Katun), 15, 37, 73(n14), 74(n32)
Xkopteil, 37–38
Xtakejil, 24
Xtojil (X-Tojil), 15, 40, 41, 44, 126, 149

Yaxcabá, 14, 34, 35, 72(n12), 74(n23); Burning of, 52, 53, 58–61, 70; exiles from, 61–63, 73–74(n22)
Yaxché, 85
Yaxuná, 59, 117
Yucatán, 19–20(n4), 181(n1); identity politics in, 11, 115; political geography of, 26–30; public education in, 79–80
Yucatecan Liberal Party (PLY), 58–59, 61, 72(n10)
Yucatecan Socialist Party (PSY), 58–59, 60, 72(nn10, 12), 73(n15), 161
Yucatec Maya, 7, 27, 114, 156. *See also* Maya
Yucatec Maya language, 7, 158(n14). *See also* Maya language

Zapata, Emiliano, 10–11; national identity and, 99–100, 101, 111(n4)
Zapatista Army of National Liberation (EZLN), 10, 11, 20–21(nn5, 7), 163; and Artisans of Chichén Itzá, 170–71
Zinacantecos, 33